COMPLETE
METALWORKING
MANUAL

R. H. Cooley

Structural Engineer

New York

Published by ARCO PUBLISHING COMPANY, Inc.
219 Park Avenue South, New York, N.Y. 10003

Second Printing, 1968

Library of Congress Catalog Card Number 66-12058

Arco Catalog Number 1406

Printed in the United States of America

Preface

THE importance for young mechanics of a general yet all-around knowledge of metalworking cannot be overemphasized. There is a growing demand in industry today for young men who have been soundly trained in the fundamental practices of metalworking. Those who wish to specialize are encouraged to go in for intensive training in the particular branch of the field for which they are best suited.

The student or apprentice metalworker may begin his training in a large, well-equipped shop under experienced instructors, who acquaint him with the method and tools used in production industry; after his training is completed, however, whether he goes to work in a commercial shop or sets up a home workshop, he will have to rely on his own knowledge of materials and methods in order to handle the jobs that come to him. This book has been designed both as a guide to machine-shop practices for the beginner and as a reference book for working mechanics. It discusses the techniques, machines, and equipment used in the industry and outlines the most efficient methods of handling jobs in a small shop, with necessarily limited equipment, by making wise use of the materials at hand.

R. H. COOLEY

Contents

1

The Shop

The School Shop

FOR maximum efficiency, a school shop should be modeled along the lines of a manufacturing plant, set up to resemble one as closely as possible. The shop room should be large enough to allow for ample space around the machines. Machines should be on their own floor standards, and each machine should have its own power drive. Adequate lighting must be provided. Large school shops may have separate rooms for various types of work; each room can be equipped with the appropriate facilities. Some schools may wish to confine shop work to one or two rooms that serve a multiple purpose.

Benches to accommodate as many students as each class assembles should be placed along the walls of the shop. These benches must be sturdily constructed and should have heavy sheet-metal tops. They should be equipped with drawers that may be locked, so that each student has a place to store his personal tools and materials for the problem he is working on.

Each student should supply himself with the small tools he will need, such as scales, calipers, hammers, and the like. As he progresses to more intricate work, he will find it desirable to have his own micrometers, thread gauges, and other precision tools. The school shop should stock only those tools that are occasionally used, such as large micrometers, surface plates, and milling cutters. Of course, each machine should be equipped with the necessary attachments to enable it to perform its various functions. Drills and other special tools should be kept in a toolroom supervised by the instructor, who issues them to students as needed. Any tool not returned or broken in use should be charged to the account of the student responsible. The toolroom, or tool crib, as it is called in some plants, should be adjacent to or should form part of the instructor's office; this office should be so situated that the instructor can observe the entire classroom without leaving his desk.

The method by which tools are charged out to the students and the type of inventory that is kept on the stock of tools are usually determined by the instructor. Small tools, such as small drills and taps, which are easily broken, should be ordered in quantity, and an ample stock of them should be kept on hand at all times. More rugged tools, such as large drills, need replacement only when they wear out.

Raw materials to be used by the students should also be purchased in quantity to insure adequate supply to classes. Storage space for raw materials should be located where it can be supervised by the instructor.

This rigid system of control of tools and materials should be maintained in the school shop, not because the students are not trustworthy, but because it will accustom them to conditions in the industrial plants in which they will later work, where similar control is practiced.

Machine Equipment

The lathe is the most important machine in a shop. Since the student cannot know what kind of lathe he will have to use in his future work, he should be trained on as many kinds as possible. The school shop should be equipped with several small lathes of the toolroom type, at least one of intermediate size, and one of large size. The number of lathes required will depend, of course, on the number of students who will use them in their shop classes. The work in each class can be spread out over the several machines so that they will all be kept busy, even when some students are working at the bench. Each of these machines should be on its own standard and should have individual motor drive. There should be at least one lathe with step-cone drive and one with geared-head drive. Each machine should be equipped with a built-in pan for the recovery of cutting oil. Modern lathes have quick-change gears, threading dials, taper attachments, and other features that will enable the students to practice using the most up-to-date equipment. Some commercial shops still use the old-style lathes, which are driven by flat belts from an overhead countershaft and have only plain change gears and no thread-cutting dials. The students should learn how to set up and cut threads on this type of lathe, on which belts must be changed from an overhead countershaft when the machine has been reversed. There should be one of these old-style lathes in the school shop.

The lathes in a school shop will receive some rough treatment at the hands of inexperienced students. Instructors do try to point out to their classes the safest and most correct way of using these and other machines, but accidents will happen, and the machines may be damaged. For this reason, it is recommended that at least one of the toolroom lathes be set up in the toolroom, where it will be used only by the instructor or the most advanced students, and so that it can be kept in accurate working order.

A small high-speed drill with a chuck capacity of $\frac{1}{2}$ inch is an important addition to any school shop. It may be mounted on its own standard or it may be of the bench variety. Since this type of drill will not handle drill bits over $\frac{1}{4}$ inch in diameter (except in relatively soft materials), there should be another drill provided for heavier work. A medium-sized radial drill will be found useful in teaching the operation of the larger drilling machines.

Facilities in the school shop should include a universal milling machine, equipped with a dividing head and several complete sets of milling cutters, including gear-cutting mills with teeth of various common sizes.

A medium-sized shaper and a large planer will also be required. These tools are found in all well-equipped machine shops, and their use should be thoroughly understood by any mechanic.

The power hacksaw would be necessary in any shop. The band cutoff saw, however, although it is used in many commercial shops where a great deal of cutting is done, is not one of the required school-shop machines. Similarly, the metal-cutting band saw, which is designed for contour sawing and which requires a special skill to operate, is not needed in a school shop.

Grinding is an operation so frequently necessary in fine machine work that a universal grinding machine with magnetic chucks should be part of the school-shop equipment.

Automatic machines, such as the turret lathe and the screw machine, are not general-purpose tools; once they have been installed by a skilled "setup man," they can be run even by an inexperienced operator. Such machines are not needed in a school shop. The makers of these tools maintain their own instructors to teach the setting up and operation of their particular machines, and thus a skilled mechanic can learn from an instructor how to handle such a machine when the need arises.

Since a knowledge of sheet-metal work is important to the students, school facilities should include a well-equipped sheet-metal shop. In this shop there should be several large benches or tables on which sheets can be spread for layout work. Necessary machines would include a sheet-metal shears of about a 60-inch capacity and a hand brake with a capacity of $\frac{1}{16}$ inch of metal. Hand-operated rolls for sheets up to 60 inches wide should be provided, as well as hand-operated beading and flanging rolls. Power-operated shears and brakes are not necessary.

Spinning and cold working of sheet metals should be taught in the sheet-metal shop, so this shop should be equipped with a spinning lathe. This should not be a heavy-duty lathe, in which the spinning tool is controlled by screw movement, but should be one on which hand tools may be used.

Every mechanic should understand pattern making: that is, the art of shaping patterns for the molds into which molten metal is poured to form castings. The school pattern shop should have ample bench capacity and a generous supply of the necessary hand tools. Several wood-turning lathes will be required, as well as a small-thickness planer about 24 inches in width and a jointer 12 inches wide. The planer and the jointer must be equipped with round cutter heads, and a guard should be placed over the cutter head of the jointer when the machine is in use. A bench drill press with wood bits is another necessary machine for the pattern shop. A ripsaw and a crosscut saw of the table variety should be provided, either combined in one or as separate machines. When separate machines are used, of course, two students can work with the saws at the same time. A band saw with 36-inch wheels and a disk-and-spindle sander are "musts."

Pattern stock may be stored in racks; from there the planks can feed onto the table of a cutoff saw of the swing or sliding type, which cuts them up as needed. Bins can hold cutoff scraps, which can later be worked into smaller parts of the patterns. All the power machines should be connected to an adequate sawdust-collecting system. A large supply of clamps, both large and small, should be available. Near the pattern shop there should be a paint room where the patterns can be shellacked.

Since pattern making entails an understanding of the foundry process, there should be a small but efficient foundry in the school shop. Students should get enough practice in foundry work to be able to design and build their own patterns. The foundry may be only large enough to allow a few students to work there at a time, under the direction of the instructor in pattern making. Since a small foundry will seldom have occasion to melt iron, a cupola furnace is not necessary. Students can solve all the problems of foundry work by using brass or aluminum, metals which have low melting points and are best handled in crucibles heated in a furnace. This furnace can be fired by gas or oil or it can be of the electric induction type. Molding sand should be stored in bins, and the foundry should have a concrete floor where the sand can be mixed and tempered. Large foundries employ mechanical mixers to turn out the sand at the right temper for the molders to use, but in a school shop the students should be taught how to wet and temper the sand by hand. Only ordinary wooden flasks are necessary. Molding machines, used to compact the sand or to withdraw a pattern, are not recommended for school purposes. By tamping the sand manually, students will learn to recognize the point at which the proper degree of compaction has been achieved; likewise, through practice in withdrawing their own patterns, they will learn how to avoid the errors of improperly finished patterns.

Blacksmithing, as it used to be practiced by village smiths, is nearly a lost art; every skilled mechanic today, however, must have an understanding of the principles of forge work and of the heat-treating of metals. In the school shop a small area should be set aside for forge work, equipped with a furnace to provide heat for forging and a muffle furnace for annealing and heat-treating steel. The instructor will find a coal-fired forge useful in demonstrating the effect of carbon, or an air blast, on the metal being heated. This shop should also have a blacksmith's vise and anvil and a complete selection of blacksmith tools. Equipment for gas and electric welding as well as gas cutting belong in this shop. If the school is to give courses in the theory and practice of heat-treating metals, there should be machines for testing the strength of metals and apparatus for examining the grain structure.

The Small Shop

A small jobbing shop and a home workshop are very much alike. Both are necessarily limited in space and amount of equipment. In the following section the equipment needed in a small shop is discussed in detail.

THE HOME SHOP

When setting up a metalworking shop at home, there are a few machines that it will be necessary to provide; certain other machines can be dispensed with at the start and added later as the opportunity arrives. Some of these you will be able to construct yourself, and these will make excellent work projects for the new shop.

There must be ample space in the shop to allow you to set up the bench and machines and provide storage space for materials. There should be a power supply that will handle four or five horsepower, and there should be a gas supply. Plan the layout of the shop so that you leave yourself enough room to assemble the work under construction. This can be done by setting up another bench or table in the middle of the shop, so that the work you are doing on it can be reached from all sides.

The Bench

You will probably construct the bench yourself to fit the space best suited for it. The top of the bench should be made of kiln-dried douglas fir, or similar wood, at least 2 inches thick. This top must be of a uniform thickness. Either of two types of working surfaces can be used. You can cover the top with ¾-inch maple flooring and then sand it to a smooth surface. For a better but more costly surface, you can have a sheet-metal shop fit a sheet of 12-gauge sheet steel to the wooden top, with the front edge of the metal turned down over the thickness of the top and with the rear edge of the metal turned up against the backboard. The sheet metal can be fastened with round-head wood screws through these turned edges, so that the screws will not protrude onto the working surface of the bench top.

The sheet-metal top is a great convenience, as sooner or later you will be overhauling some machine on the top of the bench, and oil will be spilled. The oil can easily be cleaned from a metal top, but a wooden top will absorb the oil. The metal top must be made from sheet metal that will lie perfectly flat and tight against the wooden top without any wrinkles or bulges. Tell the sheet-metal shop to use *stretcher-leveled* sheet steel. This kind of sheet has been pulled or stretched to remove all the strains worked into it when the sheet was rolled at the steel mill, and it will form a smooth, level surface.

The bench should be as long as space will allow. The legs should be made from 4-inch-by-4-inch stock, and the crosspieces at the top from 2-inch-by-6-inch stock, with all joints halved into the legs and bolted. The legs should not be over four feet apart, or else the top of the bench will be springy.

A tool rack on the top of the backboard is a handy place to store the small tools most often used, such as pliers, screw drivers, and center punches. Several drawers should be installed under the top to hold the larger tools not used so often. A shelf under the bench is also handy for storage. For the tool rack, bore holes of varying sizes to hold the tools. Three-quarter-inch holes are good for pliers and screwdrivers; $\frac{3}{8}$-inch holes are better for drifts, center punches, and the like. As some small tools may slide through the holes, some of the holes should be closed at the bottom.

In addition to the storage shelf halfway up to the drawers, there should also be one near the floor. Close off the space under this bottom shelf with a toe board set back 4 inches to give space for your toes while you are working at the bench. Small parts are often dropped on the floor and are easily lost. The toe board will prevent their rolling under the bench where it is hard to recover them.

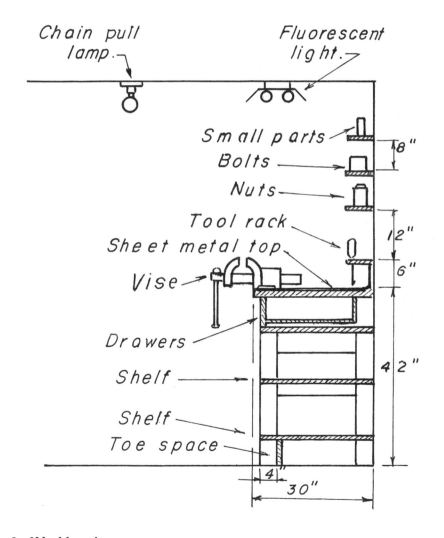

Fig. 1. Workbench

For lighting the bench and the machine tools set up on it, a row of 40-watt fluorescent lights over the center of the bench will provide adequate general lighting, but you will need light from the front of the bench, so place a row of light bulbs in chain-pull sockets about two feet from the front of the bench. The one at the vise should be at least 150 watts. For spotlighting work in a shadow, a small bulb on an extension cord should be provided. There should be duplex outlets for the portable electric tools located near the vise and near the lathe. The outlets should be grounded.

The Vise

Near the left end of the bench, bolt on a good stout machinist vise with jaws at least 4 inches wide. Do not waste money on a cheap vise, since it is going to get some very hard use and must stand up to it. Cheap vises are made of cast iron and are easily broken when they are tightened too much. A good vise is made of malleable iron, which will stand strain about as well as steel. A vise with a swivel base is very convenient, thought not absolutely necessary. Be sure the vise is bolted firmly through the top of the bench near one of the legs; otherwise the top boards of the bench will spring and give a weak base for the vise.

A vise with a small anvil built into the rear is handy, as you will often need to hammer something on a firm metal surface. Be sure never to hammer on the sliding rear end of the movable jaw, as this is liable to peen it out of shape and prevent its working smoothly in its slides.

The jaws of the vise are serrated on the face to better hold the work. The serrations will mar any finished work, so soft jaw covers of either sheet copper or sheet lead should be fitted to cover the jaws. Copper is best, as it will last much longer. Jaw covers of plywood are also handy for some types of work, such as holding a piece of wood.

Figure 1 shows an outline of the bench set-up.

Hand Tools

A complete set of wrenches of the end, box, and socket types should be provided. Several adjustable-jaw wrenches, such as the crescent type or the old-style monkeywrench, should be in your collection. Screwdrivers of various sizes and lengths, for both slotted and Phillips-head screws, are needed, as well as several types of pliers. Side-cutting nippers and needle-nose pliers will be used often.

Hacksaws are necessary for cutting metal. There should be one with 14 teeth to the inch for cutting steel, iron, brass, and the like in large cross section, and one with 24 teeth for cutting thin sections of sheet metal and pipe. A saw with 32 teeth is even better for thin sections. It is possible to change blades each time a different tooth spacing is needed, but it is much more convenient to have separate frames for each number of teeth.

It is advisable always to buy high-speed steel blades that are hardened on the cutting edge only. The soft-back blades do not break as easily, and the extra-hard teeth make the blades last so much longer that they will be cheaper in the long run. Since the hacksaw will be used most often at the vise, you should hang your saws on the wall near the vise.

Files are also very necessary tools. As it is easy to damage the teeth of a file by letting them hit a hard surface, you should provide compartments for the files in a drawer, so that they do not strike against each other. A good assortment of files would include a 10- or 12-inch roughing hand file of about 20 teeth to the inch and a hand bastard of the same size with about 30 teeth to the inch (these two files each should have one safe edge). There should be a smoothing file of about 50 teeth to the inch, and 8 to 10 inches long. A half-round bastard about 10 inches long will find wide use in your shop. You should have a large and small file of round, square, and three-cornered sections. A set of Swiss-pattern needle files will enable you to finish many small and intricate shapes. Provide handles for all your files.

Cold chisels are useful for removing large amounts of metal in a hurry. You will need several kinds: a large flat chisel for general work, a smaller flat chisel, a wide and a narrow cape chisel, and a round-nose chisel. Be sure to get the chisels from a reliable dealer who can stand behind his tools, as cold chisels will receive some very hard use.

You will need several important tools for measuring and laying out work. Have two center punches. One, called a prick punch, has a narrow, sharp point that is easy to see. The center punch has a wide, flat angle to the point that will receive and start the end of a drill. You should have a combination square with a 9-inch hardened-steel blade. You will need three adjustable heads for this blade. One is the square head, which has two sides: one at 90° and the other at 45°. The protractor head is adjustable to any angle and is graduated in degrees. The third head is the centering head. This has two arms at 45° to the blade, and the blade passes through the intersection of the two arms, so that when the centering head is applied to the end of a round bar, the blade will pass through the center.

The square head has a small, hardened-steel scriber inserted in a pocket at one end. This is a very useful tool, but it is rather small, so a larger one is well worth having. This scriber should have one straight end and one point bent at a right angle for getting into places where a straight point cannot reach.

The blade of the combination square is graduated for measuring, but you should have a smaller hardened-steel rule about 6 inches long with graduations also on the ends. It is often necessary to make a measurement in a small space where only the end of the rule can enter, and these end graduations are very important.

Two sizes of calipers should be provided. One set should be about 4-inch, and the other set 8-inch. They should be of the spring-opening type with screw adjustment. The quick-opening spring nut is a good time-saver, as it is possible to open the nut and make a rough adjustment of the calipers without having to run the nut slowly along the thread.

For accurate work you will need micrometer calipers. These are rather expensive, but a 1-inch size and a 2-inch size will be used often and are well worth the price. To go with these you should have a set of inside micrometers. These come with adjusting rods to measure from 2 inches up. For accurately measuring holes smaller than 2-inches across, a telescoping gauge should be used. This has a handle with a telescoping head operated by a spring. Several lengths of pins fit the sliding part of the head, and there is a locking nut at the end of the handle.

For measuring the depth of holes, a depth gauge is necessary. For very accurate work, a micrometer depth gauge should be used. The usual run of work in a home workshop will not require the use of a micrometer depth gauge, so one with a sliding head is good enough.

A set of feeler gauges should be provided for measuring very small thicknesses. A set of screw-thread gauges are needed to measure the pitch of threads. For setting up thread-cutting tools and for grinding the cutters and testing lathe centers, a center gauge is needed. This is a small scale with 60° notches cut in the side and end, so that the grinding can be tested.

For marking heights in layout work, a surface gauge is used. This has a flat base with an adjustable scriber; when it is set on a flat surface the scriber can mark points of equal height.

For measuring the size of small drills or wires, a drill gauge is necessary. This is a hardened steel plate with holes of various sizes, each marked with the size of the drill and its decimal equivalent.

It is often necessary to scribe a line parallel to an edge. The hermaphrodite calipers are handy for this work. These have one leg like an outside caliper to fit against the reference edge, and the other leg has a scribing point. You will also need dividers with about 4-inch legs.

A most important instrument for accurate work is the dial indicator. This has a dial graduated in thousandths of an inch and will indicate movements of a fraction of a thousandth.

Get a set of pin punches and several drifts for larger work. A set of steel stamps for letters and numbers is very useful. Letters $\frac{1}{16}$-inch high are a good all-around size.

There are many other instruments for measuring and layout work, so it would be well to get a copy of the Starrett Tool Catalogue. You can get this from your hardware store.

A set of drills is very necessary. There are two groups of straight-shank drills, each with its own stand to hold them. The smaller or numbered drills run from No. 60 up to No. 1 and fit in one stand. The larger drills, or fractional sizes, run from $\frac{1}{16}$-inch up to $\frac{1}{2}$-inch and fit the other stand. These stands are of metal with an accurate-sized hole for each drill. Straight-shank drills are held in a chuck, and ½-inch is about as large a drill as the bench drill press can handle.

For larger holes it is better to use the lathe, where the speed can be adjusted to the size of drill being used. Taper-shank drills should be used in the lathe. The taper-shank should be the same size as the centers used in your lathe. Most 9-inch and 10-inch lathes use a No. 2 morse taper. Taper-shank drills from ½-inch to 1-inch in steps of $\frac{1}{16}$-inch should be on hand. Make your own stand for the taper-shank drills. It pays always to purchase high-speed drills instead of the softer carbon-steel drills.

A set of taps and dies for cutting small threads is necessary. The type of work you intend to do will govern the range of sizes you will need. The small size of 6-32 and 8-32 are used a great deal. So are the machine-screw sizes up to ½-inch. The machine-screw sizes should be of both the fine or N.F. (SAE) threads and the standard or N.C. (USS) threads.

Three taps should be provided for each size: a taper tap for starting, a plug tap for most work, and a bottoming tap. Again it pays to buy only high-speed steel taps. You will need three sizes of tap wrenches to handle this range of sizes. Be sure to get wrenches with hardened jaws, or they will soon wear until the wrench slips on the tap.

The button dies of 1-inch diameter are a handy size. It pays to get the kind that are adjustable, so that you can cut a tight or loose thread to suit the work being done. There are several types of stocks to hold these dies. Plain stocks will get closer to a shoulder, but they are hard to get started straight. The type with adjustable guides enables you to start the thread fairly straight on the work.

Taps and dies larger than ½-inch get into much heavier sizes and are very expensive. As threads larger than ½-inch are seldom cut in the home shop, it is not necessary to provide for the larger sizes. When it is necessary to cut a larger thread, do it in the lathe. You may find use for a few of the larger taps, and these you can procure as you need them.

Pipe taps and dies are of a different nature. It is difficult to cut accurate pipe threads in a lathe. The taper of the thread can only be approximated, unless the lathe is equipped with a taper attachment. For this reason, pipe taps and dies should be part of your equipment. Solid dies are adequate for the smaller sizes, but it is almost impossible to start a solid die on a 1-inch pipe. For sizes 1-inch and larger, it is necessary to use the screw-feed type, such as the Toledo.

MACHINE EQUIPMENT FOR THE SMALL SHOP

The Lathe

The most important machine is the lathe. This tool, with its attachments, will do the major amount of the work. Home workshop lathes are made in the 9-inch and 10-inch sizes, and some even up to 12-inch. As a rule, the home workshop lathe is not as heavy or as well equipped as the toolroom lathe, but, within its limits, it will do some very fine work.

Quick-change gears are a great time-saver, but are not absolutely necessary. The plain-geared lathe can do everything that is needed. If your budget will permit, purchase a quick-change-geared lathe of the toolroom variety in a size best suited to your intended work. Get a lathe made by a well-known national manufacturer so that you can rely on his reputation to sell a good tool.

The bench-type lathe is very handy if you have room on your bench to set it up; otherwise, get one with its own standards. If set up on the bench, the bench should be well braced and rigid enough to prevent excessive vibration. Provide a capacitator-start motor of at least ½ H.P. Split-phase motors do not have sufficient starting torque to start up under load, and repulsion-start motors are not reversible. The motor should be controlled through a reversing switch.

The size of the hole through the head-stock spindle is quite important, as this limits the size of bar stock you can set up in the chucks. The smaller workshop lathes have only a ¾-inch hole and the larger toolroom lathes have a 1-inch or larger hole. Lathes with plain bronze bearings give very fine service and are the standard type used in large shops, but these bearings must be kept in perfect shape. As they wear, which they certainly do, it will be necessary to refit them to the spindle. This requires careful scraping to a perfect fit, and it may remove enough metal from the bearings to throw the spindle out of line with the ways of the bed. After a refitting of the bearings, it is necessary to carefully check and correct the alignment of the spindle. For this reason, and also because they will run at higher speeds, the tapered roller bearing is preferred for home use.

The length of the bed should be 54 inches, as this will permit turning about 36 inches between centers. The question often comes up as to which is better, a flat bed or one with "V" ways. The pressure of the cutting tool is downward and away from the work, with the greater pressure being downward. It would seem that a wide bearing surface should be used under the heavy pressure. A flat-bed lathe has such a wide bearing surface. Some large and very fine lathes have a bearing surface tilted to take the diagonal resultant of the vertical and horizontal pressures. The "V" ways give nearly as much area to resist the vertical pressure and give the same amount against the horizontal. The flat bed can be more easily ground to accurate dimensions. The ways of the better class of lathes have the wearing surfaces scraped to an accurate fit. There really are good points to both types of beds, and either will give you good service.

The face plate and the driver plate are usually furnished when you purchase the lathe. Chucks are usually bought separately. Two types of chucks will be needed, and these should be heavy-duty, as lighter chucks soon lose their accuracy. One should be of the independent four-jaw variety; the other should be a three-jaw self-centering chuck. Both chucks should be as large as the lathe will handle.

A small-drill chuck, such as a Jacobs chuck fitted to a taper shank, is handy for holding the combined drill and center reamer. This chuck should be of the ⅜-inch size. A larger Jacobs chuck of ½-inch capacity will take the straight-shank drills. You can either purchase these Jacobs chucks with the taper shank attached or get the chucks separately and make your own shanks for them.

A taper-turning attachment is nice to have, but is used so seldom that it is hardly wise to purchase one. One can be made as a work project later. Your lathe should be equipped with a compound slide for the tool holder. This slide has a limited length of travel but can be set to any angle. The tail stock can be offset for turning tapers.

Turning tools of the self-hardened steel variety are the most suitable for the home shop. The ¼-inch square size is used on most of these lathes. Three tool holders of the Armstrong type are needed. One is straight, one has a right-hand offset, and the other a left-hand offset. The cutting tools are obtained in the blank and ground to suit your needs. A parting or cutoff tool is also needed. This is a difficult tool to use, and the blades are easily broken, so supply yourself with several spare blades.

You should make a wooden tray to fit onto the right end of the lathe bed to hold the lathe tools. Divide it into compartments for the tool holders and tool bits. Place a rack with holes for the lathe centers and drill chucks at the rear side. The shanks of the centers are tapered and will bind in the holes if they go clear down to a tight fit, so put a stop bar across the bottom of the holes, so that the ends of the centers will bear on it before the taper becomes tight in the hole. Since you will have to remove this tray at times, put a wooden turn button underneath to keep it on the bed, one which can be quickly released when needed (see Figure 26).

The Drill Press

You should have a bench-type drill press with a distance of 10 inches between the drill and the back column. A motor of ½-H.P. capacity should be mounted on the drill with a double set of speed-reducing pulleys, so that the drill can run slow enough to handle drills up to ½-inch. The motor is mounted with the shaft vertical. It should have ball bearings or a special thrust bearing to take the weight of the armature. It does not have to be a reversible motor. The quill or revolving part of the drill should run on its own self-lubricated ball bearings, and the spindle should slide through the quill. There should be a depth stop to limit the depth of hole.

The table should slide on the rear column and should tilt as well as swing sideways. There should be a movable collar that clamps below the table to support it while it is being swung sideways.

To go with the drill press, you will need a drill-press vise, some bolts and dogs for clamping work to the table, and a "V" block for round work.

The Bench Grinder

A heavy-duty bench grinder is a must. This grinder should have two grinding wheels: one of a coarse grit for quick grinding on heavy work, and one of a fine grit to finish grind tools and drills. These wheels should be driven by a motor of at least ½ H.P. The type of grinder where the wheels are mounted directly on the motor shaft makes a very neat installation, but one where a separate motor is belted to a separate grinding spindle will do just as well.

The wheels should have adjustable rests for holding the work and should have adjustable guards over their tops. Grinding wheels have been known to break from centrifugal force if run above the speed marked by the manufacturer; the greatest danger, however, is that a piece of work may get caught between the rest and the wheel and break the wheel, so you must always keep the rest adjusted up to the wheel and the guard over the wheel.

The wheels will have to be trued up as they wear, so provide an emery-wheel dressing tool. One of the star-wheel type cuts very rapidly and lasts a long time. The points of the stars break down the grains of the wheel. These grains break very easily under a direct blow but last a long time while cutting.

Be sure the wheels of the grinder are in balance. If you install a new wheel and find that it is out of balance, take it back where you got it and ask for another one, as it is very difficult to balance an emery wheel. The center hole of the wheel should be lined with babbitt and bored to a close fit on the spindle.

A drill-grinding attachment is handy if you are not proficient at grinding drills by hand. It will enable you to keep your drills nearly as good as when they were purchased.

Reamers

As drills seldom produce a hole exactly to size and perfectly round, they must be finished with a reamer. For the home workshop, a set of solid hand reamers starting at ¼-inch and increasing by $\frac{1}{16}$ inch up to ½-inch and by ⅛ inch up to 1-inch will meet most of your requirements. Although you may get jobs that will require a reamer other than the ones you have on hand, it will not pay to buy a solid or adjustable reamer for the odd-sized jobs, as you may never have a chance to use it again. Many times a hole can be finish-bored in the lathe without using a reamer.

Taper-Pin Reamers

Taper pins are convenient for fastening collars, sheaves, and handles to shafts when the torque to be transmitted is small. For this sort of work, you should have an assortment of taper pins of the sizes most often used. Hardware stores sell boxes of assorted taper pins and assorted cotter pins. Cotter pins take a straight hole, which can be drilled without the use of a reamer. There is no way of fitting a taper pin, however, except by the use of a taper-pin reamer. You will need a complete set of taper-pin reamers, starting with #0, which is about $\frac{1}{8}$-inch in diameter, and increasing in order up to #5, which will finish-ream for a pin of about $\frac{1}{4}$-inch in diameter. Each reamer overlaps the one next smaller, so with a complete set you can ream and fit any size of pin.

Wire Brush and Buffing Wheel

A power wire brush is very useful for removing rust and paint from the work. It will also cut enough to remove the burr left by other cutters. Be sure to get a heavy- duty brush about 6 inches in diameter. This brush should have stiff wires firmly attached. The cheaper kinds sold in most hardware stores soon start to lose their bristles. These fly out at great speed and can do much damage to your face and eyes. Always wear your safety goggles. When enough wires have worn out to put the wheel out of balance, it will be useless and should be discarded. The wire brush will abrade the surfaces of the softer metals, such as aluminum and brass, and will leave a scratched surface.

When a polished finish is required, the cloth polishing wheel is used. This cloth wheel is charged on the rim with a buffing compound and will produce a highly polished surface. Both the buffing wheel and the wire brush can be mounted on a cheap polishing lathe, which is sold by most hardware stores and hobby shops. This can be belted to a $\frac{1}{4}$-H.P. split-phase motor. Position the starting switch so that you will not have to reach over the wheels to shut it off. If it is not positioned in this way, you may catch your sleeve in the rapidly revolving wheels. The spindle must have good bearings and should be well oiled to stand the high speed at which it runs.

The Band Saw

A most useful tool for the metal-working shop is a small band saw equipped with a metal-cutting blade. The saw can be any model of the home-workshop type, with wheels 12 inches or more in diameter. If the saw is also to be used for sawing wood, it will have to run at the high speed required for wood and should therefore be equipped with a pulley for this speed. When cutting metal, the blade must run at a much slower speed. A countershaft should be installed between the motor and the saw, so that by changing belts, the slower speed can be obtained.

For sawing thin sheet steel, a saw blade having 24 teeth to the inch and running at a speed of 175 feet per minute will do very nicely. This saw can also be used to cut thicker stock. When the work is ⅛ inch thick or over, a faster job can be done if a blade is used that has 14 teeth to the inch and that runs at 150 feet per minute. For general use in the home shop, the saw should be arranged to run at between 150 and 175 feet per minute, and blades of either 18 or 24 teeth to the inch should be used. For the few heavy jobs you will be doing, it is not necessary to have a blade of the most efficient type, but it is essential that the blade be run at near its required speed. A metal-cutting saw cuts best when running relatively slowly and with sufficient pressure to make the teeth bite and not slide over the work.

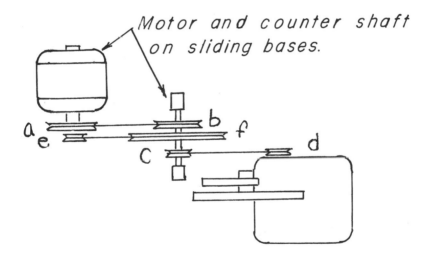

Fig. 2. Band-saw countershaft

When you know the speed of your motor and the size of the wheels of your saw, you can compute the correct size of pulleys needed to give fast and slow speeds. Multiplying the diameter of the wheels in feet by 3.1416 will give you the circumference of the wheel. To find the RPM of the saw wheels: first multiply .26 by the wheel's diameter in feet; then divide the speed of the blade in feet per minute by this number. (See also note at Table 3, p. 80.) Refer to Figure 2 for a diagram of the motor, countershaft, and saw arrangement. Pulley *a* on the motor and pulley *b* on the countershaft should be the same size. Thus, with the countershaft running at the same speed as the motor, the size of pulleys *c* and *d* can be computed to give the fast RPM for sawing wood. The size of pulleys *e* and *f* should now be computed so that, when they are combined with pulleys *c* and *d*, the slow speed for metal sawing will be obtained. Pulleys *e* and *f* should be selected so that the same belt as that used on pulleys *a* and *b* will fit them. Both the motor and the countershaft should be on sliding bases so that the tension of the belts can be adjusted.

The Portable Electric Drill

The small electric drill is one of the most useful tools in the shop. It should have a gear-type chuck that will take up to ¼-inch drills, and its no-load speed should be about 2000 RPM. Do not waste money on one of the light models built to sell for a low price. You can get a speed-reducing attachment that will enable you to use drills up to ½-inch. Also get a rubber sanding disk and a small arbor on which grinding stones and wire brushes can be mounted, for work that cannot be taken to the bench machines (see Figure 3).

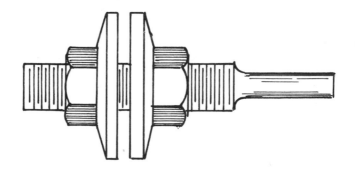

Fig. 3. Arbor for portable electric drill

The High-Speed Grinder

One of the high-speed grinders that take mounted grinding wheels with ⅛-inch shafts will enable you to do fine grinding and to sharpen taps and other tools.

Both of the portable electric tools should be equipped with cords having a ground wire, and the plugs and recepticles should be of the three-prong type that grounds the tool each time it is plugged in.

STORAGE OF MATERIALS

Sheet stock is best stored on edge in bins made of plywood. Since most of your sheet stock will be in the form of the small pieces you can get as scraps from the local iron works or from a dealer in scrap metal, your bins do not have to be large, but you should have enough of them so that the various thicknesses of stock can be stored in separate compartments. Sheet iron, such as galvanized iron, may be obtained in larger sheets, and so you should provide a few larger bins for it.

Bar stock, including pipe, can best be stored on shelves built along one of the walls. The shelves should have solid bottoms and sides high enough to prevent the bars from falling off the shelves. The shelves should be built on brackets with the near side open so that the stock can be removed from it. You will often purchase bar stock in the lengths the dealer has on hand, since his charge for cutting may be more than the cost of the extra material you get. It is always handy to have the correct size of stock on hand when you need it, so be generous in purchasing a supply. Your shelves should be long enough to handle the lengths you get. There should be several short shelves to take care of short cutoff ends.

Large bar stock, which you can get from the local machine shop as they discard it as scrap, can be stored in a bin or box made of wood heavy enough to stand large pieces being dropped into it.

Well-arranged storage bins

Small parts, such as machine screws, nuts, washers, lock washers, cotter pins, and taper pins can be stored in small glass jars. The larger nuts and bolts that are likely to break glass jars should be stored in empty coffee cans. The glass jars are convenient, as they let you see at a glance the amount and kind of each article you have. Each jar should be labeled with the name and size of the article it contains. This label should be painted on the side of the jar in large letters so that continual handling with dirty fingers will not obscure the markings. The jars should be stored on narrow shelves with the marked side toward you. Putting jars of bolts on one shelf and corresponding nuts on the shelf directly below makes it easy to locate the article you want. Do not use tops on the jars or cans—they are just something more to remove— and do not hang the jars from screw tops fastened under the shelves. It takes time to unscrew the jar and more time to replace it. You would soon get in the habit of setting the jar down until you had the time to replace the top, and this would result in a cluttered bench.

A source of very fine alloy steel is old automobile and truck axles. You can get these from junkyards, but they cannot be used in the condition in which you receive them. Parts of them may have been hardened. In any case, they will have residual strains locked in them from the use they were put to. These strains will not prevent your machining them, as will the hardened parts; but, as you remove metal from the strained piece of steel, it will relieve some of the strain, and the remaining piece will spring out of shape. You can never do accurate work with strained steel.

Another source of high-grade tool steel is old broken jackhammer drills or pavement-breaker gads that a local contractor will discard. He will sell these as junk, and you can use them for many jobs. They have been hardened and have locked-in strains due to their being finished in a cold state.

All these steels that have been hardened or that have locked-in strains can be conditioned for use by annealing, as explained in Chapter 13.

Lubricants

You will need a supply of good lubricating oil, such as the type used in your car. This can be purchased in gallon lots and transferred to a squirt can for oiling machines. A good-quality gear grease should also be on hand. You will also use a considerable quantity of cutting oil. A good sulphur-base cutting oil can be purchased in gallon lots and used from a pump-type squirt can.

A large shop will use several kinds of cutting oil. Each has its special use and can be purchased and stored in large quantities. One sulphur-base cutting oil, however, is all that is necessary for the small shop.

2

Layout Work

ALWAYS have good light on the work while you are laying out the dimensions. Use a magnifying glass, if necessary, to see that the intersections are exact.

The tools needed for layout work are: an adequate scale, such as the combination square with the square head, the centering head, and the protractor head; a set of dividers and hermophrodite calipers; a prick punch; and a center punch.

When arcs are to be drawn, make a small prick-punch mark at the center and use a magnifying glass to be sure it is at the exact center. The punch mark must be large enough to prevent the point of the dividers from slipping. A center-punch mark is not as good, since the flat angle of its sides will let the dividers easily slip.

Wherever layout marks are to be made, paint the surface with a colored marking compound. This is a thin lacquer that dries very quickly. Only a thin layer should be applied, because if lacquer is applied too thickly the point of the scriber will tear out chunks of the lacquer and leave a ragged line instead of the clean, sharp line needed for accurate work.

Sometimes, when you must work quickly, you may use a layer of chalk instead of lacquer. The chalk will not leave as sharp a line as the lacquer, so it should never be used for accurate work.

You must have a straight line or straight edge to refer all measurements to. This line can be one edge of the work that has been finished straight; or it can be an outside straight line rigidly fastened to the work, such as a straightedge clamped on; or it can be a flat surface on which the work can rest without being moved.

A straightedge is liable to slip when you are scribing a line, so always clamp the straightedge with two clamps. The mark to which a straightedge is to be set should be made so that the exact position of the mark can be seen after the straightedge has covered up half the mark. A straight line is hard to see when it is drawn near a straightedge; therefore, draw an arc, which will enable you to see the point at which the straightedge is tangent to the arc. An X or V mark shows you the intersection on the exact point (see Figure 4).

Laying off a line parallel to a reference line can be done by measuring out the same distance with a scale at two points as far apart as the work will permit and then scribing a line through the two measured points. This requires great care when measuring out to the marks and allows two chances of making an error. A better method is to set the dividers, or hermaphrodite calipers, to the proper distance and then scribe little arcs through which the line may be drawn. This reduces the chances·of error.

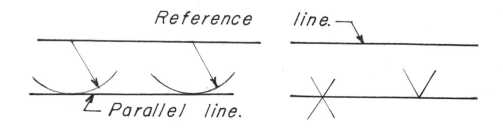

Fig. 4. Parallel lines

You will often need a line that is at a 90° angle to the reference line and that passes through a given point. If you are working from a straight edge that will take the head of your combination square, it is easy to scribe such a line. But if you cannot use the combination square, you can draw such a line with the dividers (see Figure 5). Make a small

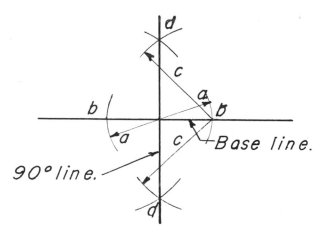

Fig. 5. 90° line

prick-punch mark on the main line where the 90° line is to intersect it. With this as a center and the dividers set to any convenient radius, *a*, scribe the arc at *b*. Make small prick-punch marks at *b* and, with any radius, *c*, draw the crossing arcs at *d*. A line drawn through these inter-sections at *d* will be at a 90° angle to the reference line and will pass through the desired intersection point.

It is sometimes necessary to lay out work to the center of a ring where you cannot actually mark the center (see Figure 6). If you can fill up

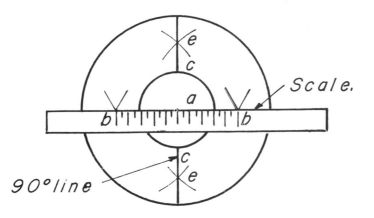

Fig. 6. 90° line in a ring

the hole with a temporary filler, do so. This may be in the form of a plug driven into the hole or of a piece of sheet metal soldered across the hole. Soft solder can easily be removed afterwards without injuring the work. When extreme accuracy is not required, a hardwood plug will do. You can scribe a line across the hardwood, but it is then almost impossible to make an accurate center-punch mark since the punch will follow the grain of the wood and may fall off center. When a punch mark is required, use the metal closure rigidly fastened in place. The top of the closure must be at the same level as the surrounding ring for accurate work. The thickness of a thin sheet of metal will not make an appreciable error, and so it can be soldered to the surface of the ring.

When it is not practicable to put a closure across the hole, a line at 90° can still be accurately drawn passing through the center of the ring (see Figure 6). Clamp a scale across the opening with point *a* exactly halfway between points *c*. This can be measured with a second scale. The clamps can then be adjusted until point *a* is at the center of the ring. Now mark points *d* the same distance from point *a* and make small prick-punch marks at points *d*. With the scale removed, the intersecting arcs at *e* can be drawn, and the line *e–e* will pass through the center of the ring and be at a 90° angle to the first line.

When laying out for drilled holes, make a small prick-punch mark at the center and from there scribe a circle of the diameter that is to be drilled. Make four prick-punch marks at the quarter points and exactly on the circumference of this circle. These are points through which the finished hole is to pass. If you notice any error when the drill starts, the error can be corrected by the outside marks, since the center mark is now gone. The prick-punch mark at the center should be enlarged with a center punch before drilling, since the wide point of the drill will not enter and follow the small prick-punch mark. For large holes, it is a good idea to draw a smaller reference circle inside the finished diameter, using the same four guide marks. The error of the drill can then be detected before you go too far. If the prick-punch marks—which should be left half on the surface and half drilled away—spoil the finish of the surface, the reference circle should be drawn and the four marks placed just *inside* the finished edge, so that they will be removed when drilled (see Figure 7).

To find the center of a shaft, use the centering head of the combination square. As there may be a slight irregularity to the surface of the

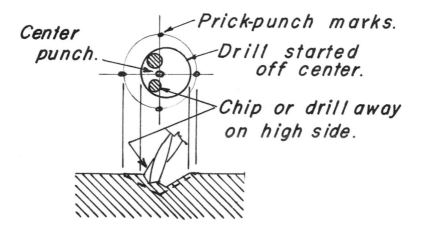

Center punch. — Prick-punch marks.

Drill started off center.

Chip or drill away on high side.

Fig. 7. Locating a drilled hole

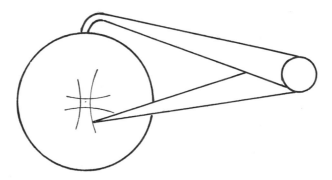

Fig. 8. Finding center with hermaphrodite calipers

shaft, many lines should be drawn from many points, all passing through the center, and the mean of their intersections taken as the center of the shaft.

Hermaphrodite calipers are best for finding the center when the surface is irregular and when the centering head cannot be used. Scribe arcs from known surfaces and take the mean of their intersection (see Figure 8).

If points on a work piece must be laid out at an equal distance from a given surface, this surface can be placed on some known flat surface, such as the table of the drill press, and the surface gauge can then be used to scribe the required line.

The surface gauge can also be used to find the center of a shaft. Place the shaft in a "V" block resting on the flat surface and scribe lines passing near the center of the shaft, turning the shaft between each mark. The mean of these lines will be the center of the shaft. By trial, you can draw four lines so that they meet exactly at the center.

When you have to lay out a hole to match another already drilled, such as the clearance hole through which a screw is to pass to fit a tapped hole, you will need to know the exact center of the original hole and its distance from some reference line. The fitting of a new flange to a mating surface that already has the bolt holes drilled and tapped is such a job. The centers of the tapped holes cannot be determined accurately, but lines tangent to the outside of the holes can be drawn. You cannot draw lines tangent to a hole that has threads in it, since the edge of the hole is different at different places on the thread, but if a bolt is screwed into the tapped hole making a tight fit, a straight edge can be held against the threads, and tangent lines can be drawn to the outside of the threads. The same applies to a smooth hole. It is difficult to see the edge of the hole, so put in a smooth plug and draw lines tangent to it.

Toolmakers' buttons, used for very accurately locating a hole to be bored, work on this same principle of measuring to a tangent to a known circle. The button is a hardened and ground ring, ground to exactly ½-inch diameter and with a ¼-inch hole through it. In use, the approximate center of the hole is laid out as usual, and a hole is tapped for a machine screw smaller than the hole in the button. The button is clamped in place by a washer under the head of the machine screw. The button can now be shifted by the amount of clearance between the hole in the button and the diameter of the machine screw, until it is in the exact position of the required hole to be bored. Measurements to the button can be made very accurately by the use of micrometers, gauge blocks, and thickness-feeler gauges, working from some known and accurately located base line. The button is clamped in its final position, and the work is set up in the lathe until the dial indicator shows the button to be running on a true center. The button is then removed, and a subhole is drilled where the machine screw was placed. This drilled hole will not be absolutely perfect, as it is next to impossible to lay out and drill a hole in an exact location. Besides, the machine-screw hole may have been slightly at error, and this will force the larger drill to follow it. The hole must be bored with a tool in the tool post until perfectly concentric, but it may be finished with a reamer.

When the two surfaces are together, the hole it is desired to meet is covered up. Unless you can scribe the holes from the far side, it will be necessary to transfer the center of the hole to the top surface of the meeting flange (see Figure 9). Draw four tangent lines on the original piece, two parallel to the reference edge and two at 90° to it (lines *b–b* and *d–d* of Figure 9). The ends of these lines are marked on the exterior surfaces, so that when the two parts are placed together they can be transferred to the top surface, and lines *a–a* and *c–c* can be drawn. These lines will be tangent to the required hole.

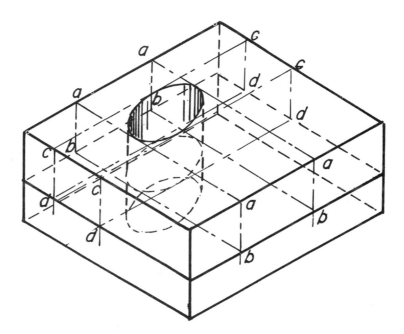

Fig. 9. Transferring a hole—straight edges

If it is not possible to extend all the lines to the exterior and thus to transfer their ends to the top surface, the lines parallel to the reference edge can be measured and laid off at the same distance, and the other two lines can be transferred from their end markings.

When the reference edge is curved, as the outside of a flange or other circular object, you cannot draw lines at 90° to it. If you can find the center of each piece, lines can be drawn through these centers and tangent to the outside of the bolt, as at *e* and *f* of Figure 10.

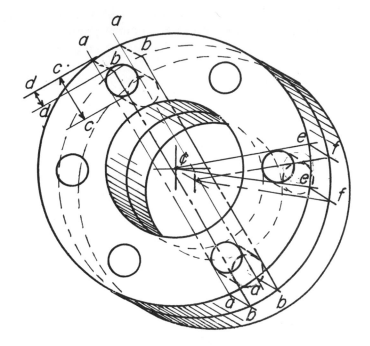

Fig. 10. Transferring a hole—curved edges

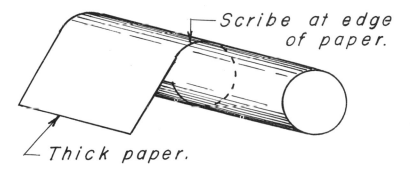

Scribe at edge
of paper.

Thick paper.

Fig. 11. To draw a line around a cylinder

The position of the mating pieces must be marked so they will be placed in the same position each time. The little transfer marks on the sides should be numbered so that they do not get mixed up when transferred. The distances c and d from the reference edge are measured for each hole, using the depth gauge or hermaphrodite calipers. The reference edges must be finished, either by machining or by filing, so they are flush for placing the transfer marks. Where there are holes diametrically opposed, lines can be drawn tangent to these two holes, as at a and b of Figure 10, and these lines can be transferred from their end marks.

To draw a line square around a pipe or shaft, use a piece of heavy paper with one straight edge. Wrap this tightly around the work so that the straight edge meets; then mark along the edge of the paper (see Figure 11).

For rough marking, use a soapstone stick, sharpened to a chisel point. This makes a mark that is easily seen, but it is not accurate enough for finish work.

For marking metal that is to be heated, as for forging, make a row of heavy prick-punch marks along the line. The punch upsets the metal around the hole, and, as it is heated, the ring around the hole will get red before the rest of the piece and can be easily seen. As it cools, the ring will get dark first and can still be easily seen.

Fig. 12. Surface gauge

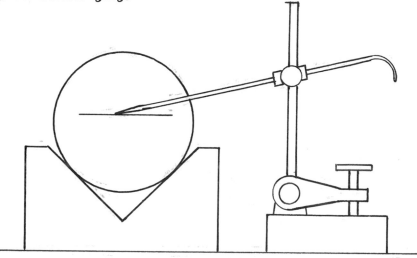

Surface gauge. The drill-press table is being used as a surface plate.

3

Bench Work

CHIPPING and filing are the two methods most often used for removing metal without the use of machine tools. Hand-scraping is a third method, often employed to produce a true flat surface on very fine work. You should become proficient in all these operations.

CHIPPING

A heavy-duty vise, the proper chisel for the kind of metal being cut, and a hammer of the correct weight are essential for doing good work. Continual hammering will tend to make the work slip in the vise: this can be partially prevented by fitting a block of wood under the work and bearing down tightly, both on the bottom slide of the movable jaw of the vise and on the bottom surface of the work. As the end grain of wood is much harder than the side grain, this block of wood should be cut from end-grain stock. Since the downward movement of the work in the vise accounts for about half the slippage, the block of wood will stop half the movement, cutting the slippage in half.

The weight of the hammer is very important. A hammer that is too light will make the cutting go very slowly and will soon tire you out, as well as doing damage to the chisel. Many light blows tend to peen over the head of the chisel, soon getting it into a dangerous condition. Working with a hammer that is too heavy will also tire you and will tend to move the work in the vise. You should select a hammer that is best suited to you. There should be hammers of various weights available in the shop.

The proper type of chisel used is also very important and depends on the type of metal being cut. The hardness and the angle of the chisel's cutting edge vary for different metals. The edge should be tempered to a medium straw color for steel and to a dark purple for brass. A hard edge will not stand up to the harder metals like steel and cast iron, but will crumble away very quickly; it can be used for soft metals, however. The chisel is forged to an edge thick enough to have the necessary strength, which is ground to the correct cutting angle. For brass and the softer metals, the included angle of the cutting edge can be 40° to 50°. For mild steel and cast iron, an angle of 60° is better; for cast steel, an edge at 70° will stand up longest. The flat chisel and the cape chisel are usually ground the same on both sides, but for some conditions, it may be necessary to grind one side to more of an angle. The round-nose chisel is ground only on the flat side.

31

The blunt angle of the cutting edge will not make cutting more difficult, since the action of a chisel is a wedging action that lifts the chip
and starts to tear it away as the cutting edge enters the metal. This
leaves the cutting edge working in metal already starting to separate,
and it has little more to do than guide the cut.

The level of the work in the vise must be adjusted to your height,
so that your striking arm can swing freely. A short man should stand on
a raised platform.

Keyways

Keyways are cut by machine at the factory, but often, in repair work,
it will be necessary to cut a keyway when the shaft cannot be set up in
any available machine, and hand methods must then be used.

To chip a keyway by hand, first accurately scribe the outline of the
slot on the shaft. After carefully locating the centers, drill a hole at each
end. the same width and depth as the slot. Be sure the holes are exactly
tangent to the sides of the slot. Clamp a straight edge along one side of
the slot. A piece of small steel angle or an angle block clamped on the
shaft makes a good straight edge, which will guide the chisel in getting
the slot started in a straight line. If a straight edge cannot be fitted, the
slot can still be started in a straight line by making very careful small
cuts. After the slot is well established, the chisel will follow it as the
slot is deepened.

To cut the slot, a cape chisel should be ground to the exact width
of the keyway, with the sides parallel. The cutting edge must be exactly
square with the sides so that there will be no tendency for the chisel to
be forced sideways by a slanting point. Hold the chisel parallel and
square with the shaft, and make small cuts, so that the sides of the slot
will come out in a finished condition. Allow for the thickness to be removed by the file when the width of the chisel is ground; then you can
dress the sides with a bent file. Since a key must be fitted tight, it is best
to allow for a little filing, as it is easier to fit a key into a tight slot than
into a loose one. Keys that are loose in the keyway will wear quickly and
may ruin the shaft.

Chipping a Surface

There are two methods of chipping a flat surface. If the amount of
metal to be removed is thin, it can best be done by removing one big chip of
the full depth. Cut on a curve so the chisel is working on the arc of the
curve; do not cut the full width of the chisel. This enables you to keep a
good chip ahead of the chisel, which will direct it in the cut (see Figure 17).

Where the amount of metal to be removed is thick, it is best to groove
the surface with a cape chisel and then remove the ridges remaining between the grooves with a flat chisel (see Figure 16).

For chipping the softer metals, like brass or aluminum, a sharper
angle of cutting edge may speed up the cut, but a 60° edge will still do
the work very well. When chipping a mild steel, you can pick up the chip
and cut a continuous curl of steel, but the more brittle metals, such as
cast iron and brass, will make chips that break off in small pieces. Since

these chips fly off in all directions remember to wear your safety goggles while chipping these metals (see Figure 13).

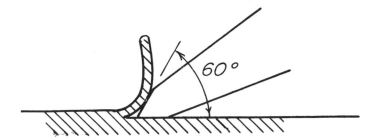

Fig. 13. Chip forming

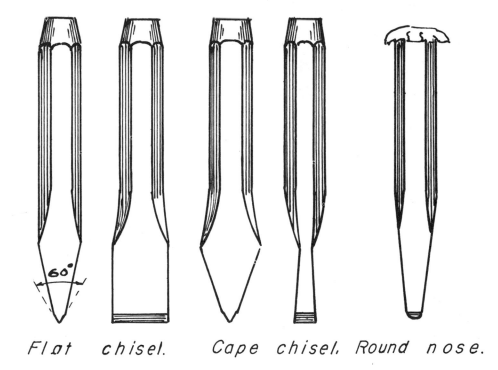

Flat chisel. Cape chisel. Round nose.

Fig. 14. Cold chisels

Fig. 15. Soft vise jaws

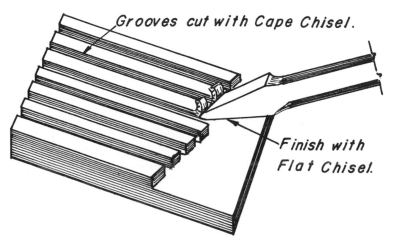

Fig. 16. Chipping with a cape chisel

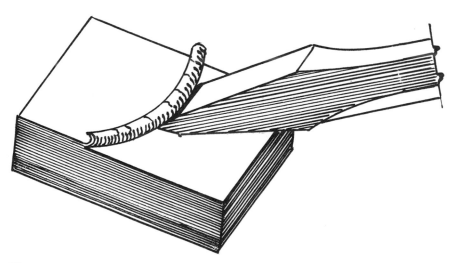

Fig. 17. Chipping with curved chip

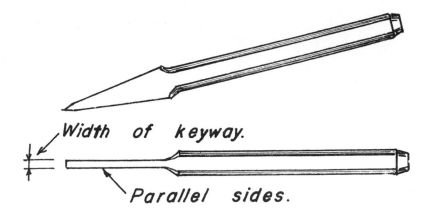

Width of keyway.

Parallel sides.

Fig. 18. Cape chisel ground to cut keyways

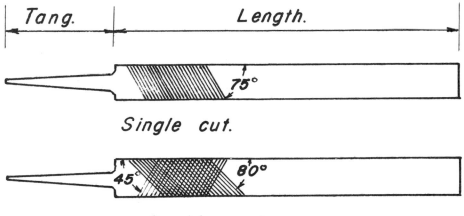

Cape chisel.

Guide angle or "V" block.

Drill end holes.

Fig. 19. Chipping a key seat

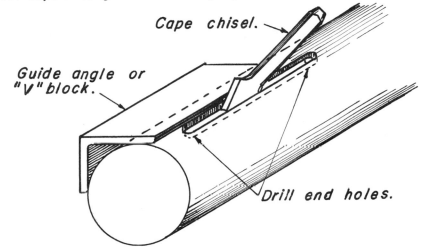

Tang. | *Length.*

75°

Single cut.

45° 80°

Double cut.

Fig. 20. Hand files

When you are using a cape chisel to cut grooves, you will find that the corners of the chisel soon get dull or break away. This slows up the cutting and prevents you from doing accurate work. For this reason, when the surface is to be finished with a flat chisel, it is better to groove the surface with a round-nose chisel or gouge. It is hard to keep a round-nose chisel in a straight line, since any error in holding it plumb will turn the top of the chisel to an angle, and the pressure of the chip on the top of the chisel, which is ground flat, will make the chisel work sideways. A cape chisel, which has the top and the bottom cutting surfaces ground parallel, will not work sideways and can be used to cut a groove to a straight line, such as a keyway. The round-nose chisel will not dull the corners quickly, as will a cape chisel.

Where the hammer strikes it, the head of a cold chisel must be kept in shape. Repeated blows will cause the end to become deformed like a rivet and eventually to curl over and split, when pieces may fly off from it with great force. To prevent this, keep the head of the chisel ground to a good chamfer. The head of the chisel must be kept soft when the chisel is tempered. If it is hard, it will shatter like glass under the hammer (see Figure 14).

FILING

The file is probably the most useful finishing tool in the shop. Its proper use is one of the most difficult for the metalworker to learn and is one in which he should become very proficient.

The blade or body of a file has teeth of a suitable type cut into it, after which it is hardened. The tang, to which the handle is attached, is left soft to prevent it from breaking. A hardened file is very brittle, and a hardened tang could snap under the side pressure needed for proper cutting action. The various operations where filing is involved make it necessary that there be a wide variety of files available. There is a type of file to suit every need, and some will do certain work better than others.

Files are named and classified according to length, sectional form, and number of teeth to the inch. The number of teeth may vary slightly with different manufacturers. The following classifications are about average:

Rough-cut	20 teeth per inch
Middle-cut	25 teeth per inch
Bastard-cut	30 teeth per inch
Second-cut	40 teeth per inch
Smooth-cut	50 to 60 teeth per inch
Dead-cut	100 or more teeth per inch

The teeth may be single cut or double cut, as indicated in Figure 20. Single-cut files have the teeth cut at an angle of 65° to 85° to the center line. Single-cut files are used on very hard metal. Double-cut files have two sets of teeth, the first being cut at 40° to 45° and the second cut at 70° to 80°. This gives a tooth shaped so that the front part slopes backward, with what is called a negative rake. The angle of the cut to the axis of the file is designed to give a slicing cut that will cause the chip to curl away from the tooth more readily than from straight-cut teeth.

Files can be obtained that are cut for the particular metal being worked on. Thus 30° and 60°-angled files are best for mild steel, while the first cut for brass is nearly 90°.

Flat files are double cut on the face and single cut on the edges, and they taper both in width and thickness toward the end. The hand file is parallel in its width and tapers slightly for about one third its length. One edge is "safe," that is, it has no teeth, and can be used in a corner where only one side is to be cut. Pillar files are narrow and rectangular in section, may be parallel or tapered, and are usually double cut. The square file is double cut on each face and usually tapers on at least one third of its length. Round files are usually single cut and, when tapered, are called rat-tail files. Half-round files are usually double cut on the flat side and single cut on the curved surface. They taper both in width and thickness. Triangular files or three-cornered files are single cut and usually tapered. There are many other types of files for special purposes.

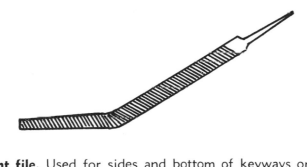

Fig. 21. Bent file. Used for sides and bottom of keyways or similar depressed surfaces.

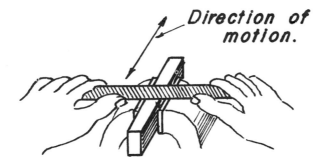

Fig. 22. Draw-filing

The needle files, sometimes called Swiss files, are a series of small files 6 to 8 inches long, made in the various shapes and having very fine teeth. They have an integral handle, and are used principally in finishing very fine and intricate work. They are easily broken, and very little pressure should be applied to them. Rifflers are files that curve upward in an arc on the ends so that the bottom of a sinking can be reached. It is often possible to bend or offset a file to allow you to reach the bottom or sides of a piece of work, as when dressing a keyway. A suitable file is heated to a dull red and bent to the desired shape by striking it with a lead or other soft-faced hammer, using a block of lead as an anvil. After shaping, the file is again heated to a dull red and quenched in water. The tang is not quenched. This will restore hardness in the cutting teeth.

The main fault in filing occurs when the file is allowed to rock on each stroke, giving a convex surface. This can only be prevented by having both arms free so that you swing from the shoulders. Use a platform to stand on so that your arms pivot naturally at the shoulders; move them as nearly alike as possible. Grasp the handle of the file in your right hand and steady the point with your left hand. Use a sliding motion toward the right for a few cuts; then slide toward the left. Turn and file in all directions with the file held flat so that only the high places will be cut. The difference in the surface finish will show you where the high places are as you reverse the direction of cut.

A file has teeth designed to cut in only one direction. Allowing the teeth to slide over the work tends to dull them more rapidly than when they are cutting, so use only enough pressure on the return stroke to guide the file into position for the next cutting stroke, which is then done under full pressure.

When rough-filing to remove metal quickly, you need a large file with coarse teeth and must apply considerable pressure to make the teeth bite. If the pressure is not heavy enough, the file will bounce on each stroke and start cutting ridges of the same spacing as the pitch of the teeth on the file. When this happens you should alter the angle of stroke of the file or else change to a file with a smaller pitch. Sliding the file sideways at each stroke will tend to prevent this cutting of ridges and will produce a straighter surface.

When filing a straight edge on a piece of stock, file crosswise with a sliding stroke, which will remove metal rapidly, and then turn the file lengthwise and work parallel to the edge. This will produce an edge free from hollows, but it may be convex with a high place in the middle. This is because it is difficult to move a file in perfectly flat strokes, and a rocking motion takes place that will reduce the ends more than the center. To correct this, apply a thin coat of marking paste—such as prussian blue ground in oil, which is used by painters for tinting paint—to the edge of the blade of your combination square. This blade is ground to a true straight edge, and when the blued edge is rubbed over the work, the bluing will mark the high places, which can then be filed until a straight edge results.

After a flat surface has been filed and tested on the surface plate to the finished condition, it should be draw-filed to produce a finished surface. Draw-filing is liable to remove more material at the center than at the ends of the stroke, so the direction of filing should be varied to equalize the cutting in all directions. After draw-filing, the surface can be polished with fine emery cloth and oil (see Figure 22).

It is best to draw-file a finished edge. Draw-filing is done by turning the file at 90° to the work and moving it sideways. This prevents the rocking motion of straight filing since it is easy to hold both ends of the file at the same level and thus to produce an edge square with the work. The file, when moving sideways in draw-filing, makes a more shearing cut between the angle of the teeth of the file and the work. Chips are not so liable to clog the teeth, and the file will finish the surface without scratching. Hollow places can develop when draw-filing, so be sure to keep a straight line. Have the edge straight before draw-filing to a finish.

An easy way to file the edge of a piece of work to a straight line is to set the scribed line even with the top of the vise jaw; this makes the top of the jaw a guide for filing. For work wider than the width of the jaw, some other piece of stock having a straight edge can be clamped on as a guide. A piece of cold rolled bar is usually straight enough for this. Of course, care must be used not to file the straight edge, but just down to it. Thin work will vibrate under the file, so you should clamp a stiff piece onto the back, with the top in line with the guiding straight edge. A pair of small steel angles make good straight edges, since they are stiff enough to clamp tight near the center. One end can be held in the vise, and a "C" clamp can be put on the other end.

Filing a flat surface is similar to filing a straight edge. After it has been chipped as near as possible to the finished dimension—if chipping was necessary—rough-file nearly to the scribed guidelines, continually testing for high spots by spreading the bluing on a true flat surface and then rubbing the work on the blued surface. Carefully file down the high spots shown by the bluing. This is best done by using the end of the file, touching only the blued spots, and preventing any rocking motion from reducing the edges.

When the rough-filing has brought the work to the required size and when the bluing shows that it is flat, the surface should be draw-filed and tested until the bluing shows a true and satisfactory surface. Keep the teeth of the file clean by frequently removing the chips that stick in the teeth with a wire brush or a file card. Your power wire brush does a fine job of cleaning a file. A hand wire brush or file card will frequently skip a chip that is wedged tight between the teeth, and these should be removed with the point of a scriber or a similar instrument to prevent them from scratching the finished surface. Rubbing chalk onto the teeth, or oiling the file will tend to prevent chips from sticking between the teeth.

The finished surface should be smooth enough to be polished with a fine grade of emery cloth. In using emery cloth, do not hold it in your hand or put pressure on it with your fingers, as this will produce an uneven surface. If the surface to be polished is large, fasten the emery cloth to a flat block of wood and use this to polish with. If necessary, it can still be tested on the blued surface plate, and the high spots can be rubbed accordingly. If the surface to be polished is small, fasten a large sheet of emery cloth to a flat surface and rub the work onto it.

Always rub in the same direction so that the finished surface, which is a scratched surface, will have the scratches parallel and the same finish throughout. Using successively finer grades of emery cloth will increase the polish of the surface. Each finer grade must remove the scratches made by the previous cloth. If a high polish is required, the cloth buffing wheel, charged with a buffing compound, will have to be used. A buffing wheel can cut enough to give a curved surface, especially on the edges, so care must be used.

SCRAPING

In former days, hand-scraping was used to produce a true flat surface. Today, in production jobs, grinding has replaced hand-scraping. For very fine work, hand-scraping is still used. Sometimes the surface is lapped. You should be familiar with both methods, since you may be working on a job that will require very fine fitting.

You will need hand-scraping tools and a true flat surface to blue and on which the work can be tested. The table of your drill press was probably ground; it is therefore a fairly good flat surface, but it may not be perfectly true. In production work, the rough castings are often ground to a finished surface without first machining them. The grinding must cut down the high spots and at the same time finish the low spots. Under the heavy pressure needed for fast cutting, both the work piece and the grinding wheel may spring away and leave a high spot. Of course, finish-grinding at low pressure will tend to remove these high spots, but you do not know how carefully the table was ground. Test it by bluing the blade of the combination square and by trying it in all directions. If it is not true, do not use it for extremely accurate work.

Shops doing fine surface finishing will be equipped with a surface plate. This is an iron casting with deep ribs on the underside to prevent distortion. The surface has been very accurately finished by scraping or lapping, and when this surface is covered with a thin coat of bluing, it can be used for testing another surface for flatness. In a general jobbing shop or a home workshop you may not find a surface plate, but the table of the drill press will serve for many jobs that do not require great accuracy.

Scraping tools can be made from worn-out files. For flat surfaces, grind the end of a flat file square across the end, making two sharp, square cutting edges. The flat side of the file should first be ground to remove the file teeth at the scraping end. The end should be slightly curved so it will cut at the center and the corners will not dig in. A long and short three-cornered scraper can be ground from an old three-cornered file. The cutting edges, after being ground, should be sharpened on an oilstone and kept sharp during use.

For scraping a flat surface, after it has been machined to the required dimension, rub the blued surface plate over it, and carefully remove the blued spots with the flat end scraper. Repeat this until the blue spots are small and evenly spaced. It is seldom necessary to continue scraping until the entire surface is evenly blued. The uniform distribution of spots of equal size will indicate a flat surface where the difference between the high and low spots is extremely small. In making your scraping cuts, cross the strokes so as to equalize the cuts and to prevent the forming of ridges.

Finely fitted plain bearings are scraped in by a similar process. The shaft is blued and the high spots removed with the three-cornered scraper. On the final fitting, the bearing should be clamped up tight to its running position. Only a very thin layer of bluing should be used since any thickness of the bluing will tend to fill the low spots and to give the appearance of a uniform surface.

4
The Lathe

THERE are many kinds of lathes. Most of the automatic lathes are designed for a particular kind of work; within their limitations, these machines can be set up to repeat any operation, requiring only to be fed with raw stock and kept properly oiled. Lathes of this type are seldom found in a jobbing shop. While the student should know how to set them up and should be familiar with their operation, skill in handling these machines is not part of a general training in machine-shop practice. The manufacturers of these machines maintain trained instructors who teach operators how to get the most out of these lathes.

The ordinary engine lathe (see Figures 23 and 24) is the machine used to turn work in most shops. It is so versatile that, with the proper attachments, it can do a great variety of work.

In all lathes, the work must be able to revolve at various speeds. There must be a cutting tool that can be controlled and that will withstand the heavy pressures required for cutting metal. This tool must move on accurate slides, both for lengthwise travel and for cross-feed. These movements are controlled by feed screws or rack-and-gear feed, and may be either hand-fed or power-fed.

The various parts of an engine lathe are shown in Figure 23, as follows:

A. Head stock	O. Compound slide
B. Spindle cone	P. "T" slot
C. Drive belt	Q. Cross-feed slide
D. Back gears	R. Rack for longitudinal feed
E. Drive plate or face plate	S. Lead screw
F. Head center	T. Hand-feed wheel
G. Tail center	U. Power-feed clutch
H. Tail stock	V. Feed selector
I. Tail-stock ram	W. Half-nut lever
J. Tail-stock ram locking lever	X. Apron
K. Tail-stock feed wheel	Y. Saddle or carriage
L. Tail-stock clamping nut	Z. Gear-change levers
M. Bed or ways	a. Feed-reverse lever
N. Tool post	b. Motor in leg

Figure 23 shows a belt-driven lathe of the ordinary type. The belt drive may be underneath (with the motor in the leg of the lathe), behind the lathe (with the motor on a bracket), or overhead from a countershaft. In any case, the various speeds of the spindle are obtained by shifting

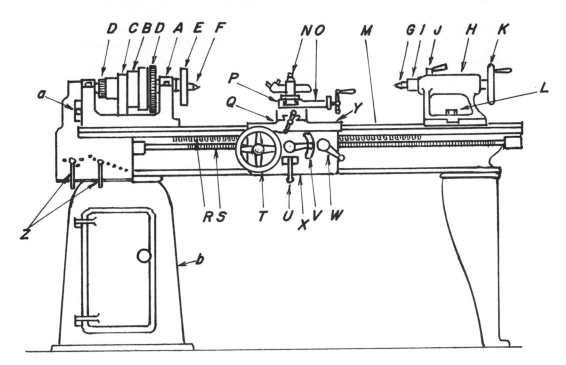

Fig. 23. Motor-driven lathe with belt underneath

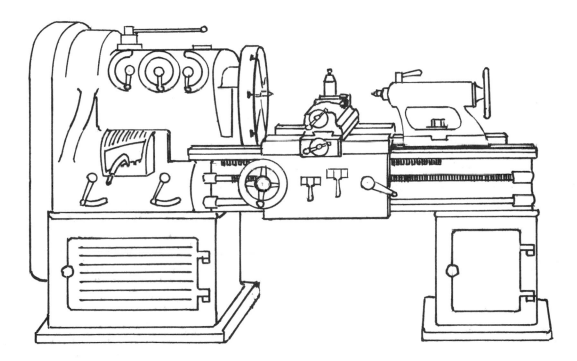

Fig. 24. Geared-head lathe

the belt to the different steps of the cone pulley. This means that there must be a way of relieving the tension and shifting the short belts used in the motor drive. Since the number of speeds available from a cone pulley is limited, back gears are used to obtain slower speeds. The more expensive lathes use a single-belt pulley to drive a change-gear box, equipped with sliding gears and a clutch to get the desired speed for the head-stock spindle. Figure 24 shows a geared-head lathe.

Most heavy-duty lathes use plain bronze bearings, but some of the smaller popular lathes use tapered roller bearings. A tapered roller bearing will keep its adjustment over a long life and will revolve at high speeds without overheating. Plain bronze bearings tend to heat at high speeds and heavy pressures.

The lathe bed is a heavy casting, well cross-braced to prevent distortion. The ways on which the carriage and tail-stock slide rest are very accurately finished by grinding or scraping. Some manufacturers use a "V" shape for the ways, and some use a flat bed. Others use a combination of flat bed and "V" ways to get as wide a bearing surface as possible under the heavy pressure of the cutting tool.

The spindle nose of the head stock is designed to take a tapered center on which the work is supported. This center fits into a tapered hole in the spindle. Since the spindle is hollow, with a hole along its full length that is larger than the tapered hole for the center, a sleeve, or bushing, fitting a larger tapered hole, is used to support the center. The smaller lathes have a thread and shoulder turned on the outside of the spindle nose to receive the face plates, or chucks, which are screwed up against the

Geared-head toolroom lathe. The top of the carriage of a similar lathe is visible in the foreground.

shoulder. The larger modern lathes use a cone-shaped nose, with a key to drive the chuck and an external thread and nut to draw the chuck up tight on the cone. This cone mounting of chucks is standardized, so that chucks made by any manufacturer may be used on any lathe equipped with a cone nose.

The cone pulley of the head stock is not keyed to the spindle but is free to revolve on the spindle. The right-hand gear of the back-gear train is keyed to the spindle, and there is a latch between the cone pulley and this gear. When the back gears are being used, the cone pulley is disconnected from this fixed gear and the cone pulley revolves on the spindle as a countershaft. When the back gears are not used, they are swung out of mesh, and the cone pulley is latched to the fixed gear so that the drive is direct from the cone pulley to the spindle.

The tail stock is arranged to be clamped to any position along the ways. It also can be moved sideways to turn tapers or to correct the alignments of the tail center with the head center. The ram or sliding part is fed by a screw and hand wheel and has a tapered hole to receive the tail center, which is hardened to withstand the wear of the revolving work. The ram has a keyway to prevent its turning, and there is a clamp to lock the ram in any position. On many lathes, this clamp is on one side and has a tendency to move the ram off center when clamped. Some manufacturers use a self-centering clamp to prevent this movement and thus increase the accuracy of their lathe. Many manufacturers use one "V" way and one flat way for the tail stock. On very large lathes, the tail stock

Large geared-head lathe. This photograph shows the separate feed rod for turning and cross-feed, leaving the lead screw for screw cutting only. The lower bar controls the main drive clutch. The reverse lever is also on the carriage. The operator has full control while standing at the carriage.

is too heavy to be moved by hand, and so a crank is supplied, which engages the rack under the ways for moving the tail stock.

The tool post is controlled by the several movements of the slides of the carriage or saddle. Several types of tool holders are fitted to various lathes. The most common one is the tool post with a rectangular slot to receive the tool. The tool is supported on a rocker or wedge that allows some adjustment of the height of the cutting edge. The lower end of the tool post fits into the "T" slot of the compound slide.

The compound slide is adjustable to feed at any angle. Its base is graduated in degrees for setting off the angles. It can be removed for the attachment of other appliances for milling or grinding operations. The feed is entirely by hand.

The cross slide is rigidly attached to the carriage and is set at exactly 90° to the ways. On most lathes, the feed is either by hand or by power.

The carriage or saddle slides on the ways on top of the bed. There is a hand wheel at the lower left-hand corner, which allows hand-feed through a train of reduction gears to a rack under the top of the bed. All these slides have adjustable gibs for freedom of movement and elimination of any backlash in the slides. The carriage also has a locking nut in the top right-hand corner, so that it can be fastened while making a facing cut.

On the front of the carriage is the apron, which holds the controls for the various motions of the carriage and cross slide. There is a clutch for engaging the power feed and a selector lever for selecting either

Small belt-driven lathe. The motor is housed in the cabinet below the head stock. The large lower lever releases the tension on the belts when they are being shifted. On the end of the head-stock spindle is the hand wheel of the draw-in bar of the collet chucks. On the wall behind the lathe is a rack containing collets of various sizes. This lathe is also equipped with a taper attachment.

longitudinal feed or cross feed. On some lathes, there is no selector lever, and each feed has its own clutch. These clutches are interlocked, so that more than one cannot be engaged at the same time. On the more modern lathes, the apron is made as a double-walled well, giving two supports to the various shafts on which the gears revolve and forming an oil reservoir in which the gears can operate. The gears that power the two feeds are driven from a sliding worm gear, riding in a spline cut the length of the feed screw. The larger lathes use a separate feed rod containing the spline rather than cutting the spline on the feed screw and reserving the screw entirely for thread cutting. Some lathes, having the separate feed rod, also have the power-feed clutch in the change-gear box with a clutch rod parallel to the feed rod, so that the clutch handle rides on the carriage apron.

The lead screw enables an engine lathe to cut screw threads of almost any pitch other than the fixed pitch of the lead screw. This lead screw is driven through a train of gears by a pinion attached to the head-stock spindle. To be able to cut right-hand or left-hand threads, it is necessary that the direction of rotation of the lead screw can be reversed. Some lathes use a set of tumbler gears at the spindle, while others use sliding gears in the quick-change-gear box. In any case, the first gear of the gear train is called the *stud gear*, and it is the same size as, and revolves at the same speed as, the gear on the spindle. The gears between the stud gear and the screw gear can be changed to give the proper ratio of screw to the spindle speed to cut the desired pitch.

Plain-geared lathes have slotted brackets that can be adjusted to take any arrangement of gears in the train between the stud and the screw.

Large automatic duplicating lathe. A template of the profile to be turned is set up on the control frame behind the carriage, and hydraulic controls cause the tool to follow the contour of the template. Once set up, it will repeat each operation.

These are covered with a swinging safety cover, and only the gears in use are set up on the lathe at one time. It is necessary to open this cover and to set up a new train of gears when a thread is to be cut or when the feed is set for turning. There is a plate attached to the lathe that tells what gears to use for the various threads to be cut.

Quick-change-gear lathes have a cone of gears permanently attached to the screw, and tumbler gears that can be shifted by two levers to give any combination of gears possible with the gear cone. These tumbler gears are driven from the stud gear by a train of gears, which can be changed to further extend the range of the cone of gears.

All lathes use a split nut, called a *half-nut,* that opens when not feeding and closes over the thread of the lead screw when cutting a thread. The half-nut is controlled by a lever near the lower right side of the apron. This lever is interlocked with the power-feed selector so that the power feed cannot be engaged while screw cutting. A dial indicator geared to the lead screw revolves when the carriage is stationary, and the marks on its top indicate when the half-nut should be closed to engage the proper thread of the lead screw. There are several marks on the indicator, and on most lathes the half nut may be engaged at any of the marks for even-numbered thread pitches; but for odd-numbered pitches, it can be closed only on the same mark used in starting the cut.

Turret lathe. On the carriage, several tools are set up. The four-armed spider wheel in front moves the carriage to the work. Each time it is withdrawn from a previous operation, the turret automatically turns to bring the next tool into position.

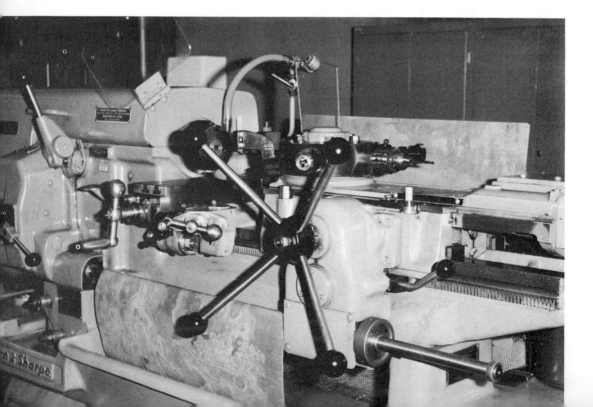

The cutting tool must be withdrawn from the cut as the tool is re-turned for another cut. To make sure that the tool returns to the same distance from the work each time. a stop is provided on the cross-feed. This stop brings the cross-feed back to the same position it was in when it made the last cut. The tool is advanced into the work by the feed of the compound slide. Some lathes have this cross-feed stop built into the cross-feed screw, while others use an external stop, which is attached each time a thread is to be cut. There is always the possibility that the tool may be drawn into the work due to the backlash in the feed screw, so some manufacturers fit their lathes with a device to prevent this draw-in.

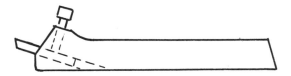

Fig. 25. Straight Armstrong tool holder

Lathe chuck mounting. Note the cone on the spindle nose and the locking ring that draws in the locking pins.

THE SMALL-SHOP LATHE

In addition to the tray on the ways of the lathe, as described in Chapter 1, you should provide a shelf on the wall behind the lathe to keep the oil cans, boring bars, and other items. The face plate and driver plate can be kept on a wooden peg projecting from the wall shelf. This wooden peg will protect the threads of the plates from damage. The two large head-stock chucks can be kept on the bench adjacent to the head end of the lathe or on a shelf under the bench.

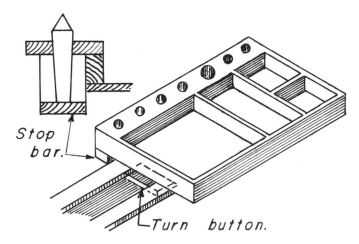

Fig. 26. Tool platform

It is handy to have three tail-stock chucks. One of these should have a capacity of ½ inch to take straight-shank drills. A smaller one of ⅜-inch capacity allows you to keep the center reamer always set up for drilling and reaming shaft centers. Another small chuck should be kept with a ³⁄₁₆-inch drill set up for drilling pilot holes for larger drills. These three tail-stock chucks should be kept in the rack on the tray with the lathe centers.

The center in the head stock is held in a bushing that can be removed to allow larger bars to pass through the spindle than would be the case with a #2 tapered center. There should be a larger hole on the center rack to store this bushing while it is not being used.

Fig. 27. Combined drill and center reamer

The Knockout Bar

You should have a rod with a weight on it to knock out the head-stock centers. The weight should be large enough to strike and remove the center bushing and should have a projection on the end small enough to drive out the center without disturbing the bushing. The outside diameter of the weight should be large enough to keep it centered in the head-stock hole. This knockout bar should be hung from a rack at the head end of the wall shelf.

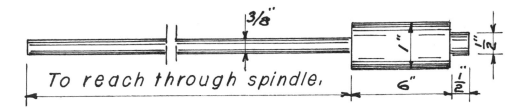

Fig. 28. Knockout bar

Center reamer. The photo shows how the steady rest is used for centering a long bar. The bar must be cylindrical to run in the steady rest.

The Center Reamer

Since the lathe center is a 60° cone, the ends of the work to be turned between centers must be drilled and reamed to this same angle to give a good and long-lasting bearing. The point of the lathe center must not touch the bottom of the hole, or it will interfere with the full bearing of the cone. The center hole is first drilled with a small drill, about ⅛-inch, and then reamed with a 60° countersink. The end of the shaft to be centered must be square with its center line before reaming. If the end is at an angle, the countersink will have to cut more metal on the high side than on the low, and will be forced away from the high side, resulting in a center out of line with the work.

The pilot drill should be run in far enough not only to clear the point of the lathe center but also to form a small reservoir for oil to lubricate the lathe center. The combined center drill and reamer does these two operations at one time. This same combined center reamer is a fine tool for starting a drill held in the tail-stock chuck. It is stiff and rigid and will start a hole without springing sideways as a more slender drill would. The end of the work should be running square, and there must be no rough spots that can catch the point of the pilot drill. This could put side pressure on the pilot and break it. A center-punch mark running out of true and making an eccentric circle would be such a spot that may break the pilot. It is convenient to have a small tail-stock chuck just to hold the combined drill and reamer; then it will always be ready for use without having to fit it up. Another small tail-stock chuck can hold a small drill, about ³⁄₁₆-inch, to use as a pilot drill when drilling larger holes.

In addition to the combined center drill and reamer, you should have as part of your equipment a 60° countersink for reaming centers and an 82° countersink for flat-head machine and wood screws.

Rests

There are two rests that should be purchased with the lathe. One of these is the *steady rest,* which is a frame that will clamp on the ways of the lathe and which has three guides that can be adjusted to bear on the

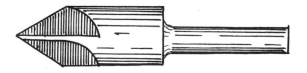

Fig. 29. Countersinks

work and to hold it on center when the tail center cannot be used. The top of the frame is split and hinged so that it can be opened to remove the work. It can only be used where the piece of work has a round part for the three guides to bear against. Plenty of oil must be used on the guides, and they must be adjusted just tight enough to guide the work but not to bind it.

The steady rest is handy for holding the end of a shaft while drilling and reaming the center in its end. For this purpose, the head end of the shaft is held in the three-jaw chuck, and the tail end is held in the steady rest. The center should be marked on the end of the shaft but not center-punched. A small prick-punch mark is all that can be used. The steady-rest guides are adjusted until the mark on the end of the shaft runs true with the point of the tail center. The punch mark on the end of the shaft used for setting up must run perfectly true. If it is off-center at all, the shaft will run concentric with the guides of the steady rest, and the punch mark will wobble in a little circle. The pilot drill of the center reamer will try to follow this punch mark, and if it is large enough to grip the point of the drill, the side pressure may break the pilot drill. Therefore, the punch mark must be small, just large enough to be seen. With the guides of the steady rest adjusted, the end of the shaft can be faced off, drilled, or turned. If there is an error in the punch mark on the end of the shaft, do not try to drill it with the combined drill and center reamer, since you may break the drill. Use a larger drill that is long enough to be flexible and follow the punch mark. This will make a hole large enough to allow the drill point of the reamer to clear and not cut. The reamer can then be used to ream the center true with the steady rest. The reamer must be held in a chuck that is steady enough so that it will not spring out of line as the drilled hole wobbles. If the chuck is not rigid enough, true up the drilled hole with a tool in the tool post of the carriage, and when it is running true, finish-ream it to a 60° angle of the center.

When it is necessary to drill and ream a center in a shaft that must run true with a bearing journal already machined, it is best to use the

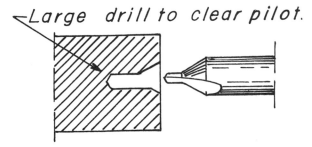

Fig. 30. Reaming a center that is out of line

four-jaw chuck to hold the head end, with the tail end set up in the steady rest. The four-jaw chuck is used because the three-jaw chuck is seldom accurate enough to prevent the head end from running out of true, and this will cause the tail end to wobble. With the four-jaw chuck and the dial indicator, it is possible to get the head end running perfectly true. The tail center can now be drilled and reamed and will be true to the journal.

Sometimes it is necessary to center a shaft where the head end cannot be held in a chuck. If this head end has a center in good condition, it can be held on the point of the head-stock center, and the tail end can be held in the steady rest. Since the shaft will not stay on the head center, it is necessary to fasten it to the drive plate, either by some form of clamp or by tying with wire. Heavy copper wire is good for this purpose.

A shaft that is not round cannot be set up in the steady rest. The jaws must have a cylindrical surface to run on. Try setting up the shaft in the four-jaw chuck in a reversed position: that is, with the end requiring the cylindrical place next to the chuck. The outer end can be steadied by a center drilled accurately at the center of the shaft. It is now possible to turn the shaft round and running true to its setting in the chuck. This round place should be close to the chuck and should be wide enough to take the jaws of the steady rest. The shaft can now be reversed end for end, with the turned part resting in the steady rest and the other end accurately centered in the four-jaw chuck. The center reamed to steady the outer end at the first setting will not be accurate with the second setting in the four-jaw chuck; and so, when the work is completed, it should be corrected by again reversing the ends in the lathe and truing up the center while it runs true in the steady rest. If this end cannot be set up in the steady rest, the temporary center should be removed or destroyed, since it cannot be reused without spoiling the work.

Another method of using a steady rest with an irregular shaft is to fit a sleeve made from a short piece of pipe over the work. This sleeve will bear on the jaws of the steady rest, and, by the use of set screws tapped through the pipe, the shaft can be centered in the sleeve. There should be four set screws at each end of the sleeve for a round shaft or three at each end for a hexagon bar.

The other rest is called a *follower rest*. This is an open-sided frame having two adjustable guides. It is bolted to the carriage of the lathe and travels with it. The two guides are adjusted to bear on a smooth, finish-turned part of the work so that it will take the pressure of the cutting tool and prevent the work from springing away from the cut. It is used to turn long flexible shafts and can be set to bear just after the cutting tool on work just turned, or ahead of the tool on a previously turned surface. In any case, the surface on which it bears must be round and straight, or it will make the work follow any error of the bearing surface. It must be adjusted after each cut to the new diameter and must not put pressure on the work, which would make it spring out of line.

TURNING BETWEEN CENTERS

Round work, such as shafts, is usually turned between centers. Any one of the methods described under the chapter on layout can be used to locate the centers at the ends. The end of the shaft should be square with the center line before laying out the center. You cannot lay out an accurate center on a rough or beveled end. If it cannot be faced off in the steady rest, grind or file the end smooth and square. If the bar is short enough, it can be set up in a chuck and the center reamer held in the tail-stock chuck. If the bar is too long for this and if you cannot use the steady rest, put the reamer in the three-jaw chuck in the head stock and support the tail end on the point of the tail center placed in the center-punch mark at that end. Then, by holding the head against the reamer by hand and feeding with the tail stock, both ends can be centered.

Be sure the center reamer is cutting at exactly 60° and that the tail center is ground to the same angle. If these two angles are not the same, the bearing surface will be a line contact and not the large surface, where the full cone of the center is in contact. This will cause a breaking down of the oil film, and the center will heat rapidly. The resulting friction will ruin both the point of the tail center and the reamed hole in the work. It sometimes happens that the heat is great enough to make the tip of the tail center fuse in the hole in the work. When this happens, it means scraping the work, as it is practically impossible to remove the fused piece. Since the fused material is much harder than the rest of the piece of work, any attempt to drill a new center will force the drill to one side, and the work will not run true. The only solution is to cut off the damaged end or to scrap the work.

Work turned on centers is only as accurate as the centers holding it. The head center can wobble, and the work will follow it and be turned eccentric to the reamed center hole. The head center should be trued up whenever very accurate work is to be done. If a soft center is used, it can be turned with a cutting tool set in the compound slide to give a 60° angle. If the center is hard, the tool-post grinder is used to true it. After the center is trued, it should not be removed until the work is completed.

The alignment of centers in the head stock sometimes goes wrong. Any chips that have not been removed from the inside of the spindle can become embedded in the tapered hole and will throw the center out of line. The spindle and the center should be marked so that the center will always be replaced in the same position. The bushing for the center must also be marked.

Work running on the tail center will run concentric to a center hole not perfect. But if the tail center is not in perfect alignment with the head center, the work will be turned tapered. The error will be twice as great as the amount by which the tail center is out of alignment.

Lathe dogs, used to turn the work when held between centers, are of many designs. All dogs, however, clamp on the outside of the work, and all have a projecting arm that can engage a slot in the driving plate or face plate and thus impart motion to the piece of work. The slot in the driving plate should be marked so that, when the work is removed from between the centers, as for testing, it can be replaced with the arm of the dog in the same slot of the driving plate. If there is any inaccuracy of the head-stock center, and if the dog is entered in a different slot, the work will be thrown off center, and the new cuts will not be concentric with the previous cuts.

The work expended in removing metal with a cutting tool manifests itself in the form of heat. This heat will cause the work to expand and will put great pressure on the lathe centers. This can quickly overheat the tail center and ruin it. For this reason the centers must be left a little loose while taking the roughing cuts. Check the centers often and adjust them as required. Adequate lubrication of the tail center is essential.

If the centers are loose, the tool will not cut a cylinder the same diameter along its full length. When the tool is at either end, the pressure will force the work away until it is tight on the center and until it has moved endwise to take up the play on the opposite center. When the tool is halfway between the ends, the play will be divided between the two centers. The result is that the work will be turned larger at the ends than at the center. This will give a false reading on the micrometer when you try at various places along the work to check for a parallel cut. Always test the centers and have them set for no play when taking a cut that is to be measured for size. Remember that as the work cools it will shrink and become loose in the centers; if the work is hot before you start taking the finish cuts, make sure that it does not become loose on the centers as it cools. The finish cuts should be light so that they will not heat up the work. This allows the work to cool as you finish it. Test your centers before the final cut.

When turning to size, it is quicker to measure the diameter with calipers than with micrometers. But a caliper measurement is not as exact as a micrometer measurement. You cannot set the calipers to an exact size from a scale. If you have some known guide to set them to, such as a gauge block or a plug gauge, you can set them with great accuracy. In taking readings with calipers, much depends on the feel. Forcing the calipers will cause them to spring and give a false reading. The feel must be the same when measuring as when the calipers were set from the gauge block.

For rough cuts, set the calipers to a slightly oversize dimension. You can take a rough measurement while the work is revolving by resting one leg of the caliper on the turned surface and by letting the other leg approach the work. Do not let the second leg touch the work while it is turning since it may jam on the work, ruin the calipers, and hurt you. The safe way is always to stop the lathe before getting as close to it as is required for measuring. It is too easy to get careless and catch your hand or your clothing in the revolving work.

As you approach the final size, shut down the lathe and take a micrometer reading. The cross-feed can then be set to remove the amount indicated by the micrometer, by using the micrometer graduations on the collar of the cross-feed screw to advance the tool by one-half the amount shown on the micrometer. Remember that the amount the tool is cutting reduces the diameter by twice the cut. Do not try to take off all that the micrometer indicates in one big cut. Take several small ones, the last one only about .0001 inch. Be sure to adjust the tail center to no play and have it clamped tight before taking these last cuts.

If you remove the work from the lathe to try its fit in some other part, be sure to return the lathe dog to the same slot in the driving plate. This is because there may be some error in the centers.

The Test Bar

The tail center is adjustable sideways and is often moved to turn tapers. It will have to be set back on center again before true cylindrical work can be turned. The rear of the tail stock is marked to show when it is on center. This mark will let you set it very close, but for very accurate work something more is needed. Make a center test bar. This should be made from alloy steel that has been annealed to relieve any locked-in strains. One end is turned to fit the Morse taper of the head stock. This should be the large taper, the same as the outside of the bushing. It must be fitted until it is tight in the spindle with no play. To turn this taper, the bar can be held on centers. Since this bar is about 16 inches long, the tail center probably cannot be set over far enough to give the required taper. The compound slide can be used to turn it. To test the angle of the taper, make four chalk marks the full length of the taper at the quarter points and insert it in the spindle, then move it a little while tight in the hole. The chalk marks will indicate where the high place is and the setting of the compound slide can be corrected until the chalk marks show that the taper is touching the full length.

With the tail center set for turning parallel, two rings are turned, one at each end of the bar. With the tool-post grinder, these two rings are ground until they are exactly the same diameter when carefully tested with the micrometers. It is not necessary that they be any given diameter, but they must be the same diameter. Of course, you have trued up the head and tail centers before grinding so that the rings are true to the bar centers.

To use this test bar to test the setting of the tail stock for cylindrical turning, place the bar on centers in the lathe and, with the dial indicator, take a reading on the ring at the head end. Without moving the dial indicator, run the carriage to the tail end and take a reading on the tail-end ring. You have to move the point of the dial indicator back with your finger so it will get onto the tail ring. If the readings are the same, the centers are set to turn parallel. If there is a difference in the readings, move the tail stock half the difference in the direction that will correct the error. Repeat until the readings are the same. Make a box to keep this test bar in, so that it cannot be damaged. Don't forget to clean and oil it after use, before putting it away.

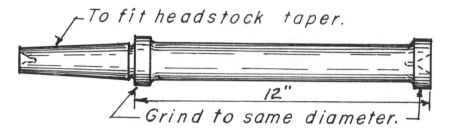

To fit headstock taper.

12"

Grind to same diameter.

Fig. 31. Lathe test bar

There may be a little wear in the lathe ways that would cause it to cut a cylinder not parallel the full length. Your test bar has proved the setting of the centers only at the point where tested. For this reason, you should always test the work with the micrometers as you take the roughing cuts to see that it is cutting parallel. This testing should be done while you still have sufficient material left, before the finishing cuts, to correct the setting of the centers.

Another cause of error is in the clamping device of the tail-stock ram. This generally works on one side of the ram. As it is tightened, it can move the ram sideways by the amount of any play in the ram. Always have the clamp tight as you make any tests and keep it tight as you make the finish cuts.

When boring a hole, the head stock must be perfectly in line with the ways of the bed or any error will show up as a taper in the hole. The test bar, when the tapered end is inserted tight in the taper of the spindle and the two circles tested with the dial indicator, will show whether it is parallel or not. Of course, the test bar must be centered in the spindle so that there is no eccentricity to it, or else there will be incorrect readings. Always take readings at the quarter points, turning the spindle a quarter-turn between readings. If these are not the same, the average of them should indicate where the true center is.

If the head stock is not parallel to the ways, it is difficult to correct the error. The bottom of the head stock casting was machined to fit the ways, and the bearings were set up parallel at the factory. The only way an error can be corrected is by filing and scraping the bottom of the casting to move it in such a way as to correct the error. This is a long and tedious job and fortunately will seldom have to be done. Unless the lathe has suffered an accident or the bearings have been scraped out of line, it should be in as good shape as when it left the factory.

Wiggle bar. This tool is used in connection with the dial indicator for accurately centering work in a lathe.

The Wiggle Bar

For setting up work in the chucks or on a face plate, a wiggle bar is necessary. You can purchase one, but you can also make one very quickly. This bar is about ⅜-inch in diameter and 10-inches long. It has a point at one end and a reamed center at the other. Both the point and the center must be concentric with the sides of the bar. The bar must be straight and should be set up in the steady rest to turn the point and ream the center, so that they will be concentric.

To use the bar, a large prick-punch mark is made at the center of the work. The point of the bar is placed in this punch mark and the other end held on the tail center. The dial indicator is placed against the wiggle bar near the head end, and the work is adjusted until there is no movement of the hand of the indicator as the work is revolved. It is easier to turn the lathe by hand if the cone pulley is detached from the spindle.

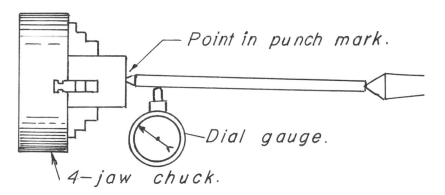

Fig. 32. Wiggle bar

Turning with Chucks

Many forms of work can be conveniently held in a chuck. There are several kinds of chucks. The ones you will have the most use for are the independent four-jaw chuck and the self-centering, three-jaw chuck. The three-jaw chuck is used for work that is round or hexagonal in shape. Bar stock can be passed through the hollow head stock and be worked close up to the chuck.

The usual type of mounting for chucks is to screw them on the end of the head-stock spindle. The rear face of the hub of the chuck fits up tight against a shoulder on the spindle. Modern production-type lathes have a special mounting on the nose of the spindle. These embody a starting portion that guides the chuck and a very large wide-angle taper that centers the chuck. These are very accurate, and the chuck always returns to center when replaced after being removed. These spindle-nose mountings are standardized, and lathes can be ordered equipped with them at an additional cost. For home workshops, these special mountings are not required. The ordinary screw-and-shoulder mounting will give very good service. The play in the screw threads was the biggest objection to this type of mounting and was the reason the cone mounting was developed. But the threads of the screw form a cone, in effect, when the chuck is tightened up to the shoulder, and thus the chuck finds its center on a cone.

The three-jaw chuck is seldom very accurate. The manufacturer will turn out a chuck accurate to .005-inch, but it will not remain this accurate. Trying to hold work beyond the capacity of the chuck can spring it out of true. Wear on the spiral that actuates the jaws will make them move unequally. Carelessness in keeping chips out of the thread and shoulder when mounting will make it run out of true. Work that projects too far from the chuck is liable to be twisted out of the chuck and damage the jaws.

Work held in the three-jaw chuck will be true to the position it was set up in, but it will not be true to some other part machined at a former setting. Where the entire work is finished at one setting, the three-jaw chuck can be used. When very accurate work must be done to run true to some part finished at a former setting, use the four-jaw chuck and dial gauge to set it true to the former setting.

Attempts to restore the accuracy of a three-jaw chuck by grinding the jaws are not always successful. To start with, the jaw must be under the same conditions as when holding work. The jaws can be tightened on a smooth cylindrical bar and then soft-soldered in that position while the bar is driven out. Theoretically this should put the jaws in a tight grip and take all the backlash out. But the jaws can be tightened only to a point where the bar can be driven out. This tension is less than that used to tighten work in the chuck to a point where it will not slip, and thus the chuck is not strained to its true working condition. Also it will only be adjusted for the position the jaws are in at that setting. For a setting where the jaws are opened farther or less, the strain on the body of the chuck will be different; so that, if the grinding does true up the jaws, it will be for that position only. The wear on the thread of the spiral will be different at different settings. Grinding the jaws for one position may make the error greater at other settings. It is better to take great care that the chuck is not damaged in use and never to try to true the jaws by grinding.

Proper care and oiling of the chucks is of the utmost importance. The manufacturers recommend that a light oil be used on the jaws and threads. This will fly out very quickly as the chuck revolves. A stiff gear grease will stay in the chuck, but the chuck must be taken apart to get the grease on the working parts, and chips tend to stick in the grease. You had better do as the maker advises and use a light oil. Chips collecting in the threads of the chuck can cause much damage. The kind of material being machined has a lot to do with the chips accumulating. Cast iron and some of the harder steel alloys crumble when cutting and form small chips and metal dust that will work into the grooves of the jaws and into the screws that actuate the jaws. After machining a metal that forms these small chips, the chuck will have to be dismantled and thoroughly washed out with a solvent, such as carbon tetrachloride, and oiled as it is reassembled.

The four-jaw chuck has four independent screws that move the jaws. The jaws can be taken out and reversed to hold either inside or outside work. While the jaws are out, it is possible to wash out the slides and screws with some of the solvent on an old brush. This is all the dismantling that can be done with the four-jaw chuck. It is hard to clean under the screws so work the brush down under as far as possible. If you have compressed air in your shop, use it to blow out the chips under the screws. An old toothbrush is very good for cleaning the slides. It can be dipped in the solvent and run down the inside of the slides.

The three-jaw chuck has a scroll or spiral thread inside that moves the jaws. As this spiral changes its diameter as the jaws move, the teeth on the inside of the jaws must be curved to fit the small diameter when near the center and to fit the large diameter when near the outer end. The teeth can be curved only one way, so that it is necessary to have a different set of jaws for inside and for outside work.

When the jaws must be changed, screw out the ones not wanted, clean the spiral by revolving it while washing with solvent on a brush, and oil both it and the new teeth. Have a small box or compartment in a convenient drawer for storing the jaws when not in use. Washing them before they are stored will keep them clean. The jaws and corresponding slots are numbered, and the numbers on the jaws and slots must match or else the jaws will not center. To insert the jaws, turn the spiral until the start of the thread shows in the #1 slot. Back it up a little so that the #1 jaw can enter until it touches the thread. Advance the spiral, at the same time pressing in the jaw to make it engage the spiral. Watch at slot #2 until the end of the spiral appears in the slot; repeat with #2 jaw and #3. Wind in on the spiral until all the jaws come even with the outside of the body of the chuck. At this point they should all be flush with the outside of the chuck. This is a test to see if the jaws are properly entered and centered. If one of them is not flush, you must wind them all out and start over again.

Never use a chuck wrench bigger than the one furnished with the chuck. The manufacturer has determined the maximum size it is safe to use with that particular chuck, so use only that size and don't take a chance of ruining the chuck by overstraining it. For the tedious job of winding out the jaws when changing them, you can make a speed wrench that is a big help. Get a piece of round, cold-rolled steel that is big enough to file a square on one end that will fit the square socket in the screws of the chuck. Then bend it to a U-shaped crank similar to that of a carpenter's bit brace. This gives you a handle to hold with one hand while winding with the other. If the sockets in the screws of the four-jaw chuck are the same as for the three-jaw chuck, you need only one speed wrench, but if they are not the same, make one for each chuck. Be sure that the arm having the square end for the four-jaw chuck is long enough to reach over the jaw when it is being removed and is in the extreme out position. If this arm is too short, the wrench will strike the jaw before it is screwed all the way out, and you will have to change to the regular "T" chuck wrench to finish removing and inserting the jaw.

When putting either chuck on the spindle, make sure all metal chips have been cleaned from the threads inside the chuck and on the nose of the spindle. A good stiff brush will remove any loose chips, but when a chip sticks in the threads it must be pried out with a sharp-pointed tool. If the chips have much oil on them, it will be necessary to dip the brush in solvent in order to remove them. Put a drop of oil on the spindle threads before screwing on the chuck. Always see that the chuck is turned up tight against the shoulder on the spindle. Use a wrench on one of the jaws to set it tight. If it is not set on tight, the chuck may spin off when the lathe is suddenly stopped or reversed. Using the chuck wrench in one of the screws to unscrew the chuck is bad practice. It wears the socket and will eventually ruin it. Use a wrench or pry-bar on the jaws to turn the chuck off. To lock the spindle while screwing a chuck or face plate on or off, throw in the back gears while the cone pulley latch is engaged. This locks the spindle, but, if too much force is used, it will throw the back gears out of mesh, and they will have to be held in. A chuck should never set up so tight that this will happen, but sometimes heavy cuts will set one on tight, and it will have to be forced off.

When centering work in the four-jaw chuck, as you approach the final setting, only very small movements of the chuck wrench are used, slacking off on the low side and tightening the high side, moving the work half the amount of the error shown on the dial indicator. The jaws on the quarter points must be tight enough to hold the work as it is moved by the jaw being tightened, but not so tight that it gives a false reading on the dial gauge. Careful work with the chuck wrench and the dial gauge will enable you to get the work exactly on the center marked with the prick punch. Of course, the point of the wiggle bar must be in tight contact with the punch mark while testing. After getting the work to the required center, tighten all four jaws equally and as tight as required to hold the work. This may spring something, the work or the chuck, so test it again with the wiggle bar and dial gauge to be sure you did not throw it off center with the final tightening. If you did, repeat until the work is tightly held and running true.

It is often necessary to set up work in a chuck so that it is held out from the face of the chuck, enabling the cutting tool to work up to the end of the piece without damaging the chuck. The steps of the jaws will give this result, as the steps are ground parallel to the face of the chuck. But where the steps cannot be used, a spacer block can be placed between the work and the chuck face. For small distances, one of the high-speed tool bits can be used. These are ground to ¼-inch square. For larger spaces, one of the chuck jaws that is not being used will work very nicely, as these are ground parallel on the sides. Insert the block between the chuck face and the work, near each jaw, and tap the work back tight against the block. Repeat with all jaws, until it takes the same force to remove the block at each jaw. In this condition, the work is as near parallel to the face of the chuck as you can get it. There is no more accurate method of measuring the distance behind the work than by the feel when you are removing the block. Be sure you have removed all the blocks before you start up the lathe.

Turning on the Face Plate

Work clamped on a face plate should always be held by two or more clamps. It is liable to slip when only one clamp is used. For clamps, use some bars of steel ½ inch by 1½ inches and 4 inches long. Drill a ½-inch hole near the center. Have an assortment of ½-inch bolts and washers of different lengths. The block used at the outer end of the clamp should be of the same length as the work at that point. If the block is not the same length, the clamp will set at an angle and is very liable to slip and become loose.

If the work must be held out from the face plate, you can insert blocks, all of the same thickness, at each clamp. These blocks will have to remain in place during the work, as the clamps hold them there. Some short pieces of cold-rolled steel, such as ⅜-inch-by-¾-inch pieces, work very well.

For centering the work, use the wiggle bar and dial gauge. First, gently tap the work to a center. You can set it up just as accurately as with a jaw chuck, but it may take a little longer. In tightening the clamps, remember that you can spring the face plate out of true with a clamp set too tight. Use more clamps with less pressure and test the centering after all clamps are tight.

If the piece of work has a surface that is already machined, this can be used to set the clamps to. If it is a cylinder, the point of the dial gauge can rest directly on the outside of the cylinder. There is also an arm that attaches to the dial indicator for reading from inside surfaces of cylinders. If it is a flat surface parallel to the plane of the face plate and turned out, the dial gauge can be used directly against it, but if the surface is turned in toward the face plate, you cannot use a dial gauge on it but must depend on the blocks between the work and the face plate to keep it true. If you can get the dial gauge on the face plate while the work is bolted to it, test the face plate to be sure it has not been distorted by the tightening of the clamps. If the dial gauge cannot be used, try a straight edge across parts where it will fit. This may indicate any distortion that may be present.

Angle Blocks

Angle blocks are very useful for setting up some work that cannot be bolted directly to the face plate. Remember to use at least two bolts between the angle and the face plate and between the angle and the work. When work is bolted to an angle, the face plate will be badly out of balance. A counterweight should be bolted to the opposite side of the face plate to correct the balance.

Several sizes of angles should be on hand. These you can make yourself. Get some scrap angles from a local iron works and machine them to a true 90° angle. To do this, bolt one of them to the face plate and the second one to the first. You are working with rough material, so the face to be machined may not be parallel to the face plate. Steel angles are not always finished to a true right angle, so you will have to insert shims under the bolts to make the face parallel. With one face finished, the angle is set up to machine the other leg. The shims will have to be adjusted so that this second leg will be exactly at a 90° angle to the first one. After one angle has been machined square, it is set up on the face plate and used to face off the rest of the angles.

With the outside faces of the legs machined, the angles can be set up in the milling attachment, and the insides of the legs can be milled parallel to the outside face. Then work can be set up on either face of the outstanding leg. Handy sizes of angles to have on hand would be one 4 inches by 6 inches by ½ inch, cut 4 inches long; one 4 inches by 4 inches by ½ inch, cut 4 inches long; and one 4 inches by 4 inches by ½ inch, cut 2 inches long. All these angles should be set up in the four-jaw chuck and have the edges finished square with the faces. Two ½-inch holes should be drilled on the center line of each leg, as far apart as possible, allowing space for the head or nut of a bolt near the inside of the outstanding leg. Other holes may be drilled for some particular job as needed.

After setting up an irregularly positioned piece of work, such as a piece bolted to an angle block, always turn the lathe by hand with the cutting tool in the cutting position, to see that everything is clear and that some part of the work does not project and strike the tool or part of the carriage. To start up under power and have the work strike something that knocks it out of line can ruin a long and tedious setup and can also do some damage to the work or the lathe. Be sure to test for all positions of the tool, as work that clears at the start of the cut may foul at the end of the cut.

Mandrels

For finish-turning, many jobs are best set up on a mandrel. A mandrel is a shaft about 8 inches long that has been hardened and ground to a slight taper, about .0005 inch per inch of length (see Figure 35). The ends are accurately centered before grinding and are reduced in diameter and flattened so that a lathe dog may be attached for driving. The work is drilled, reamed, or bored to the finished size, and a mandrel should be selected that will allow the work to be driven onto a tight fit near its center. The fit must be tight enough so that the work will not slip under the cut. Narrow work is hard to set up to a true 90° angle to the mandrel, as the width of the hole is not enough to guide it. It is necessary to adjust the work so that it runs true with no wobble before starting the cuts, and care must be used not to take such a heavy cut that the work comes loose on the mandrel, or else you will not be able to get it running true again and, if you are near the end of the work, you may not have enough metal left to get the finish cuts true. Working with the small end of the mandrel near the head stock tends to make the work crawl toward the head end and work loose.

Arbors

Sometimes the only way you can hold a piece of work is by clamping it onto an arbor. The arbor consists of a shaft with a collar at one end and a nut at the other (see Figure 33). Sleeves of various widths are used along the shaft to tighten the nut onto the work. The ends are centered and flattened to receive a lathe dog at either end. The shaft must be ground accurately to the centers, and the collar and ends of the sleeves must be face ground at exactly 90° to the axis of the shaft. Any work clamped on the arbor must be faced off so that both sides are perfectly parallel. If there is any angle formed between the faces of any of the sleeves or with the work, when the nut is tightened enough to prevent slipping of the work, it will spring the shaft, and the work will not run true. You will find that ½-inch and ¾-inch arbors are very useful in the shop.

For work that is drilled or bored to some diameter other than either ½-inch or ¾-inch, a bushing can be made to center the work on either the ½-inch or ¾-inch arbor. The shoulder on the arbor and the sleeves must be large enough to grip the sides of the piece of work, the diameter of which, of course, is greater than that of the bushing.

Select a good piece of alloy steel or tool steel to make the arbor shaft. Finish the sleeves first, then fit the shaft to a tight sliding fit by using the sleeves as a gauge to grind the shaft to size. Make the sleeves from any good material, such as soft or hard steel or cast iron. They should be of various lengths so that the position of the work on the arbor can be adjusted. Set the sleeve up in the three-jaw chuck and subdrill and ream the hole to the size of the shaft. While at the same setting, face off and grind the end of the sleeve. Use a scraper to remove the burr left by the grinding wheel on the inside. Finish all the sleeves on one end in this way.

Set up a piece of scrap in the chuck and make a spud to grind the opposite end of the sleeves (see Figure 34). This spud must be a tight-sliding fit in the sleeves so that they will not slip as they are being ground. It should be ground to size, using a sleeve as a gauge. The collar should be ground to run perfectly true. To do this, use a cup wheel in the grinder. The wheel cannot finish into the tight corner at the shaft, so an undercut should be turned on the collar to relieve the corner of the wheel and allow it to finish a complete face on the collar. As the sleeves will be a tight fit on the spud, some means must be provided to remove them. Before turning the spud, drill two ½-inch holes diametrically opposite each other, with their centers on the line of the finished collar. These holes must be deep enough to take the tips of two screwdrivers to pry off the sleeve. The sleeve is to be driven onto the spud until the end already ground is seated tight against the ground face of the collar on the spud. Use very light taps of a fiber hammer in seating the sleeve so that you will not disturb the setting of the spud in the lathe chuck.

After all the sleeves have been ground on both ends, test them with the micrometer to see that the ends are parallel. Discard any that are not parallel. It is a good idea to set up the spud in one chuck and rough out the sleeves with the other, then if it is necessary to make some extra sleeves to replace any defective ones, you will have a chuck to work with without disturbing the setting of the spud.

Assemble all the sleeves on the shaft, run the nut to them, and face off the nut. Do this with the nut close to the tail center so that, if the nut, being rough and out of true, springs the shaft when tightened, the error will be small. After facing one side, turn the nut around and face off the opposite side. Repeat this facing with little cuts each time until the nut no longer springs the shaft when tightened very tight. A better method is to turn up and thread a spud on which to face the nut. The rough nut will not bend the short spud as it would the longer shaft. It takes a little longer than facing it on the shaft, but you can harden the nut and grind the faces on the spud. You cannot grind them on the shaft without danger of damaging the thread on the shaft or of nicking the tail center.

While each sleeve is on the spud for grinding the ends, the outside should be ground so that all sleeves will be of the same diameter. Finish the outside of the sleeves to some common diameter, such as 1 inch or 1¼ inches. Then distances to the outside of the work can be measured from the outsides of the sleeves. It is important that the outsides of the sleeves run perfectly true with the shaft so that the dial indicator can be used against them to tell whether tightening the nut has sprung the shaft out of line. This is why the sleeves must be a tight-sliding fit on the shaft.

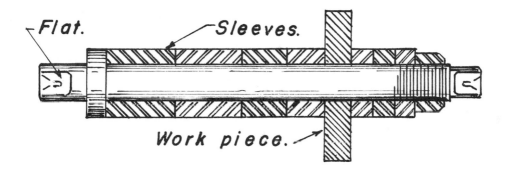

Fig. 33. Arbor

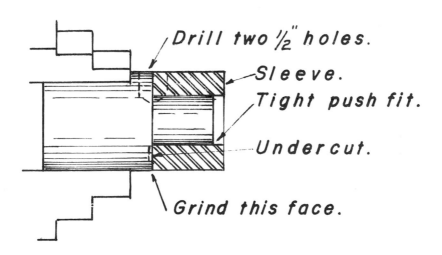

Fig. 34. Spud for grinding arbor sleeves

Put the sleeves back in the three-jaw chuck. With a scraper remove the grinding burr from the inside; then, with a fine file, slightly round the outer corner. These sharp corners can cut like broken glass.

If you have constructed a magnetic chuck, the second end of the sleeves can be ground on it. The sleeves are too small to bridge across an air gap of the chuck when centered on the chuck and will not get the full pull of the magnetic flux. Use four small pieces of steel, like four ½-inch nuts, that will bridge the air gap and concentrate the flux at the center of the chuck. The four pieces should be in tight contact with the work being ground and will hold the work firmly.

The Live Tail Center

Since there is much danger of overheating and ruining the tail center and the reamed center in the work, it is sometimes better to use a live tail center. This center has a 60° center that remains stationary in the work and itself revolves on ball bearings that are mounted on the tapered shank. This center will stand high speeds, but it is not as accurate as a dead center. Any pressure on the center will take up any play in the bearings and it will revolve accurately, but if the work is removed, as is often the case, it may not return to the same position. For this reason, both the work and the tail center must be marked so the center will always be returned to the same position in the work.

BORING

There are many types of boring bars. For small holes, the forged bar with the cutting end turned at 90° and held in a "V" block in the regular tool post is required (see Figure 36). These tools cannot project far from the tool post or they will spring away from the work. Only small cuts can be taken. The cutting edge can be ground to any of the usual forms and, after several grindings, will have to be reforged and tempered again.

For heavier work and where the depth of the hole requires it, the larger bar with inserted cutters is used. This is held in a special tool post made for boring bars only (see Figure 37). Generally there is provision made to hold at least two sizes of bars. The center of the boring bar must be on the center line of the lathe centers, as the tool post does not permit the height of the bar to be adjusted. A slight adjustment can be made by revolving the bar in the holder to put the tool in the best cutting position.

When boring with a bar held in the tool post, it is necessary to set the carriage stop so the bar will not run into the face plate or chuck, whichever is holding the work. The work must be set up leaving a small

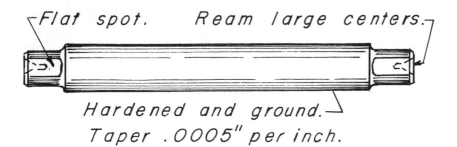

Flat spot.   *Ream large centers.*

Hardened and ground.
Taper .0005" per inch.

Fig. 35. Mandrel

"V" block in tool post.

Fig. 36. Small boring tool

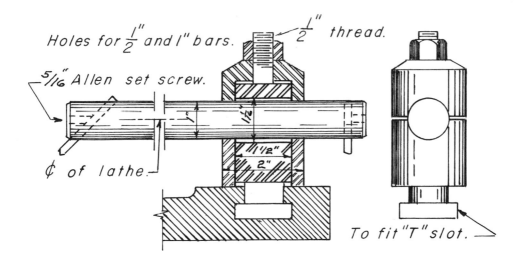

Holes for $\frac{1}{2}$" and 1" bars.

$\frac{1}{2}$" *thread.*

$\frac{5}{16}$" *Allen set screw.*

¢ *of lathe.*

To fit "T" slot.

Fig. 37. Tool-post boring bar

space behind it to allow the tool to run past the work to finish its cut. The boring bar should be the same length all along its length so that any projection will fit the tool post. One end should have the hole for the cutter at 90° and the other end at 45°. For most work the 90° end will be used, but when it is necessary to cut beyond the end of the bar, as when facing a surface or finishing a hole into a corner, the 45° end is used. For turning screw threads, the 90° end is used. To make sure the tool is cutting at 60°, the hole should be exactly at 90°, so that the tool ground to 60° can be used.

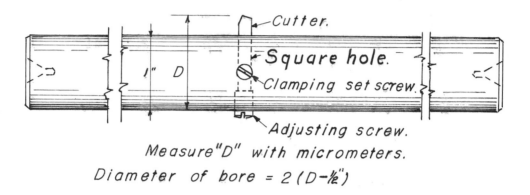

Measure "D" with micrometers.

Diameter of bore = 2 (D-½")

Fig. 38. Boring bar between centers

Some work is so large or has such a long hole that it cannot be set up on the head stock. In this case, it should be mounted stationary on the carriage, and the cutting tool should be inserted in a bar that revolves. The large engine lathes have "T" slots cast in the carriage so that work can be bolted to it, blocking and shims being used to get the correct height. Toolroom lathes and home-workshop lathes do not have such "T" slots. If the work is of such a shape that it can be mounted entirely behind the tool post, clamps can be set in the "T" slot of the compound slide or an angle block set in the "T" slot, and the work can be bolted to it. There are also bolt holes, which are used to bolt on the follower rest, and these can be used. In any case, the work must be fastened rigidly with more than one clamp to prevent its slipping.

The center of the hole to be bored must be marked on each end by laying out lines that pass vertically and horizontally through the center. Then the height can be measured and set the same at each end, and the vertical line can be lined up with the centers of the lathe.

The cutter will be at the center of the boring bar, and the bar must be long enough to allow the cutter to move the full length of the required cut without the work striking either the head stock or the tail stock. The boring bar is held between the lathe centers and driven by a dog.

The cutter must be set to the exact radius to give the finished diameter of the hole. The simplest bar will have a hole for the cutter and a set screw to hold it. The cutter is adjusted for depth of cut by tapping it either way while measuring the projection with the micrometer. More elaborate bars have a micrometer screw for adjusting the depth of cut. As you will probably make up the bar to fit the job, you can choose either type. As the bar is quite long and is weakened at the center by the hole for the cutting tool, it must be made of good alloy steel so that it will spring a minimum amount while cutting. The shape of the cutting tool, the speed of the lathe, and the depth of cut will all influence the tendency to chatter. You will probably have to experiment with all these variables to find the combination that gives chatter-free cutting.

To set the cutter to bore a given diameter, use the micrometer to measure the projection of the cutter from the opposite side of the boring bar. Subtracting half the diameter of the bar from this measurement will give the radius of the cutter, and twice this is the diameter of the hole. To make this easy, the bar should be of a diameter that is easily divided by 2, such as 1-inch, so that subtracting ½ inch would be easy. As you approach the finish cuts, remember that the bar is springing, so take very small cuts and check often.

One very important thing to remember when trying the fit of a plug or shaft in a bored hole is never to enter one without first cleaning out all the chips and oiling the hole. Without the oil, the turned surface, which is really a torn surface with a series of minute points sticking out, will turn all these little points so they will catch like hundreds of little cats' claws as the shaft is being withdrawn. It will grip the shaft so tightly that you will probably ruin both the hole and the shaft when forcing the shaft out. Always oil a bored hole.

To measure the size of a bored hole, use the inside calipers for the rough testing, but switch to the inside micrometers or the telescoping gauge for the finish cuts. In using either of these instruments, the position in which it is held will determine the accuracy of the measurement. The tool is rigid at any size it is set to, and there are two chances for error when measuring with it. It must be exactly on the center line of the hole, so that it is measuring a diameter, and it must be exactly at 90° to the work or it will be measuring too long. It is necessary to move the tool in all directions to find the correct point to measure. It helps to mark a circle with chalk or soapstone on the inside and a line passing through the center on the outside. Then by holding the instrument on the intersection of these lines, a little feeling around will give the correct measurement.

A somewhat similar boring bar to the one held between centers is one that is guided by a pilot at one end and driven by a chuck at the other end, when the work is stationary, or held in a tail-stock chuck when the work revolves. The bar is made with a pilot long enough to take the full length of the cut, and the driving end must be long enough to be held without striking the work. The cutter is inserted and adjusted as for the other bars. The pilot hole is laid out and drilled or reamed at the exact center of the larger hole. Then, without changing the setup, the pilot is inserted in the pilot hole, which guides the cutter to bore in exact alignment with the pilot hole. This is called line boring or line reaming.

The cutter in the boring bar must have room for the chips to get away or they will jam and give a false cut by forcing the bar to spring away from the work. For small holes, use a small bar to get side clearance and grind the cutter with more side rake to throw the chips away from the tool. The tool cuts on the leading edge, and this will prevent the chips from jamming. For larger holes, where there is plenty of clearance, the cutter is ground with more back rake, and the cutting point is set on the center line of the lathe.

TAPER TURNING

Three methods are used to turn a taper in a lathe. For long tapers of a small angle, using the offset tail stock is the quickest. Knowing the length of the work between centers, the amount of the tail-stock offset can be computed to give any taper per foot, within the capacity of the offset. The centers are working out of line for this work and so are making a line contact, which may cause the tail center to heat. Watch it and correct the pressure and oil as necessary. As the lathe dog driving the work is operating at an angle to the head stock, the work will not turn uniformly. At one position the dog will be close to the driving plate, and as the driving leg of the dog is parallel to the center line of the work, the driving leg will be nearer the lathe center than when it is diametrically opposite. For a given angle of revolution of the driving plate, the lathe dog will travel farther when in the outer position than when nearer the center. The result is an irregular turning of the work. The lead screw is turning uniformly with the head stock and advances the cutting tool at a uniform rate, but the turning of the work is irregular, making the amount of metal removed by the tool more on one side of the work than on the opposite side. This can cause long work to spring away from the cutter on the side of the heavy cut, giving an oval shape to the work. The finished cuts must be very light to prevent the springing of the work and to assure a true circular cut. This irregular turning when using a lathe dog to drive tapered work makes it impossible to turn tapered threads with an offset tail center. They would come out wavy, what are called "drunken threads."

For short tapers with a large angle, the compound slide can be set to give the required taper. The feed will be by hand, as there is no power feed on the compound slide. The compound is graduated in degrees, so that the taper per foot must be converted to degrees to be set directly by the graduations. As it is nearly always necessary to try the fit of a taper in a hole, make four chalk marks at the quarter points, then enter the work and move it slightly in the hole. The chalk marks will show where the work is touching, and the setting of the compound can be corrected as needed. Tapers longer than the feed of the compound cannot be cut at one setting, although it is possible by careful work to move the carriage to a new position and cut an extension of the taper. Never move the work until the taper is completed.

A taper-cutting attachment will cut long tapers of a greater angle than can be done by offsetting the tail center. The attachment is a guide bar that can be clamped to the rear of the lathe bed at any angle shown on the graduations on the bar. A slide on the bar is attached to the cross slide of the carriage, which is disconnected from its feed screw. The taper bar then controls the movement of the tool, which will cut a line parallel to the bar. The amount of cut, or the position of the cutting tool, is roughly adjusted by the clamp to the slide bar, and the fine adjustment is made with the compound slide. True taper threads can be cut with this taper attachment, as the work is on aligned centers and turns at a uniform rate.

Table 1 gives the half-angles for changing a given taper in inches per foot to degrees.

LATHE TOOLS

There are many types and kinds of cutting tools for lathes. For the small workshop the self-hardening high-speed tool bit held in an Armstrong-type holder will be the most useful. The tool holder comes in three forms: a straight tool, a right-hand offset tool, and a left-hand offset tool. These tool holders take high-speed cutting bits, which are held in place with a set screw in the tool holder. The cutting bit comes in blank form and is ground to the requirements of the work being turned. There are also forged tools that are shaped and hardened for special cutting. These will seldom be used, except for the small boring tools.

Different materials require different shapes of the cutting edge. The diagrams in Figure 41 show the various angles for grinding the bit. Figure 40 shows how the tool is ground. Table 2 gives the angles for several kinds of materials. A special tool is the cutoff or parting tool. This has a thin blade that can be extended to the depth of cut required. The blade comes with vertical side clearance and is generally used without any top rake. The blade must be set exactly at 90° to the work, with the cutting edge on the center line. The cutting edge can be ground square across or with a right- or left-hand bevel. With a square grind, the burr left when the tool breaks through will generally remain on the piece cut off. A right-hand bevel will leave the burr on the cutoff piece and the face of the remaining stock clean. The left-hand bevel leaves the burr on the stock and the cutoff piece clean. Grind the cutting edge to suit the way you want the burr to form.

The cutoff tool has a tendency to bind on the sides of the cut when it gets in deep. The pressure will spring the tool until it digs in and wrecks something; either the work will be ruined, or the blade will be broken. Relieving the sides of the blade so that the cutting edge is wider than the rest of the blade stops this binding on the sides and is very important in deep cuts. But this grinding away of the width of the blade reduces its cutting width as the cutting edge is sharpened. This is very wasteful of the blade, as it soon grows too narrow and will have to be scrapped. There are two ways of getting around this trouble. If the cut is not too deep, two grooves can be cut side by side and overlapping into each other. Work a little in one and then in the other, so that the blade is always in a groove wider than the blade. This cutting of two grooves makes the blade cut on one side at a time, and it will spring away from the cut. The farther out the blade is, to make deep cuts, the more flexible it is, and the more it will spring. It will soon have cut a tapering groove with the bottom narrower than the top. You cannot make the flexible blade take a side cut unless the top is given a side rake to hold it into the cut. But this side rake would prevent it cutting on the opposite side of the groove, so it cannot be used. However, it will be possible to work in quite deep by this method, and it is safe. The groove will be quite rough on the sides and will have to be refinished after the cutoff. A better method is to use a short projection of the blade, cut in as far as possible without binding, and then finish with a hacksaw. The hacksaw can be used while the work is slowly revolving and will do a good job. Or the work can be taken out of the lathe and finished by sawing on the metal-cutting band saw. This operation is outlined in Chapter 7, METAL SAWING.

Never try to cut off a piece that is held in a chuck without using the tail stock to steady it. The pressure of the tool will gradually make the piece work out of the jaws, putting side pressure on the blade until it catches and twists the work out of the chuck. The tail stock will prevent this. Figure 39 shows the grinding and setting of the cutoff tool.

CHATTERING

Chattering is a trouble caused by many conditions, some acting singly and some simultaneously. If the work is long and slender, it will spring away from the cutting tool and may start to vibrate. The follower rest should be used to steady the work. This rest is bolted to the carriage and travels with it. The rest has two adjustable guides that bear on the work and steady it. The guides must bear on a part of the work that has been turned concentric with the lathe centers, and must be adjusted after each cut to the new diameter. The speed of the lathe has a good deal to do with starting vibrations. Chatter is less with slow speeds. The depth of cut also affects it. If the tool can be kept cutting deep, it will have less of a tendency to vibrate. On large diameters, the amount of power required to take a deep cut may be beyond the capacity of the lathe or motor and smaller cuts are required, which may start the vibrations. The shape of the cutting tool also is a factor. A broad cutting edge in contact with the work will chatter more than a narrow one. A round-nosed tool also chatters more than a sharp-pointed one. A tool cutting on its side as it advances into the cut, with ample side and top rake, does not vibrate as much as one cutting on the end. The side cutting

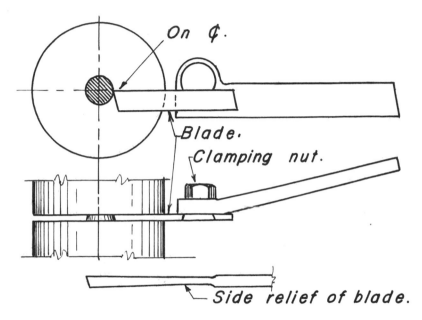

Fig. 39. Cutoff tool

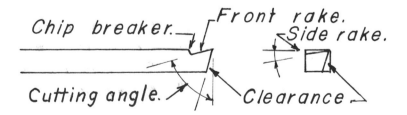

Fig. 40. Tool grinding

tool does not leave as smooth a finish as one that cuts on the end, so the best combination is a tool ground with a small radius between the side edge and the end edge, and set so that the end makes a small clearance angle with the finished surface. This puts the end edge almost parallel to the finish and the small ridges caused by the feed, and this slight angle will hardly be seen. The tool is cutting on the side and the small radius, and the end is doing the finishing. If chatter starts, it may be necessary to try several remedies before the right combination is found. In spite of what some have said, the back gears have nothing to do with chatter. A properly cut set of gears mesh without any interference of the teeth and give a smooth action.

Table 1

Half-Angles for Tapers

Taper (inches per foot)	Taper per inch	Angle (degrees and minutes)	Taper (inches per foot)	Taper per inch	Angle (degrees and minutes)
$\frac{1}{32}$	.00260	0–09	$1\frac{3}{16}$	.09896	5–39
$\frac{1}{16}$	.00520	0–18	$1\frac{7}{32}$	.10156	5–48
$\frac{3}{32}$	.00781	0–27	$1\frac{1}{4}$	.10417	5–57
$\frac{1}{8}$	.01042	0–36	$1\frac{9}{32}$	.10677	6–06
$\frac{5}{32}$	.01302	0–45	$1\frac{5}{16}$	.10938	6–15
$\frac{3}{16}$	.01562	0–54	$1\frac{11}{32}$	.11198	6–23
$\frac{7}{32}$	.01823	1–03	$1\frac{3}{8}$	.11458	6–32
$\frac{1}{4}$	.02083	1–12	$1\frac{13}{32}$	.11719	6–41
$\frac{9}{32}$	.02344	1–21	$1\frac{7}{16}$	.11979	6–50
$\frac{5}{16}$	.02604	1–30	$1\frac{15}{32}$	.12240	6–59
$\frac{11}{32}$	.02865	1–38	$1\frac{1}{2}$	.12500	7–07
$\frac{3}{8}$	.03125	1–47	$1\frac{17}{32}$	.12760	7–16
$\frac{13}{32}$	.03385	1–56	$1\frac{9}{16}$	.13021	7–25
$\frac{7}{16}$	.03646	2–05	$1\frac{19}{32}$	.13281	7–34
$\frac{15}{32}$	.03906	2–14	$1\frac{5}{8}$	.13542	7–43
$\frac{1}{2}$	.04167	2–23	$1\frac{21}{32}$	.13802	7–52
$\frac{17}{32}$	.04427	2–32	$1\frac{11}{16}$	.14063	8–00
$\frac{9}{16}$	.04688	2–41	$1\frac{23}{32}$	.14323	8–09
$\frac{19}{32}$	.04948	2–50	$1\frac{3}{4}$	.14583	8–18
$\frac{5}{8}$	.05208	2–59	$1\frac{25}{32}$	.14844	8–27
$2\frac{1}{32}$	.05469	3–08	$1\frac{13}{16}$	.15104	8–35
$1\frac{1}{16}$	.05729	3–17	$1\frac{27}{32}$	.15365	8–44
$2\frac{3}{32}$	.05990	3–26	$1\frac{7}{8}$	.15625	8–53
$\frac{3}{4}$	.06250	3–35	$1\frac{29}{32}$	.15885	9–02
$2\frac{5}{32}$	.06510	3–43	$1\frac{15}{16}$	.16146	9–10
$1\frac{3}{16}$	.06770	3–52	$1\frac{31}{32}$	.16406	9–19
$2\frac{7}{32}$	.07031	4–01	2	.16667	9–28
$\frac{7}{8}$	.07292	4–10	$2\frac{1}{4}$	.18750	10–37
$2\frac{9}{32}$	.07552	4–19	$2\frac{1}{2}$	.20833	11–46
$1\frac{5}{16}$	.07813	4–28	$2\frac{3}{4}$	.22916	12–54
$3\frac{1}{32}$	.08073	4–37	3	.25000	14–02
1	.08333	4–46	$3\frac{1}{2}$	.29167	16–16
$1\frac{1}{32}$	.08594	4–55	4	.33333	18–26
$1\frac{1}{16}$	.08854	5–04	$4\frac{1}{2}$	.37500	20–33
$1\frac{3}{32}$	.09115	5–12	5	.41667	22–37
$1\frac{1}{8}$	.09375	5–21	6	.50000	26–34
$1\frac{5}{32}$	.09635	5–30			

When given the taper, to find the corresponding angle:
1. Divide the given taper per foot by 2.
2. Find the corresponding half-angle in Table 1.
3. Multiply this angle by 2 to get the included angle.

When given the angle, to find the taper per foot:
1. Divide the included angle by 2.
2. Find the corresponding taper in Table 1.
3. Multiply this taper by 2 to get the taper per foot.

When given the taper per foot, to find the tail-center offset:
1. In Table 1, find the corresponding taper per inch.
2. Multiply this by the length in inches.
3. Half this amount is the center offset.

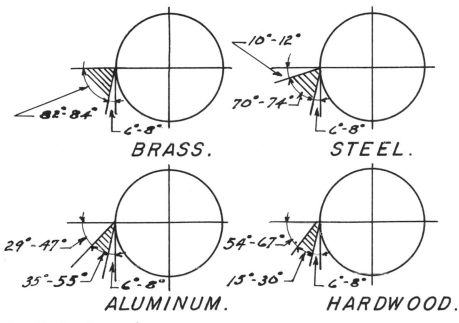

Fig. 41. Cutting angles

Table 2

Tool Grinding with High-Speed Steel Tools

Material	Clearance angle*	Front rake	Side rake	Nose radius
Aluminum	8-10	45	12-18	$\frac{1}{16}$
Bakelite	10-15	0	0	$\frac{1}{16}$
Brass	6	0	0	$\frac{1}{64}$
Cast iron	6	8	14	$\frac{1}{16}-\frac{1}{2}$
Hard steel	6	8	14	$\frac{1}{16}-\frac{1}{2}$
Soft steel	6	8	22	$\frac{1}{16}-\frac{1}{2}$
Copper	18	20	30	$\frac{1}{8}$
Commutators	10	22	15	$\frac{1}{32}$
Phosphor bronze	10	5	0-2	$\frac{1}{16}$

* All the above angles are given in degrees.

With the Armstrong tool holder, the cutting bit is set at an angle that approximates the front or top rake, so this does not have to be ground for most materials. For aluminum, a positive rake should be ground to increase the rake of the tool holder; for brass and bakelite, a negative rake is needed to get the zero rake required.

The correct grinding of all lathe tools is very important. Tools of carbon and high-speed steel are usually ground by hand. For this work, a grinding stand with two wheels set up on it is very handy. One wheel is a coarse-grained wheel for roughing, and the other is fine-grained for finishing. Both wheels must be fitted with work rests that can be adjusted up close to the wheels. Many accidents are caused by having the gap between the rest and the wheel so large that the work can be drawn into it and jammed against the wheel.

The face of the wheels must be straight across and smooth, without any ridges. Use the wheel-dressing tool to condition the face of the wheel, if it is not true. The tool must be kept moving across the face of the grinding wheel to prevent grooves from being formed, as would happen if the tool was held too long in one place. Very little pressure should be used so as not to overheat the tool. It is permissible to cool the tool in water if it is not too hot, but an overheated tool cooled in water is liable to develop small cracks that will cause the cutting edge to crumble under work.

Rough-grind the tool to approximate shape on the quick-cutting wheel and finish to a sharp edge on the fine wheel. The grinding wheels leave a small wire edge on the cutting edge, which will crumble away and leave a small rounded edge to do the cutting. Whetting the cutting edge with a hand whetstone will remove this wire edge and make the tool stand up longer when cutting. The cutting edge can also be improved by whetting with the hand stone without removing the tool from the lathe. Be sure to wear your safety goggles while grinding.

Carboloy-tipped cutting bits can be purchased that will fit into the Armstrong holder, but these are very expensive and hard to grind. In the larger shops, where speed in removing material is required, carboloy tools are used, and a special diamond grinding wheel equipped with tool-grinding holders sharpens them to the exact angles for the work being done. It will not pay to use these tools for small-shop-work: but, if you get a casting with a hard spot that takes the edge off a high-speed steel cutter, you will need a carboloy tool. Machine shops use these tools in sizes too large to fit your tool holders, but they are large enough and strong enough to be used as solid cutters in a holder made for them. After several grindings the hard tip is reduced in size so that it is no longer useful for the heavy work of the large shop, and the entire tool is retired to have a new tip brazed on it. You can probably get some of these retired carboloy tools from the local shop, which will still have enough of the carboloy tip remaining to do a lot of work for you. By taking plenty of time, these tools can be sharpened on your regular grinding wheels. The carboloy facing is very hard but extremely brittle.

It will stand up to a great deal of pressure when backed up by the shank of the tool, but the tip will break if reverse pressure is put on it. Be careful not to let the work turn backward when the tool is in contact with it, or the tip will break. Any other similar pressure will also break it. Figure 42 shows a simple tool post to take these carboloy tools. As the top of the cutting tool should be on the center line of the work, after the block has been faced to size and the center bolt fitted, block it up so an end mill in the three-jaw chuck will mill the slot for the cutting tool with its top in the center line. If you cannot get any of these discarded carboloy tools, it will pay to get one small tool to fit the Armstrong holders and grind it for the hard spot when you need it.

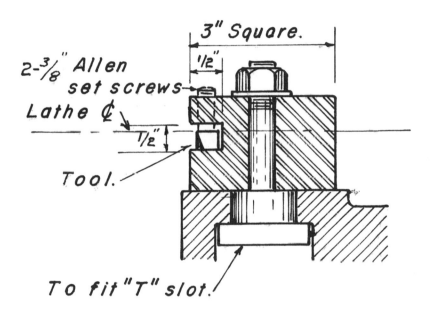

Fig. 42. Carboloy tool holder

Figure 42 shows a simple square block of steel, finished all over, and with a bolt through the center. The head of the bolt is square so that it will not turn and will fit to the "T" slot. Slots for cutting tools can be milled on all four sides so that four cutters can be set up at a time. Each slot should have two ⅜-inch Allen set screws with flat or half-dog points.

CUTTING SPEEDS

Cutting speeds, which vary with the different materials, are measured in feet per minute (fpm) along the surface at the cutting tool. The following is a list of some of the cutting speeds used:

Cast steel	50 fpm
Bronze	70 fpm
Cast iron	70 fpm
Malleable iron	100 fpm
Mild steel	100 fpm
Soft brass	200 fpm
Aluminum	300 fpm

By manipulating the cone pulley and back gears of your lathe, you can obtain several speeds (in RPM) for the spindle in the lathe. When you know the speed of the motor, you will be able to work out speeds for the spindle at each of the several positions of the belt on the cone and settings of the back gears. A table of lathe speeds in RPM should be mounted on the wall near the lathe. You should also copy Table 3, which

Table 3
Diameters with Relative Circumferences*

Diameter (inches)	Circumference (feet)	Diameter (inches)	Circumference (feet)	Diameter (inches)	Circumference (feet)
½	.131	3½	.92	8	2.10
¾	.196	4	1.05	8½	2.22
1	.26	4½	1.18	9	2.36
1¼	.33	5	1.31		
1½	.40	5½	1.45		
1¾	.45	6	1.56		
2	.53	6½	1.83		
2½	.65	7	1.83		
3	.79	7½	1.95		

* The lathe speed in RPM can also be found by using the following formula:

$$RPM = \frac{feet\ per\ minute}{.26 \times diameter\ in\ inches}$$

where: $.26 = \dfrac{\pi}{12}$.

gives the circumference in feet for various diameters, and place it alongside the table of RPM. Using these two tables, you can quickly select the most efficient speed for the material you are working with. Divide the required speed in feet per minute by the circumference in feet, as given in the table; then select the nearest speed in RPM from the speed table. The formula is:

$$RPM = \frac{\text{feet per minute}}{\text{circumference in feet}}$$

The cutting speed will vary with not only the type of material being cut, but also the shape and rigidity of the piece of material. Work that is difficult to hold in a chuck or on a mandrel, or work too large for the capacity of the lathe, may have to be cut at a speed lower than one given in the table. Maximum speed is also not advisable if the tool tends to heat and become dull too rapidly. The table gives cutting speeds for average conditions. Experience will soon teach you when to modify the cutting speed or the shape of the cutting edge. A little cutting oil will often allow a speed higher than does dry cutting. Try it.

Chip Forming

When turning a ductile material, like mild steel, the chip is formed primarily by shear, and the chip curls up the face of the tool and forms long spirals. The chip may be separated from the work by the wedging action of the tool. In this case, the point of the tool does very little cutting, the least power is consumed, and a good finish is left (see Figure 43).

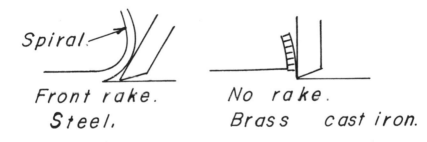

Spiral.

Front rake.
Steel.

No rake.
Brass   cast iron.

Fig. 43. Chip forms

With brittle materials, the cutting tool can have little or no rake, as there is no wedging action, and the chip crumbles in small pieces in front of the tool. This applies to cast iron and brass.

Where the chip curls up the face of the tool, a great deal of friction takes place, which heats the tool. Lubrication with a cutting oil will reduce this friction and tend to keep the tool cool. Applying the cutting oil to the work piece from a squirt can does not keep a good oil film under the chip. The heat of the chip will drive the oil film away from the cut, leaving the tool dry. Just spreading the oil on the work ahead of the cut is also not enough. It is necessary to keep applying it right at the tool: use it sparingly, but use enough to keep oil on the cutting tool at all times.

When you work with certain metals, such as aluminum, you will notice that heating of the tool causes a deposit to form on the cutting edge. Use oil to free the tool of this deposited material, which tends to dull the cutting edge.

SPECIAL LATHE CENTERS

There are often jobs that cannot be set up on the standard lathe centers, and for these special centers are needed. For setting up work with a large hole, such as a piece of pipe, the cone center is used (see Figure 44). This is a cone made to turn on a shank that fits in the tail stock. The head end of the work is usually held in a chuck. This cone center is not very accurate. The hole in the work may not be a true circle, and the cone will bear more on one side. This tends to let the work wobble on the cone, and the finished job will be subject to these wobbles.

A better method is to braze a piece of scrap across the hole and ream a center on this piece. Use soft solder if the work is brass, or silver solder if it is steel or cast iron. The piece of scrap can then be melted off the finished work at low heat that will not injure the finished piece. However, there may be jobs where the large cone center will help, so it will be worth your while to construct one. The shank is fitted to the tail stock, and the head end is finished for a bearing in the cone. There must be a shoulder on the shank to take the pressure of the centers. This shank should be made from alloy steel, but it does not have to be hardened. The cone is made of cast iron, which is a good bearing material for running on the steel shank. Make several cones of different sizes to fit the one shank. Ream the holes and mount them on a mandrel to turn the outside. The bearing should be a tight-running fit when properly oiled.

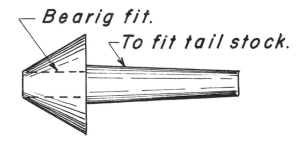

Fig. 44. Cone center

Another handy fixture is the extension center. This is simply a tail center about three inches longer than standard centers so that it can reach in to mate with a center hole hidden by some projection on the work piece that would strike the tail stock if a standard center was used. Because of the long overhang of this center, the force of the cutting tool can make it spring, so only light cuts should be taken with it. It is useful to steady work set up in a chuck that is of an irregular shape and that projects so far from the chuck that it is liable to be torn out of the chuck. This center should be made of tool steel so that it can be hardened and ground to the 60° angle.

Another handy tail center is a flat plate on a taper shank, often called a drill pad. It is used to feed work up to a drill held in the head stock chuck. A variation is to fit a "V" block on a taper shank so that round stock can be drilled in the lathe. The center of the "V" should be in alignment with the center of the shank.

FITS

There are several classes of fits between a hole and a shaft. These have been standardized by the American Standards Association for use in production work. They have divided the fits into eight classes. For your work in the home shop you will not need all these classes. They give formulae for computing the allowance and the tolerance of the shaft and the hole. All these formulae involve the use of the cube root of the diameter. Since extracting the cube root of some odd fractional size is not easy, these formulae are useful only to the designer, who can make the computations in his office and record them on the drawings of the finished part.

The numbers in the first column of Table 4 are the classifications of the American Standards Association.

The limits shown in Classes 6 and 8 are positive.

In making shrink fits, it is necessary to work fast, as the work will cool quickly and if it is not in its final position you will never be able to correct it, unless it is possible to heat the hole and not heat the shaft. Sometimes this can be done by protecting the shaft with wet cloths and using a small flame from the torch on the hole. Better be sure your dimensions are correct before heating. Have a shoulder on the shaft to position the hole. Have a pipe sleeve handy that will slip over the shaft to push the hot hole down into place. It may be a little tight, and you cannot move it while trying to place it with the tongs. Be ready to tap it a few blows if necessary. Care must be used in shrinking a cast-iron hole on a shaft. Cast iron will not stand much tension, and since the shaft is larger than the hole it will expand against the hole as it cools, putting great tension in the surrounding cast iron, which may crack it. Use the smaller of the two limits in Table 4 for cast iron.

Table 4

Hole and Shaft Fits

Nominal Diameter	Up to 1/2-in.	9/16-in. to 1-in.	1 1/16-in. to 2-in.	2 1/16-in. to 3-in.	3 1/16-in. to 4-in.
CLASS 1 LOOSE FIT (WITH ALLOWANCE FOR RUNNING)					
High limit	—.0010	—.0012	—.0017	—.0020	—.0025
Low limit	—.0020	—.0027	—.0035	—.0042	—.0050
Tolerance	.0010	.0015	.0018	.0022	.0025
CLASS 2 FREE-RUNNING FIT					
High limit	—.0007	—.0010	—.0012	—.0015	—.0020
Low limit	—.0012	—.0020	—.0025	—.0030	—.0035
Tolerance	.0005	.0010	.0013	.0015	.0015
CLASS 3 MEDIUM-RUNNING FIT					
High limit	—.0005	—.0007	—.0007	—.0010	—.0010
Low limit	—.0007	—.0012	—.0015	—.0020	—.0022
Tolerance	.0002	.0005	.0008	.0010	.0012
CLASS 4 PUSH FIT					
High limit	—.0002	—.0002	—.0002	—.0005	—.0005
Low limit	—.0007	—.0007	—.0010	—.0010	—.0010
Tolerance	.0005	.0005	.0005	.0005	.0005
CLASS 6 DRIVING FIT					
High limit	.0005	.0010	.0015	.0025	.0030
Low limit	.0002	.0007	.0010	.0015	.0020
Tolerance	.0003	.0003	.0005	.0010	.0010
CLASS 8 PRESS OR SHRINK FIT					
High limit	.0010	.0020	.0040	.0060	.0080
Low limit	.0005	.0015	.0030	.0045	.0060
Tolerance	.0005	.0005	.0010	.0015	.0020

ECCENTRIC TURNING

When part of the work is to be eccentric to the main center line, first turn the main part and then offset the work by the amount of the eccentricity. If the work is such that it can be held in a chuck, the four-jaw chuck can be used, unless the offset is greater than the jaws can take.

When the offset is large, two of the jaws, the ones at 90° to the axis of the offset, may be so far from the center line that they cannot grip the work. Then the work must be clamped to the face plate in the offset position, using an angle block if necessary.

Where the work is held between centers, a new set of centers are drilled and reamed at the required offset. If the diameter of the shaft is large enough to take the second set of centers, they can be drilled in the work. Where the second hole would not be permitted, a cup must be fitted over the ends and the offset centers drilled in the cup. Where the second centers lie outside the ends of the shaft, flanges must be fitted at each end and the offset centers drilled in the flanges (see Figure 45).

This is the condition when turning a crankshaft. Since it is essential that the second set of centers be parallel to the main center line, the work is set on a flat surface, and the height of all the centers is then marked with the surface gauge. In turning a crankshaft, only small cuts can be used, and the tools much be narrow enough to work between the throws of the crank pin without striking them. The Armstrong tool holder will be too wide for a small shaft, so forged tools will have to be used.

The pressure lengthwise from the lathe centers must be taken by fitting blocks between the crank throws and the end flanges, or else the shaft will spring from this pressure and be turned out of true. For the same reason, the blocks must not be wedged in so tightly that they spring the shaft in the opposite direction. When fitting the blocks, have the work set between the centers and use the dial gauge to indicate when the wedges start to spring the shaft. Hardwood blocks are suitable, or else little jackscrews can be made by threading the inside of a pipe to take a cap screw that can be adjusted to length. The head of the cap screw should be turned to a flat cone so that it will bear on one spot at the center, otherwise it may bear on a corner and be impossible to tighten.

Large crankshafts are usually made from forgings. Sometimes a special ductile cast iron is used. For drop-forged or cast shafts, the space between the crank throws is open and ready for turning. With hand-forged shafts or small shafts cut from solid stock, this space must be cut out by sawing down the sides and drilling across the end.

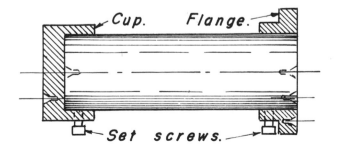

45. Eccentric centers

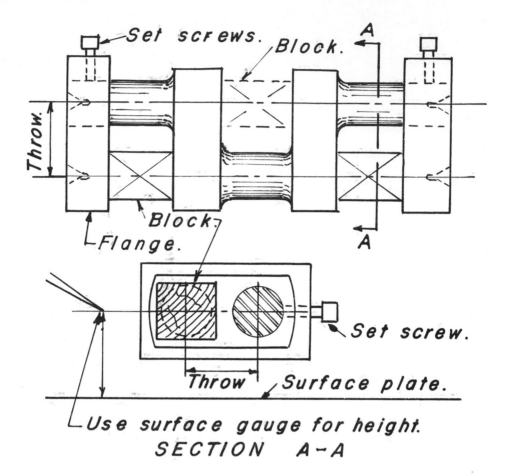

Set screws. *Block.* A

Throw.

Block.

Flange.

Use surface gauge for height.

Set screw.

Throw *Surface plate.*

SECTION   A-A

Fig. 46. Section A-A of crankshaft

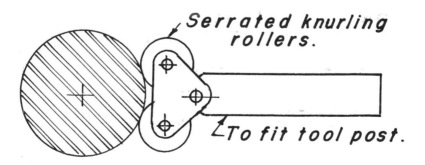

Serrated knurling rollers.

To fit tool post.

Fig. 47. Knurling tool

KNURLING

Knurling is the process of making a serrated surface on round work for the purpose of getting a better grip on a handle, for ornamentation or for making light press fits where a small amount of torque is to be transmitted from a shaft to a flange or pulley.

The knurling tool consists of two hardened grooved wheels mounted in a pivoted frame, so that when they are pressed against the revolving work, the grooves will form little ridges and hollows on the work (see Figure 47). For most work, two knurling wheels are used, having right- and left-hand spiral grooves. The marks cross and make a diamond pattern.

The knurls do not cut and remove any metal. They upset the metal between the ridges so that the knurled part is larger than the unknurled part. If the knurled part is pressed into a hole where the unknurled part was a loose fit, the result will be as tight as a light-driving fit. If only one roller is used, the grooves will be diagonal and not diamond-patterned. If these knurls are hardened before pressing into the hole, the ridges will cut little mating grooves in the hole and form a series of small splines that will transmit a considerable amount of torque.

To use the knurling tool, the work must have adequate centers at each end to stand the heavy pressure. The work is revolved at slow speed, and the tool is mounted in the tool post so that its center is in line with the lathe centers. The reason the two grooved wheels are on a pivoted arm is so that the pressure will be evenly divided between them. If they were rigidly held, one wheel would cut deeper than the other and spoil the diamond pattern. When a single wheel is used it is rigidly held in the tool shank.

Getting the pattern well started is the most important part of knurling. The knurl wheels are revolved by their contact with the work, and the number of marks made on the work may not be an even number. The pitch of the marks on the knurls is fixed and may not go an even number of times into the circumference of the work. The grooves cut by the knurl must be deep enough to pull the ridges of the knurl into the grooves cut by its last revolution. This means deep cutting on the first time around. If the full width of the knurl was in contact with the work, tremendous pressure would have to be used to cut grooves deep enough to make the knurls track to a full pattern. Start knurling with the wheels only partly cutting by using only about one quarter the width of the knurls. Use sufficient pressure to get the pattern well established on this small cut and then feed the knurls along the work until the full surface is knurled. If the knurls do not pick up the pattern on the first revolution, they will start a second pattern in between on the second revolution, thus spoiling the pattern.

If a knurled surface in the form of a ring is to be cut, turn a raised diameter the width of the ring and large enough so that the knurl teeth will be entirely outside the smooth surface on each side. The knurls can then start on one edge and will not mark the smooth surface. The raised part does not have to be as high as the full depth of the knurled pattern, because, after the pattern has been started at the edge, the tool can be moved to the center, and sufficient pressure can be used to complete the pattern. The knurls also upset the pattern so that a smaller raise than the depth of cut can be used. For a wide-knurled surface, a slow power feed can be used after the pattern has been well started.

5

Thread Cutting

CUTTING threads, either with chasing tools, such as taps and dies, or in the lathe, requires more skill and practice than most other metalworking operations.

TAPS

The tap is used to cut internal threads. There are many forms of taps used in manufacturing work, but the hand tap is the only one used in a home workshop. Three taps are used for each size of thread. The *taper tap* is used to start the thread. This has a long taper ground on the point that will enter the drilled hole and act as a pilot to guide and center the tap. Even with this self-guiding feature, you must hold it in line with the hole or it will start crooked. The tapered end will try to get it back to the center of the hole, and this will bend the tap and is liable to break it.

Because of the long taper of the starting, or taper, tap, it cannot reach very far into the hole, and so a tap with a shorter taper, called a *plug tap*, is used after the thread has been started with the taper tap. For holes that are drilled clear through the piece of work, the plug tap can finish the thread, but, for blind holes, a *bottom tap* is used to finish to the bottom of the hole. This tap is square across the end without the taper, just a small chamfer.

It is possible to start a thread with a plug tap by carefully guiding it and using sufficient pressure. It is not possible to start a thread with a bottom tap. If your budget does not permit the purchasing of the three taps, get a plug tap and a bottom tap.

Taps are easily broken and must be handled very carefully. Never use a tap wrench too large for the tap and do not force it as it cuts a chip. After the chip has formed, turn the tap backwards until it breaks the chip. With very small taps, it helps to run the plug tap in as far as it will stand without breaking, then back it out and cut with the bottom tap until it reaches its limit. This way, each tap cuts less metal each time and is less liable to be broken by twisting. It takes longer, but is worth the extra time by saving broken taps. It helps to have two small tap wrenches so that the two taps can be left set up in the wrenches. Bending a small tap sideways is one of the easiest ways of breaking it. Turn the tap with the fingertips of one hand and use the other hand to steady the first by resting your wrist on the vise.

When tapping a hole where the tap must line up with a clearance hole, place the two parts together and tap the thread through the clearance hole, which acts as a guide. If the two holes are not in line, the tap will be forced against the tight side of the clearance hole and will cut threads that will allow the screw to enter the threaded lower part. These part threads cut in the clearance hole may prevent the screw from clamping the two parts tight, and it may be necessary to remove them with a round file.

When a thread must be exactly parallel to a drilled hole, it is best to start the tap in the drill press before the work has been released from the clamps used to drill the hole. Insert the tap in the drill chuck and adjust the chuck so that the tap will slip if it is biting too hard. Use a short rod that will fit into the key holes of the chuck to turn it, at the same time using a little pressure on the drill-press feed to start the tap. The entire thread can be cut this way, which is rather slow; or, after it is well started, the work can be removed from the drill press and the thread finished by hand in the vise.

If it was necessary to move the drill-press table to remove the drill and insert the tap, make sure it is returned to the exact position used to drill the hole. Adjust the collar on the column so that the table will not drop down and fix the turn indicator to its position, before moving the table. If there is no turn indicator, make a chalk mark on the column. This same method of starting a tap in a drilled hole applies to holes drilled in the lathe. In this case the tap is placed in the tail-stock chuck, and the work is turned by hand, using a wrench on the chuck jaws to turn with and feeding with the tail stock.

Larger taps, like pipe taps, cannot be held in the drill-press chuck. These taps generally have a center reamed in the head end, and a 60° stub center can be set up in the drill press to line up the tap. Then the tap is turned with a wrench on its square end. This stub center is a piece of $\frac{1}{2}$-inch stock turned to a 60° point. It does not need to be hardened, although it would last longer if it were hard. This stub center is very useful in locating a punch mark under the center of the drill. Set the stub center in the drill chuck and center the work under it before clamping to the table.

Many firms supplying drills have printed cards showing the size of hole to be drilled for taps and the clearance holes for threads. These also show the size of drills and their decimal equivalent. Get two of these cards, one showing the tap drills and the other the decimal equivalents. Mount them on the wall near the drill press. We are including these two tables in this book, but as the book may seldom be handy when you need it, and as your hands may be greasy at the time, you will seldom refer to the book. If you cannot obtain these printed cards, take the time to copy these two tables and mount them on the wall. Cards mounted on the wall should have a clear plastic cover over them to keep them clean.

DIES

Dies are used to cut external threads. The small button dies of 1-inch diameter are very handy for threads up to ½-inch, but for threads over ½-inch, larger dies are required. Even the button die of 1-inch for ½-inch threads is so narrow that only a few teeth can cut the thread. This size is very useful for rerunning a thread that has been damaged.

Only one die of each size is needed. One side of the die has a taper for starting and is used for cutting the thread. The other side has the full thread clear to the face of the die, and the die can be turned this side to the work to finish the thread up to a shoulder.

It is difficult to start a die square with the work. If it is not started square, it will try to follow its own threads, while at the same time running off-center to the work, which tries to force it back to center. The result is a very crooked thread. There are die stocks that have three adjustable fingers on the starting side. These can be set to bear on the work and guide the die square. You should also have a plain die stock to finish threads in close quarters where the stock with the guide is too wide to use.

When you purchase the dies, get the kind that are split on one side so that the size can be adjusted. There are a lot of these button dies sold at bargain stores that are not true to size. These can cause a lot of trouble by cutting an odd-sized thread. Get dies made by one of the recognized, nationally established firms, so that you will be sure of getting good ones. It is often required to cut a thread a little under size, say, for a free-running nut, and the adjustable die can do this. It is also possible to cut an undersize thread by rerunning the thread with the die held at an angle. This makes the die cut some off the side of the previously cut thread, but it will not be a true and even thread, and is to be used only when an adjustable die is not at hand and never where accurate threads are required.

For cutting threads in the lathe with these button dies, use a die holder that fits in the tail stock. This has a guide portion on which the die can slide as it feeds onto the work. The thread is started by putting pressure on the die with the tail stock. After it is started, the die will feed itself. The lathe can be run under power, using the slowest speed of the back gears. On completion of the thread, the lathe is reversed and backed off the die. When backing off the die, be sure to remove the amount of feed used to start the die, or the die will stop backing off when the free travel is used up and will chew up the threads. It is best to unclamp the entire tail stock from the bed as you start to back off; you can then be sure the die can work all the way off without doing any damage. A little sulphur-base cutting oil should be used on both taps and dies. With brass and aluminum, the taps and dies tend to stick to the metal unless oil is used.

THREAD CUTTING IN A LATHE

Threads that must be accurate with some turned part must be turned in the lathe at the same setting used to turn the work. For this work, a proper cutting tool is set up in the tool post, and the lead screw is geared to the head-stock spindle to give the required lead to the thread. The gears to use for each thread are shown on a plate attached to the lathe by the maker. But you should know how to gear the lathe without the plate. There is a gear of a known number of teeth permanently attached to the head-stock spindle. This gear is followed by a set of gears used to reverse the rotation of the lead screw. After the reverse gears is another gear, which is the same size as the one on the spindle called the stud gear and which revolves at the same speed as the spindle. If a train of gears is set up between the stud gear and the lead screw, the lead screw can be made to revolve at any desired speed. The lead screw has a thread of a fixed number of threads per inch. If the lead screw can be made to advance the cutting tool one thread-space, or thread-pitch, per revolution of the work, the result will be a thread of that pitch. The rule for finding the ratio of teeth in the lead-screw gear to the teeth in the stud gear is to multiply the pitch of the thread to be cut by the teeth in the stud gear and divide by the pitch of the lead screw, which will give the number of teeth in the lead-screw gear. As an example:

> Required: to cut a thread of a pitch of 10 threads per inch.
> Stud gear has 32 teeth.
> Lead-screw pitch is 8 threads per inch.

$$\text{Screw teeth} = \frac{\text{required pitch} \times \text{stud teeth}}{\text{lead-screw pitch}} \quad \text{or} \quad \frac{10 \times 32}{8} = 40$$

A gear with 40 teeth on the screw will cut a thread with a pitch of 10 threads per inch.

It sometimes happens that the gear required is not available, and then a compound setup must be made. On an intermediate stud, set up two gears to drive the lead-screw gear at half-speed and use a screw gear of half the teeth, or compound for twice the speed and use a gear of twice the teeth.

To check the gear train:

Pitch of lead screw, multiplied by the product of all the driving gears, divided by the product of all the driven gears will give the pitch of the thread to be cut.

With lathes equipped with quick-change gears, most common threads can be set up by moving the required gears, but when it is necessary to cut a thread of an odd pitch, the train of gears between the stud gear and the quick-change-gear box will have to be changed. As as example, metric threads can be cut on a lathe having a lead screw with the pitch in inches by using the ratio of 50 on the stud to 127 on the screw. This is because there are 127 centimeters in 50 inches.

Tail-stock die holder

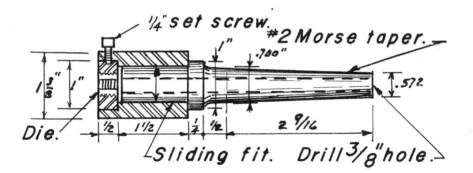

Fig. 48. Tail-stock die holder

The cutting tool is ground with a point making a 60° angle. This angle can be tested in one of the "V" notches of the thread-cutting gauge. The compound slide is set to an angle of 60°, and the tool is set square with the work, using the "V" notch of the thread gauge to set the tool. The point of the tool must be at the same height as the lathe centers. The tool is run up to the work with the cross feed, and the cross-feed stop is set to always bring the cross feed back to the same position after backing out the tool to return for another cut. The compound slide is used to feed the tool into the work. By feeding the tool on the 60° angle to which the compound slide is set, the tool cuts on one side only, and it can be given a side rake to make the chip clear the thread groove. If

Lathe set for thread turning. The compound slide is set to 60°, the feed selector is set at neutral, and the half-nuts are closed by the lever at the lower right side of the apron. The thread dial is shown geared to the feed screw.

the tool is fed in square with the work, it will have to cut on both sides. No side rake can be used, and the two opposing chips will interfere and jam in the cut.

The carriage is attached to the feed screw by closing the half-nuts. There is a safety interlock between the friction feed for turning and the half-nuts for thread cutting, so the two cannot be engaged at the same time, which would wreck something. At the end of each cut, the half-nuts are opened, and the tool is withdrawn from the cut, so that the carriage can be returned to the start for another cut. If the tool is not withdrawn from the cut, the backlash of the feed gears would leave the tool out of line with the thread and if the lathe were reversed, the tool would damage the thread. If your lathe is not equipped with a thread-cutting dial, you will have to reverse the lathe to return the tool to the start for another cut. Without the thread dial, the half-nuts cannot be opened until the thread is completed.

The thread-cutting dial indicator is a dial geared to the lead screw. When the carriage is stationary, the dial revolves, but when the carriage is cutting a thread, the dial is still. There are several graduations on the dial, each numbered. As the dial revolves, the half-nuts are closed when the correct number comes up to the index mark. For most even-numbered threads, there are several places on the dial that can be used to close the half-nuts; but, for odd-numbered threads, there is only one position, and the half-nuts must always be closed on the same number used to start the first cut. After making the first cut, return the tool until it nearly touches but does not cut and try the several numbers on the dial to see which ones track the tool in the first cut. Then any of these can be used for the rest of the job.

In starting the first cut, close the half-nuts on the number 1 line of the dial and feed the tool with the compound until the tool just scratches a fine line, indicating the thread. Shut down the lathe and test this line with the thread-pitch gauge to see that the lathe is cutting correctly. The cross feed of the carriage must always be up tight to the cross-feed stop before moving the tool with the compound feed. At the end of the cut, if the thread just fades out, it is necessary to withdraw the tool while the feed is still on so that the thread will finish with a taper. To do this requires working at slow speed, and it helps to put a chalk mark on the work so that the tool can be backed out at the same place each revolution.

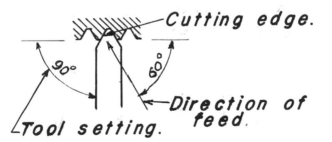

Fig. 49. Cutting threads

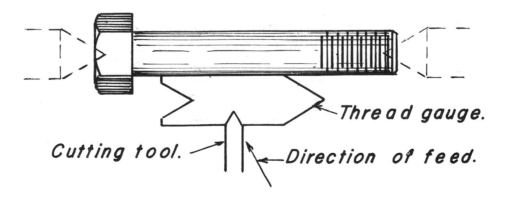

Fig. 50. Setting thread tool

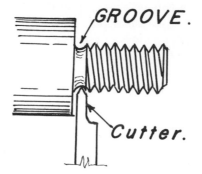

Fig. 51. Stopping against a shoulder

When the thread finishes close to a shoulder, turn a small groove next to the shoulder as deep as the bottom of the thread so that the tool can finish in this groove, leaving a complete thread up to the shoulder so that the nut will tighten up tight to the shoulder. It is wise to set the carriage stop so that the tool cannot run into the shoulder. The cutting tool should be ground so that the point will be in the groove while the side clears the shoulder. Where it is not necessary that the nut run up tight against a shoulder, the tool can cut its own finishing groove if you open the half-nuts at the same place each time and if you let the tool cut a complete circle each time before withdrawing it.

To use successfully any of these methods of finishing a cut, you must work quickly with both hands: back the tool out with one hand while you open the half-nuts with the other. When you return the tool for another cut, advance the compound slide by the amount of the chip. Never change the setting of the cross-feed stop after you have started to cut a thread or you will throw the tool out of alignment with previous cuts.

To find out how far to advance the compound in order to cut a required depth of thread: refer to Table 6, at the appropriate *DD* column (short for *double depth of thread*); then look across to the 60° column at the right of it. Before you start the first cut, with the tool barely touching the work, set the micrometer collar on the compound feed at zero. If the tool were traveling square with the work, you would advance the tool as far as half the double depth of thread (that is, half the amount given in the *DD* column). In this case, however, since the tool is traveling on the 60° angle of the compound, you must divide half the *DD* figure by the sine of 60°, or .866; the resulting figure will be the amount by which the tool is to be advanced on the compound slide. When it has advanced as far as the amount given in the *60°* column, the thread should be at its finished diameter.

Since there is always some springiness or backlash in both the cutting tool and the work, you will have to take several finishing cuts with the tool at its final setting, without advancing it any deeper, so that it can work out the oversize cutting. When possible, keep handy a nut of the required size that has an accurate thread, and use this to test the new thread. If the work is driven by a lathe dog while on centers, be sure the slot in the driving plate is marked so that the dog will be replaced in the same slot each time after removal for testing.

Use plenty of cutting oil when cutting steel. Brass and cast iron can be cut dry, but aluminum tends to stick to the tool and leave a rough surface unless a little oil is used.

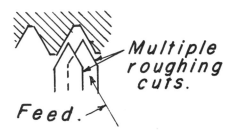

Fig. 52. Roughing out a large thread

When cutting large threads, which tend to overload the tool on a single cut, it is wise to run through with a roughing cut, keeping well within the space of the finished thread, and then reset the tool to make the finishing cuts of the full-size thread. Trying to cut a large thread by using the full width of the tool and a small depth of cut is not advisable, as it will probably cause chatter due to the tool's not biting enough to steady it (see Figure 52).

Multiple threads require that the lead screw be geared to the pitch of one of the threads. When this is finished, disengage the gears to the feed screw and turn the screw one half a revolution for a double thread or one third a revolution for a triple thread. For this to be done, the gear on the lead screw must have a number of teeth that is divisible by the number of threads. Then mark the starting tooth and count off the required number of teeth to move the screw. This requires that the train of gears from the stud to the screw must mesh at the same tooth each time, so all gears must be marked and replaced at the correct tooth.

Thread Forms

The *American standard thread* is a 60° angle with one eighth of the depth of thread cut off the top and bottom of the thread. As this flat part will vary with every pitch of thread, it is necessary to grind a separate tool for each pitch. The width of this flat part can be set off on the micrometer and the grinding fitted to it. As a full "V" thread will work at the root of the thread, it is possible to cut threads with a sharp "V" point that will work with the American standard thread. This leaves the diameter at the root of the thread smaller than for the American standard and reduces its strength, but for many jobs it is entirely adequate.

There are several other thread forms used in the United States. The *Acme thread* has a side slope of $14\frac{1}{2}°$ or an included angle of 29°. This is the thread used on lead screws where the half-nuts must have clearance for entering. It is commonly used on all feed screws on machine

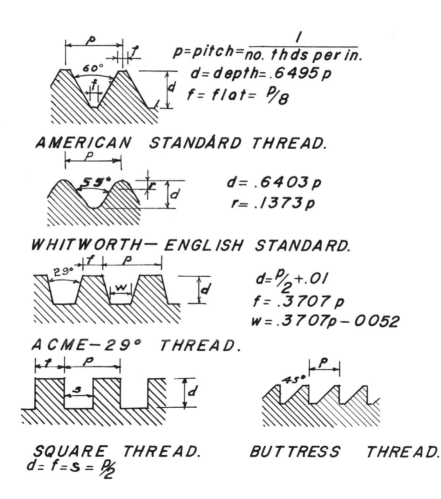

Fig. 53. Screw thread forms

tools. Another thread form is the *square thread*. This is a strong thread, and, since its bearing surface is less than that of the other forms, the friction is less. It is used on jacks and vise screws where the load is heavy. A third form of thread is the *buttress thread,* which is straight on the pressure side but sloped at 45° on the back side. It can be used only where the pressure is from one direction, as with quick-opening vise screws. All of these threads require tools to be ground to their individual shapes; and, as the cuts are large, it is best to rough out the thread with a smaller tool. These tools require that the sides have sufficient relief to clear the sides of the thread due to the spiral angle.

The American standard pipe thread is similar to the American standard machine thread, except that it has a taper of ¾ inch per foot. It is not possible to cut a pipe thread accurately on a lathe unless a taper attachment is used. It can be approximated by varying the depth of cut along the length of thread, but this will not produce a leakproof thread. It is best to rough out the thread in the lathe and finish with a standard tap or die.

Left-hand threads are cut the same as right-hand ones, except that the feed of the lead screw and the angle of the compound slide are reversed and the rake of the tool is changed so that the tool is cutting off the advancing edge.

Internal threads are cut with a boring bar with the proper shape of cutter inserted. The feed of the compound slide is outward on each cut, and the carriage stop must be set so that the bar cannot accidentally run too deep into the work. Remember to oil the work before trying a nut on a thread, as you do when you are fitting a plug into a hole. If entered dry, it may seize and ruin the work when backing out.

Table 5

Machine-Screw Threads

Screw size (inches)	Thread series	Tap drill	Clearance drill
2/64	NC	#50	#42
2/56	NF	50	42
4/40	NC	43	31
4/48	NF	42	31
6/32	NC	36	26
6/40	NF	33	26
8/32	NC	29	17
8/36	NF	29	17
10/24	NC	25	8
10/32	NF	21	8
12/24	NC	16	1
12/28	NF	14	1

Table 6
Fractional Thread Sizes

Screw size (inches)	Thread series††	Tap drill	"V": DD*	60°†	USS: DD*	60°†
¼–20	NC	7	.086	.050	.065	.037
¼–28	NF	3	.062	.035	.046	.027
$\frac{5}{16}$–18	NC	F (¼)**	.096	.055	.071	.042
$\frac{5}{16}$–24	NF	I ($\frac{9}{32}$)	.073	.042	.054	.031
⅜–16	NC	$\frac{5}{16}$	.108	.063	.080	.047
⅜–24	NF	Q ($\frac{11}{32}$)	.072	.042	.054	.031
$\frac{7}{16}$–14	NC	U (⅜)	.124	.071	.093	.054
$\frac{7}{16}$–20	NF	$\frac{25}{64}$	.087	.050	.065	.037
½–13	NC	$\frac{27}{64}$	.133	.077	.099	.057
½–20	NF	$\frac{29}{64}$	.087	.050	.065	.037
$\frac{9}{16}$–12	NC	$\frac{31}{64}$	.144	.084	.108	.067
$\frac{9}{16}$–18	NF	$\frac{33}{64}$	.096	.035	.072	.027
⅝–11	NC	$\frac{17}{32}$	.157	.091	.118	.068
⅝–18	NF	$\frac{37}{64}$	.096	.035	.072	.027
¾–10	NC	$\frac{21}{32}$	.173	.100	.130	.075
¾–16	NF	$\frac{11}{16}$	.108	.063	.081	.047
⅞– 9	NC	$\frac{49}{64}$	.192	.110	.144	.083
⅞–14	NF	$\frac{13}{16}$	.124	.072	.093	.054
1– 8	NC	⅞	.217	.125	.163	.094
1–14	NF	$\frac{15}{16}$	.124	.072	.093	.053
1⅛– 7	NC	$\frac{63}{64}$	.247	.143	.186	.107
1⅛–12	NF	$1\frac{3}{64}$	.144	.084	.108	.067
1¼– 7	NC	$1\frac{7}{64}$	.247	.143	.186	.107
1¼–12	NF	$1\frac{11}{64}$	.157	.084	.118	.067
1⅜– 6	NC	$1\frac{7}{32}$	.288	.167	.217	.125
1⅜–12	NF	$1\frac{19}{64}$	.144	.084	.108	.067
1½– 6	NC	$1\frac{11}{32}$	.288	.091	.188	.068
1½–12	NF	$1\frac{27}{64}$	.144	.084	.108	.067
1¾– 5	NC	$1\frac{9}{16}$	.347	.200	.259	.150
2–4½	NC	$1\frac{25}{32}$	.385	.225	.289	.167

* *DD* means *double depth of thread*. Deduct this amount from the external diameter to find the diameter of the root of the thread, which is the size to which a nut for an internal thread must be bored.

† Use the appropriate *60°* column to determine the amount that the compound slide must advance, when set at 60°, to cut to the root of a thread.

** Drill sizes in parentheses are the fractional sizes nearest to the lettered sizes.

†† NC means *National Coarse Series*. NF means *National Fine Series* or *SAE Series*.

Many of the Whitworth threads, which are standard in Great Britain and Canada, were very similar to the United States standard or Sellers thread. On November 18, 1948, a standardization committee representing Canada, the United Kingdom, and the United States agreed on a common standardization of screw threads for their respective countries and called it the United Thread Standard. This means threads used in these several countries are interchangeable. These unified threads are very nearly the same as the existing United States standard threads.

Table 7

Tapered Pipe Threads

Pipe size (inches)	Tap drill	Clearance drill	Threads
$\frac{1}{8}$	R ($\frac{11}{32}$)	$\frac{7}{16}$	27
$\frac{1}{4}$	$\frac{7}{16}$	$\frac{9}{16}$	18
$\frac{3}{8}$	$\frac{37}{64}$	$\frac{3}{4}$	18
$\frac{1}{2}$	$\frac{23}{32}$	$\frac{7}{8}$	14
$\frac{3}{4}$	$\frac{59}{64}$	$1\frac{3}{16}$	14
1	$1\frac{5}{32}$	$1\frac{7}{16}$	$11\frac{1}{2}$
$1\frac{1}{4}$	$1\frac{1}{2}$	$1\frac{3}{4}$	$11\frac{1}{2}$
$1\frac{1}{2}$	$1\frac{47}{64}$	2	$11\frac{1}{2}$
2	$2\frac{7}{32}$	$2\frac{1}{2}$	$11\frac{1}{2}$

The NC series was unified from $\frac{1}{4}$ inch to 4 inches, and is called the UNC series. The NF series was unified from $\frac{1}{4}$ inch to $1\frac{1}{2}$ inches, and is called UNF. There are two exceptions where these UN sizes are not the same as the US series. The $\frac{1}{2}$-inch-13 NC, while still used, has been changed to the $\frac{1}{2}$-inch-12 UNC, and the 1-inch-14 NF has been changed to the 1-inch-12 UNF.

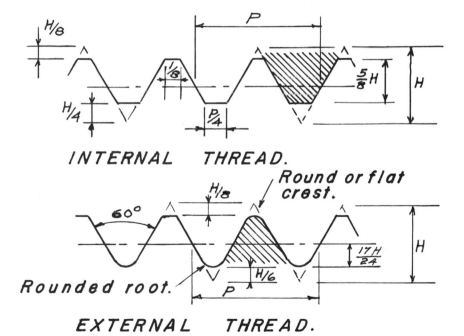

Fig. 54. Unified thread forms

The original 55° angle of the Whitworth thread has been changed to 60°, and the rounding off of the top and bottom now nearly equals the flat top and bottom of the American standard thread. Whitworth threads will now fit American standard threads with very little interference. For all practical purposes in the home workshop you can use the "V" thread for pitches of $\frac{1}{20}$ or less and the American standard thread for larger pitches.

When testing the fit of a thread to a nut, be sure the shapes of the threads are the same. The tops of the threads you have just cut are a sharp 60°, while the nut may be of the United States standard type with one eighth of the height of the threads flattened off. To be sure, run a flat file over the points of the threads you have just cut, reducing them by one eighth, so that the nut will fit the sides of the threads and not bind on the points.

As most threads cut in a lathe have the 60° shape of thread, and since the compound is set to feed the tool at this 60° angle, it is convenient to keep the compound set to this angle. It is then ready for thread cutting; and, since it is feeding at an angle, it also gives a slow motion to the advancing of the tool for either cylindrical turning or facing.

The 30° angle is used for truing the lathe centers, and a 45° angle is used for chamfers. These three angles, 60°, 45°, and 30°, should be prominently marked so that the compound can be set quickly to the desired angle. For general turning, keep it on the 60° mark.

6

Drilling and Reaming

DRILL PRESSES

THERE are three types of drill presses found in most jobbing shops, each designed for a specific type of work. The smallest of these is the *high-speed sensitive drill,* now almost superseded by the popular bench drill. It is equipped with a gear-type chuck that will take drills from the smallest up to the ½-inch size. A large range of speeds can be obtained by changing the belt drive. Drill feed is by hand lever. An adjustable stop limits the depth of hole.

High-speed drill press

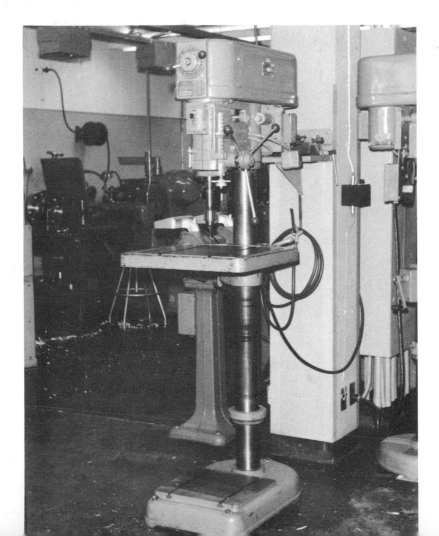

The heavy-duty drill press is mounted on its own base with the drilling quill rigidly attached at the top of the column. The column may be either round or box-shaped with ways for the table to slide on. The table is adjustable for height by means of a jacking screw. It may be arranged to be tilted for drilling at an angle. On round column models, the table can be swung sideways. The spindle has a socket for a Morse taper so that taper-shank drills can be set up in it, or a Jacobs-type chuck mounted on a taper shank can be used with straight-shank drills. The speed of the spindle is adjustable by belt-shifting on cone pulleys or by gears, or by a combination of both. Feed is by hand lever or hand wheel and by power. The power feed is adjustable for slow or fast feeds. Depth of hole is regulated by a stop on hand feed or a power kick-out on power feed.

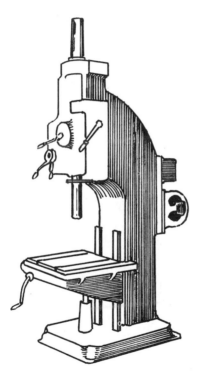 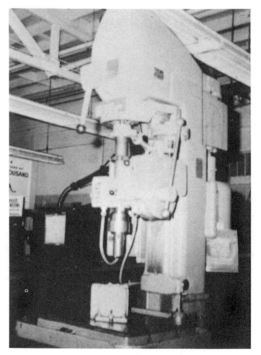

Fig. 55. Heavy-duty drill press

The radial drill press has the spindle mounted on a sliding head carried on a swinging arm mounted on the column, which is round to allow the arm to swing. The work is set up and clamped to the machine base, which has "T" slots for this purpose, and the drill is positioned by raising or lowering the arm and by swinging it and moving the spindle out on the arm. When the drill is in the correct position for drilling, all motions

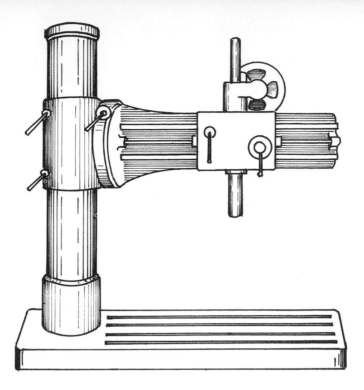

Fig. 56. Radial drill press

Small radial drill press

are clamped against any movement and the drill is fed by the movement of the spindle through the quill. Angle drilling can be done by revolving the head on the arm. The machine is different from the rigid-column heavy drill in that the work is stationary and the drill is movable to position, while with the rigid-column drill the drill is stationary and the work must be positioned under the drill. The radial drill can handle large and heavy castings much easier than the rigid-column drill. All of its adjustments are similar to the ones described for the rigid-column drill press.

In addition to these three universally used drill presses, there are many special machines designed to do specific jobs such as multiple drilling or drilling at several angles at one setting. These are all production machines and are not found in the average shop. Instruction in their use is left to the manufacturer of each special machine.

There are many kinds of drills, each designed to do some specific job, but for the home workshop the common twist drill is the most useful. Under the chapter on SPECIAL TOOLS, we will take up the construction of special drills.

DRILL GRINDING

The condition of the cutting lips of the drill has a great deal to do with how well the drill performs. The drill must be sharp and the two lips ground to the same angle, bevel, and length. Unless the lips are the same length, the long lip will do most of the cutting and the drill will be forced away from the long lip until the short lip does its share. This will make the drill cut an oversize hole. After the points of the cutting lips enter the work, the sides of the drill will guide it, and the drill will tend to work back toward the center, with the result that the hole will be larger at the start than at the finish. If the angle is not the same on both cutting edges, either the center point of the drill will be off center or the outer points of the lips will not be the same length, which will give the same results as though both lips were not ground to the same length.

To drill a true hole, the drill must be perfectly ground. It is almost impossible to hand grind a drill and get it perfect. An experienced mechanic can make a pretty good approximation of it. For holes that do not have to be exact, hand-ground drills do very well. You can tell fairly well the condition of a drill by holding it up to the light and observing the angle and length of the cutting lips. These can be tested by one of the several gauges made for the testing and grinding of drills. Another test is to look directly at the end of the drill. The two cutting lips must be parallel. Any error of angle or length will move the edge down the angle of the spiral and will throw the edges out of parallel. New drills, as received from the maker, are machine-ground and will cut a true hole. You can get a drill-grinding attachment for your bench grinder, so that you can machine-grind your own drills at home. With careful work these do a good job.

There is another place the drill will cut an odd-size hole and that is when it breaks through the last of the cut. If the work is thin, the point will cut through and allow the drill to chatter in the cut. The result is an irregular hole. The outer points of the lips will try to find their own center; and, as there are only two lips, they will dig in and form two slots through which the drill will jump, pulling the work up the spiral of the drill. Even if the work is fastened down, as it certainly should be, there is enough backlash in the drill-press quill to allow the drill to jump ahead. With a thick piece, the drill is not so liable to catch and force the work up the spiral. In any case, a ridge of a smaller diameter than the drill is left at the finish end.

It was explained in Chapter 2 how the four prick-punch marks are located on the circumference of the desired hole. The problem is to make the drill cut exactly tangent to all four of these marks. The center-punch mark must be accurately located and large enough so that the point of the drill can enter it and be a guide for starting the drill. The point of a large drill is very wide and will not enter a center-punch mark unless the mark is larger than the point of the drill. You have used a prick-punch mark in laying out the center of the hole, so now you must open it up to a larger punch mark that will take the point of the drill. The center punch has a much flatter angle to the point than the prick punch and will enlarge the mark, but even if you accurately center it in the small punch mark, if it is not held perfectly plum and struck with a perfectly centered blow, it is liable to be driven off center. Enlarging the prick-punch hole by using a small drill that will center in it and that is large enough to take the larger drill is a more accurate method. The large point of the drill requires much pressure to make it remove metal. The action is scraping with a very negative rake angle and is not a cutting action as is the rest of the cutting lip. This heavy pressure can be relieved by first drilling a pilot hole large enough to take the point of the drill and then opening it out with larger drills. A more accurate hole will be drilled if several smaller sizes of drills are used so that the hole is enlarged in steps and not all at one cut. This is also easier on the drill press as such great pressure is not required as with one large drill.

After drilling the pilot hole, start the larger drill and cut a small crater until the edge approaches the four guide marks. The finish-size drill should be used when checking the guide marks. If the guide marks are all the same distance from the edge of the crater, the drill is cutting true to the center. But if it is off center, the drill must be drawn back toward the center by cutting away some of the crater on the high side. This can be done by chipping with the round-nose chisel or by using a small drill in the electric hand drill to drill away a little metal on the high side. Try the larger drill again and see if its crater is centered on the four guide marks. This correction of the centering must be done and finished before the crater reaches and eliminates the guide marks. This is the reason it is sometimes well to scribe more than one concentric circle and punch a group of guide marks inside the larger ones. The small pilot hole is not large enough to make the larger drill follow it if it is slightly out of line. In enlarging the hole to its final size, use drills ground to the same angle as the one used to make the test crater. These will then follow the test crater and result in a hole being as near to its required position as it is possible to produce by drilling, except by the use of a hardened drill guide to accurately control the drill. As a drill will spring sideways, there is always the chance of some error. A hole that has to be placed on an exact center can only be produced by setting it up in a lathe and boring it, or by the use of an adequate drill guide. As a drill does not cut a perfect hole, it is necessary to finish with a reamer. This applies also to a hole bored in the lathe, where it may be perfectly centered but the reamer will produce a smooth hole exactly to size.

The angle of the cutting edges varies with the kind of material being drilled. For general-purpose drilling, the included angle of the cutting lips is 118°, and the lip-relief angle is 12° to 15°. For hard materials, a blunter point is required; for softer materials, a more acute angle. For soft cast iron, an included angle of 100° is better, and for wood the included angle is 60°. For general work in the home shop, general-purpose grinding, as you will receive the drill from the store, is suitable for most of your work. In drilling brass or copper, this grinding is liable to let the drill bite in too fast and take up the backlash of the drill press, resulting in the drill grabbing and breaking it or the work. This is especially dangerous when drilling with the hand-held electric drill. To prevent this, the cutting lips can be ground on the face of the cutting edge to give a scraping action to the cut. This same grinding of the face of the cutting edge is also used on very hard material, as it allows greater pressure to be applied to the cutting edges.

This face grinding will not ruin the drill for use on mild steel or cast iron, but it will slow up the cutting action. You can regrind the drill after it has been face-ground or let it be worked off as the drill is resharpened. Of course, if you expect to do a great deal of drilling in brass, you can purchase extra drills and keep them ground for drilling in brass, but the general-purpose grinding will be the most useful.

Needless to say, a drill is not intended to be used on hardened steel or chilled cast iron. Carbide-tipped drills can be had for that kind of work, but they are too expensive to be stocked in a home workshop. Get them as you need them when faced with drilling of hard material.

Cast iron requires no lubrication of the drill, but for drilling steel a good cutting oil will help. Also with brass and copper, the material seems to bind on the drill, and, if the hole is deep, a little lubrication helps. With aluminum, the metal tears with a rough surface, and the drill will do a better job if lubricated. In commercial work, various types of cutting oils or cooling compounds are used, varying with the material to be drilled. These are usually pumped to the work and recovered in troughs built into the machine. For your work, a sulphur-base cutting oil, which any hardware or plumbing-supply store can supply, will be most useful. Since your machine tools are not equipped for pumping and recovering, the cutting oil is fed to the work from a squirt can, one of the pump type being best for this work.

Take care that the outer corners of the cutting lips do not get dull. As soon as they start to wear smaller than the rest of the drill, they will start rubbing and not cutting, and the resulting friction will heat the drill until the temper is drawn and the drill is ruined. Be sure the drill is sharp before starting and, if it pulls hard or is noisy in the cut, take it out and sharpen it. Be sure enough pressure is applied to keep the cutting edges always under metal. If they slide over the work they will heat up and soon dull.

The position of the hole is important when drilling. It is not possible to start a hole on an inclined surface, as it will force the drill sideways. Always provide a flat surface, such as a boss or depression, to start the hole. Sometimes a drill can be started on an inclined surface by using an end mill the size of the drill, or larger, to mill a flat surface for starting.

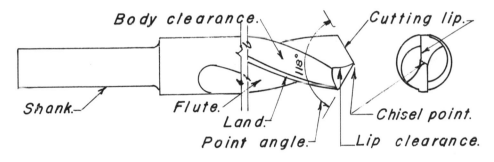

Fig. 57. Drill terms

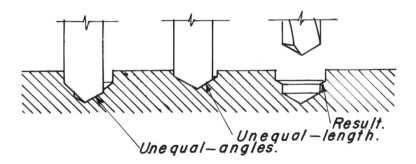

Fig. 58. Incorrectly ground drills

The end mill will be cutting more on the high side and will tend to be forced away from that side and will leave a spot not centered on the drill hole. This will force the drill off center. The end mill must cut a surface large enough to take the entire diameter of the drill.

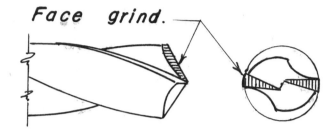

Fig. 59. Drill ground for brass

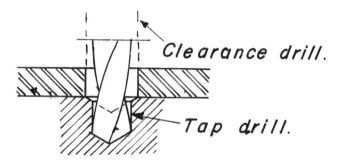

Fig. 60. Lining up drilled holes

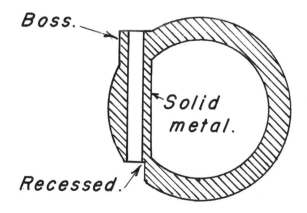

Fig. 61. Drilling on an inclined surface

A drill can be started on an inclined surface by drilling a small way normal to the surface. This will form a crater that will take the point of the drill on the side of the crater when starting to drill at the angle to the surface. You can not locate a hole accurately by this method, as there is no way to lay out the center or the guide marks, and as the drill will not be cutting evenly in this irregular hole, it cannot be controlled.

See that the drill cuts in solid metal the full depth of the cut. If it runs out of the cut on one side, it will force the drill in that direction, and a crooked hole will result. This applies also to when a drill finishes its cut through an inclined surface. The drill will try to run away from the side still cutting, and the sides of the drill will be forced to cut on the side flutes, forming an oval hole. The drill is also liable to catch on the inclined surface as it breaks through and break the drill. Where it is required to drill through from one side and out the other of a curved surface, see that there is a flat surface for the beginning and end of the hole. If the casting has not provided the flat spots, lay out and mill such places before attempting to drill the hole.

Automatic drill press. A punched tape is fed through reels on the front of the cabinet on the right of the drill press. This tape, through the hydraulic system, controls all movements of the drill press.

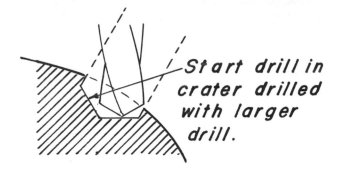

Fig. 62. Starting a drill on an inclined surface

Where two holes are to line up, such as the tap hole and clearance hole of screw threads, two methods can be used. Where possible, the tap size can be drilled clear through both pieces at one time while the parts are clamped together. The clearance hole can then be enlarged after the parts are separated. Where the tap hole cannot be drilled first, drill the clearance hole, and, with the two parts clamped together, use the point of this drill to cut a crater to start the tap drill. This will center the tap drill on the clearance hole.

Where a series of holes are to be drilled, each overlapping into the next, the drill must be prevented from running sideways into the overlapping hole. The first hole can be plugged with a piece of scrap metal so the drill will always be cutting in solid metal, or else a guide for the

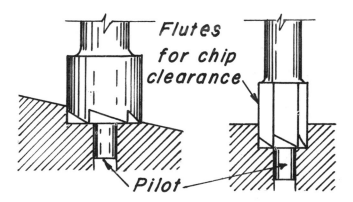

Fig. 63. Spot facing (left). **Countersinking** (right).

drill can be used to prevent its moving sideways into the first hole. This guide can be moved to the location of each hole. If the holes are deep, the drill will bend and run into the first hole after it gets below the guide. This may break the drill. For deep holes, the guide method is not as good as the plugs, but for shallow holes it works very well. The guide will last longer if hardened, but if it does wear to an oval shape, if placed right, it will still guide the drill, and a soft guide can be used. Where it is not possible to plug the holes or use the drill guide, the holes should be laid out just a little farther apart than the diameter of the drill so that it will always be cutting solid metal.

Many holes require the outer surface to be square with the drilled hole. This applies where a bolt head is to bear on the surface. This surface is milled flat after the hole is drilled with a spot-facing tool. This tool has an end like an end mill, but has a guide pin in the center the same size as the drilled hole. This guide pin keeps the spot-facing tool centered on the hole and prevents its jumping sideways as an end mill will do when it cuts on one side only. When the heads of bolts or machine screws must be flush with or below the surface, the hole is countersunk with a tool similar to the spot facer. In this case the tool is cutting in a deep hole. Unless it is provided with grooves on the sides, either spiral or straight, the chips cannot get out and will clog the cutting teeth. The tool would then have to be withdrawn and the teeth cleared.

It is very important that the work be held still while drilling. No work should ever be held in the hand without some tool to hold it with. Sometimes a large wrench can be used to hold the work, and smaller objects can be clamped in the drill-press vise. There is always the possibility that the drill may catch as it breaks through at the finish and the work be forced up the spiral of the drill. This can pull the work out of a wrench so it would be out of control when it reaches the top of the drill and would start spinning with the speed of the drill. Always clamp the work to the drill-press table and be sure the table is clamped to the column. Always use at least two clamps on the work. With one clamp, there may be a high spot under the work that forms a pivot, and while it seems tight when tried by hand, under power it may slip and spin around on this pivot spot. The two clamps will prevent this.

The drill-press table probably has several grooves cast in it to take the bolts of the clamps. Sometimes the work piece has holes tapped for screws on the bottom side, and these can be used to clamp the work. It is seldom that these tapped holes will fit the slots of the table when the work is positioned to drill the hole. If the work cannot be clamped from the top, as its shape often prevents, it can be bolted to a sub-base through the tapped holes and then the sub-base positioned and clamped to the table. The sub-base may be a piece of scrap or an angle block.

Drilling a hole at an angle also requires a similar procedure. Round work that cannot be held in the drill press vise can be clamped in a "V" block on the sub-base. A line should be scribed across the end in line with the drilled hole, and this line is set square with the table by testing with the combination square. It must also be positioned with the center-punch mark under the point of the drill. This requires two places to be aligned and tested before the clamps are tightened. With the work and "V" block clamped to the sub-base, the vertical line can be set square with the base, and the whole thing positioned under the drill. Thus only one part has to be aligned at a time. This method does use more clamps, but it saves time, and each part of the setting can be checked and corrected without disturbing the other.

The column of the drill press should be equipped with a collar under the arm supporting the table, which can be clamped to hold the table when it is loosened from the column to be moved sideways. It is often necessary to swing the table out of the way when changing drills, and there should be a stop or indicator that will clamp to the column so that the table can be returned to the same position.

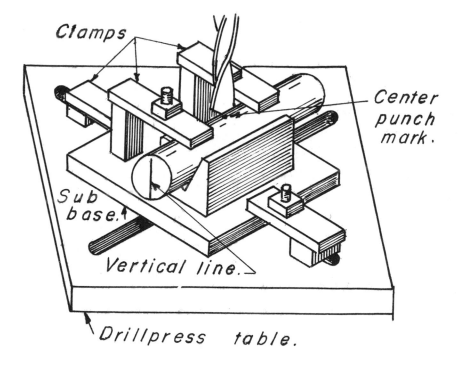

Fig. 64. Setup on a Sub-base

Setup on a Sub-base. Mark a vertical line on end of work to align work and drill. (left)　　　　　　　**Drilling at an angle** (right)

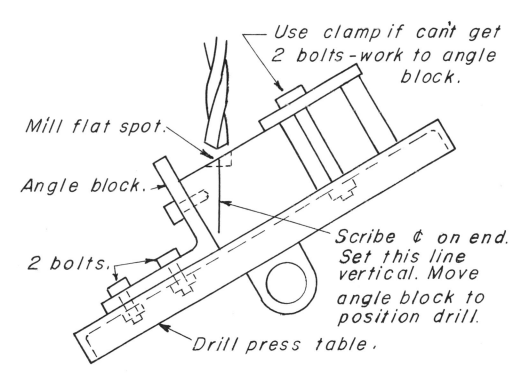

Use clamp if can't get 2 bolts – work to angle block.

Mill flat spot.

Angle block.

2 bolts.

Scribe ¢ on end. Set this line vertical. Move angle block to position drill.

Drill press table.

Fig. 65. Drilling at an angle

The speed at which the drill revolves is very important. The smaller the drill, the faster it should revolve. Table 8 gives the speeds for high-speed steel drills in various metals.

Table 8

Cutting Speeds for High-Speed Steel Drills*

Drill size (inches)	Brass	Cast iron	Mild steel	Stainless steel
1/16	12,000	6,000	4,800	3,000
1/8	6,000	3,000	2,400	1,500
1/4	3,000	1,530	1,200	1,000
3/8	2,000	1,000	815	500
1/2	1,530	760	610	380
5/8	1,220	610	490	300
3/4	1,000	500	400	250
7/8	875	440	350	220
1	760	380	300	190

* The speeds are in RPM.

Knowing the speed of the motor driving the drill press and the sizes of the various pulleys of the belt-changing system, it is easy to compute the speed for each combination of pulleys. A table of the drill speed should be made up and posted on the wall behind the drill press for quick reference. This table should be covered with clear plastic to keep it clean.

To find the required speed, the speed of the driver is multiplied by the ratio of the pulleys. Thus, to get a speed of 1200 RPM from a motor running at 1720, the ratio is 1200 divided by 1720 or .70. Then a set of pulleys having the ratio of 7 to 10 will give the desired speed. The smaller pulley would be on the motor.

It is a difficult job to remove a broken drill in a hole. If the end is projecting sufficiently, try brazing an extension on it with silver solder. Trying to turn the broken drill with a wrench or pliers will probably only crush it and make matters worse. Annealing the broken end may prevent crushing it, unless it is cracked down inside the hole. If it is broken below the surface and the holes made by the flutes are open, try making a forked tool to fit in the holes of the flutes and use it as a screwdriver to back out the broken drill. This tool should fit the size of the drilled hole so that the hole will guide it. Use the shank of the broken drill to make the tool. Anneal it and file the points to fit the broken part of the drill, then temper it to a blue color. If harder than a blue color, it will be so brittle that the points will snap off. If the work piece will stand being heated to a high temperature, it can be heated to a red heat and allowed to cool very slowly. The broken drill may then be annealed soft enough to be drilled out with a new drill.

REAMERS

Since a drilled hole is seldom true to size or alignment, a reamer is used to finish the hole. There are many kinds of reamers, but only two types are needed in a home shop. The usual one and the type that should be kept in stock is the hand reamer. This reamer has flutes of the finish diameter, followed by an afterguide ground to the same diameter as the finished hole. The entering end of the flutes is ground to a slight taper so that the tool can enter and enlarge the hole. The hand reamer is turned with a tap wrench, or other wrench, at a slow speed and with little pressure. A wrench pulling from only one side, such as an end wrench or a crescent wrench, is liable to pull the reamer sideways; and, as it can cut on the side, an oval hole can result. The slight angle of the tapered point makes the reamer bite into the material very easily, so too fast a feed will make the reamer cut a chip too large to handle. Never turn a reamer backwards. The flutes should be kept always cutting metal as they will dull rapidly if allowed to slip over and not cut. Turning the tool by hand with the correct size of wrench will enable the operator to feel the condition of the cut.

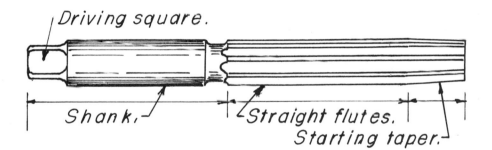

Fig. 66a. Hand reamer

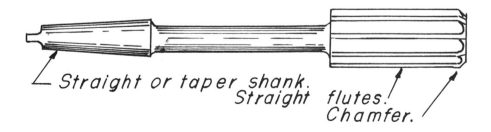

Fig. 66b. Chucking reamer

The flutes are either straight or spiral. The straight flutes are usually spaced unequally to prevent chattering. Spiral flutes are not so liable to chatter and are evenly spaced. A right-hand spiral tends to pull the reamer into the work, and less pressure is needed to feed it. A left-hand spiral opposes the feed and tends to prevent the reamer from jamming in the cut. If a reamer is turned backward to loosen it in a jam, it may leave ridges in the hole that can start chattering. As soon as you feel the cut getting heavy, ease off on the feed, but keep turning, always forward, until the reamer is cutting freely again.

The tapered part of the flutes do all the cutting, and these have the back of the lands relieved to a sharp edge or a very narrow land, so that they can bite into the cut. The straight part of the flutes may or may not have the lands relieved. This part does not do any cutting but guides the reamer in line with the finished hole, as does the afterguide without the flutes. If the hole is drilled crooked, the tapered point will tend to follow the curve. As it cuts from all sides, it will stay in the center of the hole where the cut is even on all sides. This will force the straight part of the flutes sideways, and they will do some cutting, making an untrue hole.

The second type of reamer is the chucking reamer, intended to be used in a lathe or other power tool. This reamer has short flutes and no taper at the entering end. Instead, the points of the flutes are beveled at a 45° angle so that they do the cutting on the beveled end. This chucking reamer is called a fluted reamer when the lands of the flutes are relieved, and a rose reamer when the flutes are not relieved. The shank can be either straight for holding in a chuck, or tapered to fit the Morse taper of the tail stock. This reamer will remove a larger amount of metal than the tapered-end hand reamer without biting too much or jamming. Its cutting action is similar to that of a many-fluted drill, and it will stand more pressure on the feed.

The shell type of reamer is similar to the chucking reamer except that it has a detachable shank that can be used on several reamers of other sizes. It is mainly used in large production shops and is of little interest to the home worker.

The hand reamer can be used in the lathe if proper precautions are taken. The RPM must be very slow, about half that of a drill of similar size. A small reamer can be held in the tail-stock chuck, but a larger reamer will have to be centered on the point of the tail center. To prevent the reamer from turning, use a tap wrench or lathe dog. As the tapered point of the hand reamer tends to grab into the work, some means of preventing its running into the work too fast must be provided. A reamer held in a chuck is safe because it is always under the control of the feed screw of the tail stock. But a reamer on the tail center is free to run in too fast. If it pulls off the point of the tail center, it will be forced sideways by the tap wrench or lathe dog and will be twisted out of the work. This may break the reamer and ruin the work. To prevent this, set up a blank tool in the tool post, bearing on the side of the tap wrench or lathe dog so that the tool can hold back the reamer. Then the carriage is moved at the same speed as the feed of the reamer, always keeping the blank tool tight to prevent the reamer from running in. Never try to withdraw the reamer all the way out of the hole while the lathe is running. It is liable to catch in the hole and cause a bad accident. As soon as the reamer is free from the cut, shut down the lathe and remove the reamer safely.

Either a hand reamer or a chucking reamer will cut on the side if forced off center by a crooked hole or a hole that is off center. If the hole being reamed is not running true with the reamer, the reamer must be free to follow the hole. A floating drive must be used. This permits the reamer to move off center enough to prevent side pressure from causing the flutes to cut on the sides, thus keeping the finished hole concentric with the drilled hole.

Hand reamers should not be expected to remove more than .002 inch. This is about the depth of the tool marks if the hole was bored in the lathe. For a drilled hole, a drill should be selected that will leave this amount to be removed. Chucking reamers will remove a larger amount, as they cut only on the short beveled end. The points of the flutes of a hand reamer can also be beveled similar to a chucking reamer, and it will then enter and enlarge a hole where a greater amount of metal must be removed. Rose reamers have heavier lands and stronger flutes and can be used to remove large amounts of metal, such as when truing up a cored hole in a casting. They will also cut a crooked hole if forced sideways, so they must be used with a floating drive for untrue holes. For holes not true, such as cored holes, it is best to run through with a rose reamer of a smaller size to straighten the hole and then finish with a reamer of the exact size. The best method for cored holes is to set the work up in the lathe where the hole can be roughed out with a boring bar and then reamed to finished size. This way you will need only the finishing reamer of either the hand or chucking type.

Cast iron is usually reamed dry, but most other metals require a little lubrication. The action with brass and aluminum is similar to that explained under DRILLING. The metal tends to stick to the tool unless lubricated.

A special type of reamer is the taper-pin reamer. These are built in a series, so that the next larger one overlaps the cut of the last, smaller one. This enables you to cut a continuous tapered hole until the exact size for the taper pin being used is arrived at. Taper pin reamers are small and should always be used with the smallest tap wrench that will fit the reamer. Drill a straight hole as small as the small end of the taper pin, while both the shaft and the surrounding piece are fastened, so that there will be no movement between them while you are drilling and reaming. The reamer is fed very slowly into the hole, always turning in the same direction. Remove the reamer often to clear it of chips that may become caught in the flutes. Test the taper pin for fit at frequent intervals, as it is easy to ream it too far. The pin will drive in quite a distance when it is driven tight in the hole, and this distance must be allowed for in the reaming. Try driving it tight and then backing it out so that you will know how much to allow for driving. Test it often, especially as you approach the final size. These small reamers are very delicate, and care must be taken to see that they do not bite too much and that they are not bent sideways. Steady your hand as you use them.

Another special reamer is the combined drill and center reamer, used to ream the centers in shafts for setting up in the lathe. Since, this reamer has a small pilot drill followed by a 60° reamer, the hole and the center are drilled and reamed at the same time. The small pilot drill is very easily broken, so be careful not to force it too much and to see that it is running true with no side pressure put on it. This reamer, when held in the tail-stock chuck, makes a very good starter for drilled holes in work set up in the lathe. If you make a center-punch mark to center the work, be sure the mark is running true. A center-punch mark is large enough to surround the pilot drill; and, if it wobbles, it can put enough side pressure on the pilot drill to break it. It is best to use a prick-punch mark for setting up, so that the hole will not be big enough to damage the pilot drill in this manner.

A very important thing to remember when using a chuck on a lathe or a drill press is never to leave the chuck key or the wrench in the chuck after using it. It is too easy to forget that it is there and to start up the machine without removing it. The key or wrench will be thrown off with great force when the machine starts, and someone or something may be hurt.

DEEP-HOLE DRILLING

Drilling a true deep hole—that is, a hole more than twenty times as long as its diameter—is an operation that is seldom required in a home shop. However, you may occasionally have to drill a very deep hole the far end of which must be aligned with respect to the starting end. For this work a standard twist drill will not be accurate enough, and a special drill must be used. This drill can be any of several types, all of which work on the principle that the body of the drill guides the cutting point as it runs in the part of the hole already finished. Such a drill is similar to a rose reamer in that it cuts only at the end while the body guides the point.

For very long holes, you will need a special machine to guide and feed the drill, while circulating a coolant through the hollow shank of the drill to flush out cuttings. One- or two-flute drills are often used for very deep holes. You can make one of these drills for use in the home shop: remember, however, that a homemade tool will not circulate a coolant and so must be withdrawn frequently to allow you to remove the cuttings. To make the deep drill, turn a piece of tool steel to the required diameter and then mill one or two flutes on the end. The cutting lips are ground in the same way as those on a twist drill. After the tool is hardened, it should be ground to the exact diameter of the finished hole. Since the cutting end has no center, the tool will have to be held in the steady rest while you grind the outside. The shank should be rigid with the cutting end so that the end will start straight in the hole. (Before you begin work with this tool, drill a starting hole a short distance in, using a twist drill; this will serve as a guide to the deep drill when it starts.)

When the far end of the hole can be a little out of line with the starting end, and when the hole is large enough to allow you to use a drill with an extension, you can put the hole through by using several drills of different sizes. A small pilot drill can be sweated into a small tube, or into a hole drilled in the end of a steel rod. This rod, being of a larger diameter than the pilot drill, will not be able to enter the opening made by the pilot drill. A larger drill on an extension is then used to enlarge the hole until the smaller pilot drill, with its extension, can re-enter the enlarged hole and continue, until it is again stopped by the large extension. This is repeated, using larger and larger drills on the extension shanks until the required diameter of hole is reached. The hole can even be reamed on an extension if it is large enough. The completed hole can be finished true to size, but it may not be perfectly straight. For the larger drills, a driving socket may have to be filed on the end of the extension, if sweating in with soft solder will not transmit sufficient torque. It is best to select drills in stepped sizes, so that the larger ones will not be cutting more than the solder will stand. This will also give a more accurate hole. Soft solder should be used, as its low heat will not ruin the drill for other work after it is removed from the extension.

7

Metal Sawing

SHOPS that specialize in contour sawing have band saws especially designed to saw metal. These machines are equipped with brazing or welding devices, enabling them to do inside sawing and welding right at the machine. They also have fences and guides similar to those on a woodworking circular-saw table, which guide the work. The speed can be regulated to suit the work being done. In the home workshop, a simple woodworking band saw with the speed reduced will do all you require.

To saw thin sheet steel, use a blade having at least 24 teeth per inch and run it at 175 feet per minute (fpm). For work over ¼ inch thick, a blade with 14 teeth and running at 150 fpm will cut more quickly, but the 24-tooth blade will do very well. Do not try to cut thin sheet metal or thin pipe with a 14-tooth blade. When two teeth of a blade are not cutting at the same time, the teeth may be stripped from the blade, ruining it. If you have only one metal-cutting blade, let it be of the 24-tooth variety.

Curves can be cut in metal as well as in wood. The radius of the curve depends on the width of the blade. A blade ¼ inch wide is the handiest to use. It will cut straight lines nicely and will cut curves of ¾-inch radius. A ⅜-inch blade will stand up to more pressure and will cut a curve of 1½-inch radius. Blades wider than ⅜ inch and narrower than ¼ inch will not fit the saw guides of the band saw in the small home shop.

Cutting curves will tend to ruin the set of the blade, especially when cutting on the outside of the curve. It is best to alternate the direction of cut when making curves, so as to equalize the loss of set. When a blade loses the set on one side, it will no longer cut a straight line; when it loses the set on both sides, it will bind in the cut and will not cut to a line. Therefore, in either case, you will have to discard the blade and use a new one. The saw shops keep the material for these blades in long lengths, and they will cut and weld one to your required size for very little money. Since accidents do happen, and you might break or ruin a blade in the middle of a job, you would be wise to have a spare blade on hand.

For cutting wood, a blade having 6 to 8 teeth per inch and running at 4500 fpm will handle all your work. The blade width should be ¼ inch or ⅜ inch.

For cutting internal holes, the saw blade must be cut and passed through the drilled pilot holes and then rewelded. This is a job easily done on the commercial machines that have welding equipment attached, but for the home worker such a job would require that he take the cut blade and the work to a saw shop to have them weld it in the hole. As it would not pay to have your own welding equipment, you obviously should

Metal-cutting band saw. Note the lubricating feed to the saw blade and the blade-welding apparatus on the column, left.

Band cutoff saw. The wheels are set at an angle to produce a good depth of cut. The blade is twisted in the guides so that it will cut on a vertical plane.

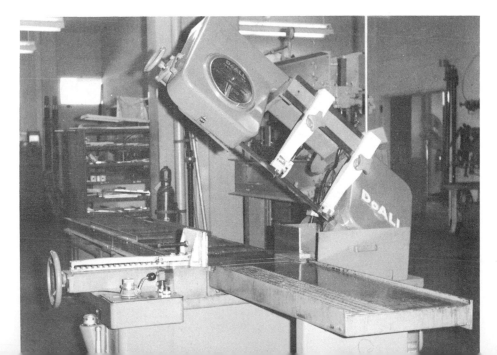

not attempt to do internal sawing where the blade must be cut. Use a method from the days before band saws were developed, such as drilling, chipping, and filing.

Where the job will permit it, an internal hole can be sawed by cutting a saw kerf through from the outside and, after sawing, welding or brazing up the saw kerf (see Figure 67). Where the work is to be machined after sawing, this welding of the starting kerf will not be objectionable, if the weld metal penetrates clear through. Allowance must be made for the distortion of the work due to the heat of welding.

When cutting up to a small radius corner, be careful when breaking through into the drilled hole. The saw will be cutting on one edge and is liable to bind in the cut. On starting the cut on the far side of the corner, first nib out a space wide enough so that the blade can start into the cut parallel to the finished line.

When cutting a curve of smaller radius than the blade will stand, make several radial cuts before starting the curve cut. With these radial cuts close together, the scrap can be removed with short tangent cuts, which will approximate the required small-radius cut.

The metal-cutting band saw will handle a large portion of the metal cutting done in your shop. Of course, it will not cut a piece larger than the throat of the saw. The blade must have enough tension so that it will not sag between the upper and lower guides, and the guides must be adjusted to keep the saw in position without bending it out of line. Do not force the blade, as this will cause the blade to bend and run out of true. Use only enough pressure to make sure the teeth are biting into the work and not sliding over it. Before starting to cut a piece of metal the condition of which you are not sure of, test the metal with a fine file to see if it is soft enough to saw. This will prevent you from ruining the blade.

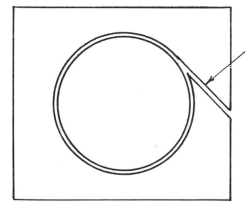

Starting kerf- weld solid on completion.

Fig. 67. Sawing inside hole

The table of the saw is adjustable for cutting bevels; however, since the pointer of the graduated bevel scale under the table is not very accurate, the angle should be checked with the protractor head of the combination square. There is a stop screw under the table that brings the table back to zero after it has been used, and the setting of this stop screw should be checked with the square head of the combination square.

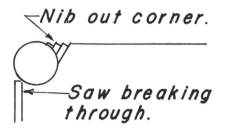

Fig. 68. Sawing into a corner

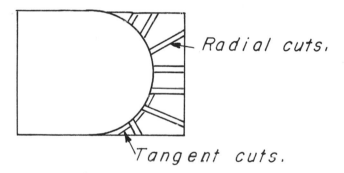

Fig. 69. Sawing a small radius

8

Grinding and Lapping

GRINDING involves the use of a rotating abrasive wheel to remove material. The grinding wheel may be a natural object, like a grindstone, or a manufactured wheel, built up of grains of a natural or manufactured abrasive. These grains are held together by some cementing adhesive, which is called the bond.

Natural Abrasives

Of the natural abrasives, corundum, a natural aluminum oxide, is a very hard crystalline substance. The ruby and sapphire are colored varieties of corundum. Emery is an impure corundum and is much used in emery cloth. Other natural abrasives are garnet, quartz, and flint. These are all used in making sandpaper. Commercial diamonds, called *borts,* are often used where very hard materials are to be ground. Diamond dust is used in lapping and polishing.

Manufactured Abrasives

Silicon carbide and aluminum oxide are the two most popular artificial abrasives. Silicon carbide is the hardest of all manufactured abrasives, exceeded in hardness only by the diamond. The grains are sharp and readily graded for size, but are very brittle. It is best suited for grinding very hard materials.

Aluminum oxide is stronger and less brittle than silicon carbide, but is not as hard. Its impact strength is quite high, and it can be used to grind all materials of lesser hardness.

WHEEL MANUFACTURE

Grindstones, which are cut directly from sandstone deposits, are used only for grinding glass and sharpening cutlery. Manufactured wheels are made by combining grains of the abrasive material of the proper size with a bonding agent. Grain sizes from 8 to 600 are used. The size of the grain is determined by the mesh of the screen used to sort the abrasive. Grains finer than 200 are called *flours*. The bond may be shellac, rubber, or resinoid; or it may be a type of glass formed by mixing clay and feldspar with the abrasive and baking at a high temperature. Since the various abrasives used in wheels do not differ widely in hardness, the hardness of a wheel depends on the strength of the bond. In all wheels, the abrasive is first mixed with the bonding material, and then, after the wheels are dried, they are baked for a time, at a temperature suitable to the bond being used. The wheels are then trued up, balanced, and bushed with lead, and are given a running test at speeds 50 percent above their allowable speed.

Grain Size

Commercial grain sizes are designated as follows:

Coarse	6, 8, 10, 12, 14, 16, 20, 24
Medium	30, 36, 46, 54, 60
Fine	70, 80, 90, 100, 120, 150, 180, 220, 240, 280, 320, 400, 500, 600

The grain size required depends upon the type of work and the intended finish. Coarse and medium sizes are usually used for roughing and semifinishing; fine sizes, for finishing.

Wheel Bonds

The abrasive grains are like a cutting tool, and the bond is like a tool post holding the tool. The bond must be strong enough to allow the grain to do its cutting. The amount of bonding material used determines the hardness or softness (strength) of the wheel, since the abrasive remains the same both in strength and volume. As particles of abrasive become dull, the bonding material breaks away, releasing the dulled particles and exposing sharp grains. The following are the four most used bonds:

Vitrified bond: A clay. The wheel is burned in a kiln to produce a glass similar to crockery. Most wheels use this bond, since its strength and porosity give it high cutting rates.

Silicate bond: A baked bond, commonly known as "water glass." It releases the abrasive grains more easily than the vitrified bonds, and is used where the heat of the grinding must be kept to a minimum, as in grinding edged tools.

Resinoid bond: A synthetic organic compound that can be used in various structures, from hard, dense, coarse wheels to soft, open, fine wheels. It cuts cool, removes stock rapidly, and can be run at high speed.

Rubber bond: Gives a strong, dense wheel and is extensively used for extremely thin wheels.

Bond designations are as follows:

B	Resinoid
E	Shellac
O	Oxychloride
R	Rubber
S	Silicate
V	Vitrified

Wheel Grades

[Not manufactured]	A, B
Very soft	C, D, E, F, G
Soft	H, I, J, K
Medium	L, M, Ń, O
Hard	P, Q, R, S
Very hard	T, U, V, W, X, Y, Z

Wheel Structure

The spacing of the grains on a wheel is called its structure. Wheel manufacturers designate the various wheel structures by numbers from 1 to 15: #1 is dense, and the higher numbers mean that the structures are more open and porous.

SELECTING A WHEEL

The cutting action of a wheel for any particular job will be determined by the type of abrasive used, the grain or size of the abrasive, the bond strength or grade of the wheel, and the grain spacing. The factors you should consider when selecting a wheel are as follows:

1. The kind of material to be ground.
2. The amount of material to be removed by the grinding.
3. The finish you wish to obtain.
4. The area of contact between the wheel and the work.
5. The type of grinding machine you are using.

The area of contact will be determined by the diameters of the wheel and the work and by the depth of cut.

When choosing a grinding wheel for a specific job, all these points must be taken into consideration. Details are given in the outline below. The student must remember that the specifications apply to average conditions and that circumstances can modify certain of these rules.

1. *Type of abrasive*
   a. Materials with high tensile strength require aluminum oxide.
   b. Materials with low tensile strength call for silicon carbide.

2. *Grain size (size of particles)*
   a. Soft materials require coarse grain.
   b. Hard, brittle materials require fine grain.
   c. Fast cutting requires coarse grain.
   d. Fine cutting requires fine grain.
   e. A small area of contact calls for fine grain.
   f. A machine subject to vibration requires a very fine grain.

3. *Grade (strength of bond)*
   a. Hard material requires a soft wheel.
   b. A small area of contact requires a hard wheel.
   c. A machine in poor condition or subject to vibration requires a very hard wheel.
   d. The higher the relative speed of the wheel and the work, the harder the wheel must be.

4. *Structure (grain spacing)*
   a. Soft, tough, ductile materials will clog a wheel with a close structure; and so require one with widely spaced grains.
   b. For removing a large amount of material, use a wheel with wide spacing.
   c. Fine finishing requires close spacing.
   d. Surfacing requires wide spacing.
   e. For cylindrical operations, use medium spacing.
   f. A rigid, vibration-free machine can use wide spacing.

5. *Bond*
   a. A high finish is best obtained with a wheel having a shellac, rubber, or resinoid bond.
   b. Thin, cutoff wheels use a shellac, rubber, or resinoid bond.
   c. Large solid wheels use silicate bonding.
   d. Wheels running at less than 6500 surface feet per minute (sfpm) need a vitrified bond.
   e. Wheels running at more than 6500 sfpm need a resinoid bond.

The student should note the interrelation between some of the above factors and should make a careful study of all the requirements when choosing a wheel for a job. When a conflict occurs, good judgment must be used in order to select a compromise wheel that will be best suited to all the conditions.

Grinding wheels are ordinarily operated at 6500 sfpm, but many operations require either higher or lower speeds. For roughing, wheel speeds up to 9000 sfpm are common. Wheels must be specially made for use at these high speeds, and are speed-tested for safety by the manufacturer.

A wheel selected for a *work speed* of 125 sfpm to 150 sfpm will generally give good results.

Recommended Wheel Speeds

Internal grinding	2000–6000 sfpm
Machine knife grinding	3500–4500 sfpm
Cutlery grinding (large wheels, offhand)	4000–5000 sfpm
Surface grinding	4000–5000 sfpm
Snagging, offhand grinding (vitrified)	5000–6000 sfpm
Wet tool grinding	5000–6000 sfpm
Cylindrical grinding	5500–6500 sfpm
Grinding with cutoff wheels (rubber, shellac, or resinoid)	9000–16000 sfpm

GRINDING MACHINES

There are four principal types of grinding machines: cylindrical, tool, surface, and centerless. Each of these operations, except for centerless grinding, can be performed on a universal grinding machine. There are, of course, special machines for particular jobs, such as crankshaft grinding and cylinder grinding, but these machines are not found in jobbing shops and will not be discussed here.

Universal grinding machine. A separate motor is used to revolve the work. The upper table, containing the head and tail centers, can swivel for grinding tapers.

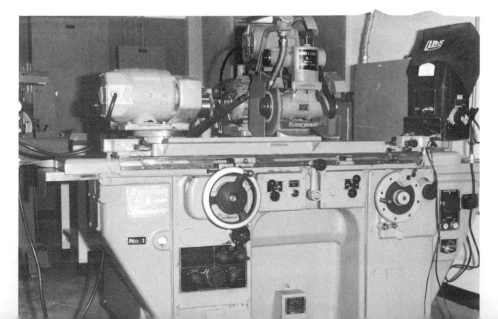

The *universal grinding machine* has a bed like that of a lathe, except that the grinder bed is turned over, with the ways underneath, where they are protected. The grinder dust is very abrasive and would soon ruin the ways of the bed if they were exposed, as in the usual engine lathe. The whole bed of the grinder travels. On the top of this bed is a swivel bed with "T" slots for clamping on of centers for cylindrical grinding or a magnetic chuck for surface grinding. The grinding wheel is mounted on a column behind the bed for vertical movement and attached to a sliding arm for horizontal adjustment. The feed of the wheel is controlled by a hand wheel having a very slow movement for fine feeds. The head center has a power feed for revolving cylindrical work, and the bed has a power feed for traversing. This machine is capable of accurately finishing a great variety of work that is held rigidly on the bed and passed in front of the grinding wheel.

The *centerless grinder* works on an entirely different principle. This machine consists of a large grinding wheel with a smaller, regulating wheel opposite it. The work is held at the proper grinding position on a blade or rest between the two wheels. The rotation of the work is controlled by the regulating wheel so that, by setting this wheel at a slight angle to the axis of the work, the work can be fed across the cutting wheel at the required speed (see Figure 70). This machine will do very accurate grinding and is used extensively for grinding of shafting and piston pins, which can be fed into it in a continuous stream.

The centerless grinder does not require any maintenance of center holes and centers nor the use of driving dogs, and it can be used for long shafts without the danger of deflection, allowing very rapid removal of material.

Two types of *surface grinders* are in general use. One employs a traveling bed that passes the work back and forth under a cylindrical wheel, which is fed across the work. The other type of surface grinder uses a large, circular bed, which revolves the work under a flat wheel, usually of the segmented type, and having a diameter a little greater than half the diameter of the bed. Since the machine can be made very rigid, great pressure can be used, allowing rapid removal of material. For this type of machine, since the area of contact between wheel and work is very long, a soft, open wheel is required.

WHEEL TRUING AND DRESSING

In order to produce good work by grinding, it is necessary to true and dress the wheel often. The terms *true* and *dress* are sometimes used interchangeably, but they actually refer to two different operations. To true a grinding wheel is to cut it, both grain and bond, so that the periphery is made truly concentric with the axis. To dress a wheel is to cut, break down, or crush it in order to open the face, so that its cutting action may be used to the limit. Dressing a wheel may or may not make its periphery absolutely true with the axis.

In most cases, a wheel is trued with a commercial diamond, or bort, which is the only material hard enough to cut through the abrasive in a wheel when it is rotating at high speed. Using a diamond, you can rough-true a wheel (open the face for quick cutting); you can true it so that it will produce a good finish; or you can dull its face so that it will product a high finish. Any of these results can be obtained by varying the depth of cut of the diamond and the rate of traverse across the face of wheel.

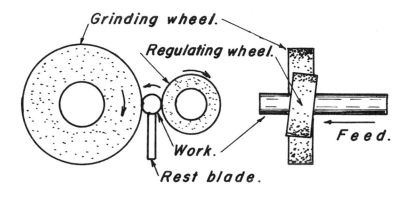

Fig. 70. Centerless grinding

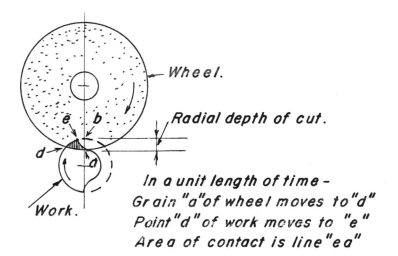

Fig. 71. Area of contact

Diamonds can easily be damaged by too deep a cut or too fast a traverse. When using a diamond submerged in a coolant, the depth of each cut should not exceed .001 inch at a time, and the traverse, not faster than 10 inches per minute. If the work is to be ground dry, the wheel should be trued in a dry condition, using slower cuts.

Diamond truing tools should always be set at an acute angle to both the wheel face and the direction of rotation. The point of the diamond must be at the center height of the wheel. Pointing the diamond down at about a 10° angle will prevent chatter; using an angle of about 30° to the face of the wheel will prevent diamond marks on the surface of the wheel, and the wear on the diamond will tend to make it self-sharpening. To keep a diamond sharp, it should be turned frequently. When a diamond gets dull, it will be forced away from the wheel and will not cut a true surface. A good job of truing cannot be done with a dull diamond. Diamond nibs must be held in rigid supports to prevent vibration, and they must be arranged so that they can be easily turned to present a new face to the wheel.

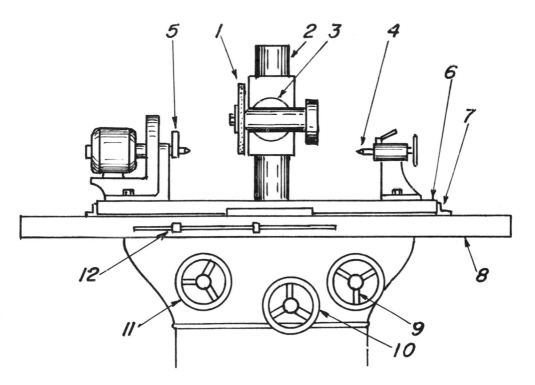

Fig. 72. Universal grinder. The principal parts are: (1) grinding wheel; (2) column; (3) cross-slide arm; (4) tail center; (5) live head center; (6) swivel table; (7) swivel-table lock; (8) main table; (9) cross-feed hand wheel; (10) vertical hand wheel; (11) longitudinal-feed hand wheel; (12) power-feed carriage stops.

Dressing a grinding wheel can be done by using steel cutters or an abrasive dressing wheel, or by crushing. The steel cutters are either star-shaped disks or a solid cylinder with slots, mounted on a free-running bearing. In use, the tool is rapidly traversed across the face of the wheel, while the wheel spins the cutters at high speed. The points of the cutters break down or crush the grains and the bond, thus quickly changing the shape of the wheel. Abrasive dressing wheels are mounted on ball bearings. They are held at an angle of from 5° to 7° with the face of the wheel and rapidly traversed by hand. The angle between the two wheels brings about an abrasive action between them that wears away both wheels until the high places are removed. Both the steel cutter and the abrasive dressing wheel will give a faster cutting surface than the diamond dresser.

Crusher dressing requires a formed crushing roll, which is pressed with great force against the face of the grinding wheel and turned one revolution at slow speed. This crushes and breaks down the bond and produces a very true grinding surface. It is much used for contour grinding and thread grinding.

To counteract the heat generated in grinding and also to carry away the grinder dust, most grinding is done with a suitable coolant sprayed on the work and wheel. A filter in the return line of the coolant adds much to the quality of the finish.

GRINDING IN THE SMALL SHOP

The tool-post grinder is a very useful machine, and there should be one in every home metalworking shop. It consists of an electric motor of about ¼ H.P. and a ball-bearing spindle on which grinding wheels can be mounted. The grinder is mounted on the compound slide of the tool post. The spindle and motor should be equipped to take pulleys of various sizes so that the speed of the grinding wheel can be adjusted according to its size. The spindle should turn in a counterclockwise direction, as you face the end on which the grinding wheel is mounted. This will direct the sparks downward, so that the removed metal can be captured and will not fly all over the stop. The motor is mounted in such a way that the belt tension can be adjusted for each set of pulleys used. The motor should have a balanced armature that will run without vibration. The bearings of the spindle should be of the double-sealed, permanently greased type that can run smoothly for a long time before needing adjustment.

There should be two spindles fitted to the same bearings. One spindle is short, permitting the grinding wheel to be set up close on the left end; the other spindle should be long enough to extend about 6 inches into inside work. An overhang longer than 6 inches is not practical for this size of grinder, as the machine is liable to start vibrating if there is the

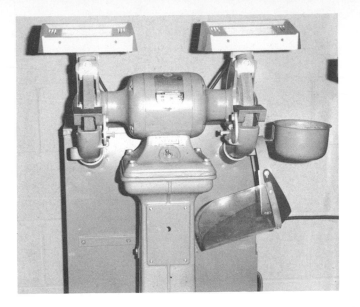

Tool grinder. Note guards over the wheels; cup of water for cooling the work; and safety eye shield, hung where it cannot be overlooked.

slightest imbalance. The long spindle, intended for internal grinding, uses only small-diameter wheels and will run very fast. At the right-hand end of the short spindle, there should be a left-hand thread, so that grinding wheels can be mounted on either end. Some tool-post grinders are designed to do internal grinding deeper than 6 inches. These have an extended housing for the bearings, so that one bearing is near the wheel and one is near the center to prevent vibration.

Each time a wheel is mounted on one of the spindles, it must be trued up while running at full speed. Hold a diamond tool rigidly against the wheel, taking light cuts with the diamond until the wheel has an even cutting face over-all. The appearance of the face will indicate when it is true, since the color will be darker where the diamond has not cut away any low spot. A good way to hold the diamond is to mount it in the tail-stock chuck or the head-stock three-jaw chuck and then feed the wheel across its point. If it is held in the tail-stock chuck, the tail-stock ram must be locked in position, as any looseness here will let the diamond vibrate, and it will not cut a smooth surface on the wheel.

A holder for the diamond must be made so that, when it is gripped in the chuck, the point will be slanting downward at a 5° angle and sideways at a 30° angle. This will prevent vibration of the diamond and will make the wear on the diamond tend to keep it sharp (see Figure 73). The point of the diamond must be at the exact center of the grinder and should be turned frequently to equalize the wear.

The diamond is hard enough to cut the tops off the grains of abrasive on the wheel, and the rate of traverse of the diamond across the face of the wheel will govern the wheel's cutting characteristics. A quick traverse

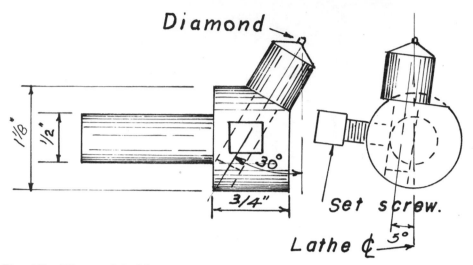

Fig. 73. Diamond holder

will leave a more open grain structure to the wheel, so that it will cut more quickly for roughing but not smoothly enough for finishing. For finishing, a very slow traverse with small infeed is used, which will leave all the grains cut to an even, smooth surface that will not be as sharp but will cut very smoothly. This smooth surface will become glazed very quickly if heavy cuts are taken with it.

Since roughing cuts are taken by the advancing edge of the wheel, the edges of the wheel must be trimmed or chamfered to run true, or else they will chop at the work as they advance into the cut. Truing the wheel with a diamond also slowly wears down the diamond; and, unless it is turned frequently in its holder, it will wear to a blunt point, which will cause it to spring away from the wheel instead of cutting it. You cannot do a good job of dressing a wheel with a dull diamond. Take care of your diamond and see that a sharp point is presented to the wheel each time it is dressed.

A diamond cuts the grains, but a star-shaped dressing tool crushes the grains, leaving an open surface to the wheel, which will cut very much faster than a diamond-dressed wheel. Such a wheel will not glaze as quickly, but it will not cut smoothly enough for finishing. For shaping the grinding wheel so that it will cut to a contoured pattern, the star dresser is the best tool to use. A final surface can be given by using a diamond mounted in a hand tool, and the face of the wheel is worked to fit a template of the desired pattern.

The work should revolve slowly in the opposite direction to that of the grinding wheel, and the traverse should be fairly fast, with light cuts. The grinding will generate a great deal of heat, which will make the work expand lengthwise, putting increased pressure on the tail center. This must therefore be kept thoroughly lubricated and should be adjusted frequently to prevent damage to the work or center. In commercial grinding, the grinding machines are equipped to use a coolant on the grinding wheel, which keeps the work cool; but work ground in your lathe will have to be ground dry. Work slowly and let it cool often.

If there are any locked-in strains in the material from former operations, the heat will change them as metal is removed, and the work will spring out of shape. When this is happening, you will observe that a cut is not concentric with the last cut. Work that has been hardened, because the heating and quenching was not uniform, will have these locked-in strains. All you can do in such a case is to let the work cool off and then take very small cuts that will not heat up the work. It will still spring, but working slowly will tend to minimize the error. Be careful with your hardening operation.

The sparks and particles removed from the work will be directed down onto the bed of the machine. This material is very abrasive and, if it gets under the slides of the saddle or cross feed, it will do a great deal of harm to them. The slides should be covered to protect them. Paper towels or old newspapers fitted under the work and weighted down so that they will remain in place will do a fine job of keeping the area clean. Since the movement of the slides will disturb the paper covering, watch it and adjust it to any movement as you work. Also put a small dish under the grinding wheel to catch the sparks. Fill this dish with oil or water, and the sparks will collect in it and not bounce around.

When you are grinding an inside job, however, you cannot use this water bath to catch the sparks. When possible, fit a vacuum cleaner to suck in the sparks. The nozzle of the hose from the vacuum cleaner should be fastened to the carriage in such a way that it will pick up the dust and stay in the same position as the grinder moves. If you cannot collect the grinder dust, cover the area around the lathe or other tools that may be injured by this dust, and keep them as clean as possible. Before using them after you uncover them, wipe them clean with an oily rag.

For grinding small internal holes, the small wheels mounted on $\frac{1}{8}$-inch shanks and held in a special collet chuck are used. For larger holes, there are mounted wheels having $\frac{1}{4}$-inch shanks. You will need collet chucks to handle both $\frac{1}{8}$-inch and $\frac{1}{4}$-inch shanks. These chucks are described in Chapter 20. The collet chucks screw onto the end of the grinder spindle and must be very accurate and in perfect balance. The small wheels must revolve very fast or else they will be worn away faster than they can cut. To get this high speed, you will need a second tool-post grinder having a high-speed motor of small power and a belt that will stand such high speed. The large grinder cannot run fast enough. For larger internal holes, small wheels mounted directly on the main spindle are used.

Cup wheels are handy for many grinding jobs, and you should have one or two sizes on hand; but they are poor cutters to use when facing off a flat surface. The axis of the spindle must be set at a narrow angle to the face being ground. If set at exactly 90°, both sides of the wheel will be cutting, and this will cause chatter to start. In large grinding machines, where very rigid construction is used, the cutting wheels of surface grinders can be set at 90°, but the wheels are large enough so that they cut from only one side. The tool-post grinder wheel is too light to be used at 90°. Setting the axis at a narrow angle causes the cutting edge of the wheel to form an arc with a very long radius in contact with the work. This causes a great deal of friction on the cutting area, and the wheel soon glazes over and springs away instead of cutting. A freshly dressed wheel will cut satisfactorily if the surface to be ground is small; but if it is at all wide, the wheel will glaze before the cut is finished and would have to be withdrawn from the cut and dressed with the diamond. It would then be impossible to set the wheel to cut exactly in line with the previous cut, and the surface would not be ground true. For grinding a small edge, as when sharpening a reamer, a cup wheel or a saucer wheel will work very well; but for facing a large surface, use the circular wheel and grind from its face.

Grinding wheels vary for different metals. As a rule, the softer the metal, the harder the wheel. The speed of the grinding wheel and the RPM of the work have a great deal to do with how the wheel cuts. The arc of cut regulates how much each grain of the wheel will cut. Cutting on a long arc will cause chips to clog the grains before they can finish the arc. These chips then rub on the rest of the arc, causing heating and glazing of the wheel. Anything that increases the length of arc will increase the amount of chip removed; or, in other words, increase the

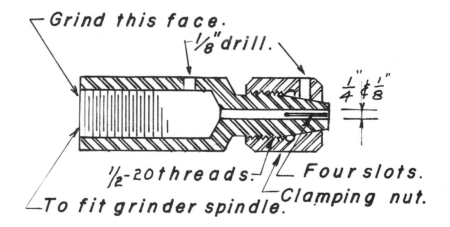

Fig. 74. Grinder collets

depth of cut. Increasing the *work* speed or decreasing the wheel speed will increase the length of arc and will therefore give the effect of a harder wheel. A hard wheel will tend to glaze more quickly than a soft one.

In commercial shops, the grain, bond, and binder can be selected so as to give maximum results and the finish desired. In your home shop, you will not have a large selection of wheels and you probably have only one wheel of the right size and type to do the job. It may not be the very best wheel for the job, but it will have to do. The RPM of the wheel is fixed, but the speed of the lathe can be adjusted. By changing the speed of the lathe, you can make the wheel cut hard or soft (within the limits of the lathe speed) and so handle a large variety of work.

In general, for cylindrical grinding, use a work speed of 125 sfpm to 150 sfpm and a wheel speed of 5500 sfpm to 6500 sfpm. For internal grinding, a wheel speed of 2000 sfpm to 6000 sfpm is best; for surface grinding, use a wheel speed of 4000 sfpm to 5000 sfpm. The reason for this variation in wheel speeds is that the arc of contact varies, depending on whether the work is cylindrical, outside or inside, or flat (see Figure 71).

The rate of traverse affects the surface finish. A slow traverse rate makes the wheel cut mostly on the leading edge, which will then wear faster than the center of the wheel. The wheel will soon get out of round and start to cut roughly. Light cuts must be taken so that the center of the wheel can also do some cutting. For rough work, a traverse as long as three quarters to seven eighths of the width of the wheel will keep it cutting over its full width and wearing evenly all over. For finish cuts, where only very small cuts are taken and the wear on the wheel is not great, a slow traverse, as long as one eighth to one quarter the width of the wheel, can be used. This will produce a better finish. The wheel should be dressed with the diamond before starting the finish cut; and several passes should be made, without changing the cut, until sparks stop forming, or "sparking out," as it is called.

Work driven tight on a tapered mandrel may put a strain on the mandrel that will cause it to run out of true. The finished work will then be as much in error as the mandrel; so check the mandrel with the dial indicator to see that it is running true before starting to grind the work. Work that is clamped between collars on an arbor may spring the arbor, if the sides of the work or the faces of the collars are not perfectly parallel. Test the arbor with the dial indicator to be sure. Work held in the jaws of a chuck may be distorted by the pressure of the jaws. Work clamped on a face plate can also be distorted, or the face plate can be pulled out of true, by the clamps. Check for any of these conditions after each setup and do not proceed with the grinding until they are corrected.

Long, slender work will spring away from the grinding wheel and thus will not be the same diameter along its full length. To prevent this, a follower rest must be used. This rest is different from that used

External grinding. Paper protects the lathe bed, and a pan of water collects the grinder dust. The grinder shown is the larger, more powerful type.

Internal grinding. The small grinder has a high-speed vacuum-cleaner motor, flat belt, and collet chuck for small mounted grinding wheels. Paper covering of the bed is essential.

to turn slender work in the lathe. A cutting tool in the lathe tends to lift up the work as well as push it away, but a grinding wheel tends to push it down and away. Therefore, the follower rest must have one of the adjustable guides under the work as well as one behind it. These guides must be adjusted with great accuracy. Use the dial indicator to make sure that the work is not moved out of line by pressure from the guide.

The cutoff wheel is very useful. This is a wheel ⅛-inch thick with a rubber or resinoid bond. It will not break readily if it is bent sideways. A rubber-bond wheel should be run at 9000 sfpm, and a resinoid wheel at 16000 sfpm. The resinoid wheel is better for dry grinding. At this speed, the wheel will heat the work ahead of it and make the cutting easier. Such a thin wheel may vibrate or flutter while running free; but when the cut has been well established, it will run steadily and cut to close tolerances—to within .020 inch. Even when the material is very hard, the cutoff wheel will go through it easily. It is not possible to take very deep cuts with this wheel, however, and several small passes must be made with it when the piece to be cut is thick. The sides of the wheel must be exactly at a 90° angle with the center line of the work, or else it will rub against the sides of the groove and heat up rapidly. The face of the wheel will then soon be worn down to a rounded edge, causing the wheel to wander in the cut and heat up too quickly. Frequent dressing of the wheel face is therefore required.

A grinding wheel is mounted on a spindle between large collars, and there should be a piece of blotting paper under each collar. If there is too much play, or space for free motion, between the hole in the wheel and the spindle, take up this play by wrapping gummed paper around the spindle. If such play is allowed to remain, the wheel will settle to the bottom of the space whenever the collars are tightened and thus be thrown out of balance and off center. Dressing the wheel will not restore the balance, as the weight of the wheel will still be off center. A grinding wheel that is out of balance cannot be used for finish work. In large shops, such wheels can be set up on knife edges and brought back into *static* balance by application of weights under the collars; but they may still be out of *running* balance.

In the home shop, you can balance a wheel only by trial and error. This method is a great waste of time, however, because the wheel will be thrown out of balance again the first time it is removed after the balancing. If you purchase a new wheel and find that it is out of balance, take it back and exchange it for another one. If it gets out of balance while you are using it, throw it away.

When making a finish cut, always feed in the same direction. Since there is always a small amount of backlash in the slides of the lathe, if you reverse the feed, the wheel may cut more or less deeply than on the previous traverse. This will prevent you from getting an exact reading of the final size on the micrometers. To return the wheel to the starting point for another cut, first shut it down; then prevent it from rubbing against the work by holding back on it, to take up the backlash. If there is enough backlash to spoil cutting done in the reverse direction, there will be enough so that you can hold the wheel away from the work. Don't force it enough to change the setting of the wheel.

LAPPING

Lapping is an abrading process for refining the finish and dimensions of a piece of work after some previous operation. The following features are basic to this process:

1. Loose abrasive is used between work and lap.
2. Lap and work are not positively driven, but are guided by contact with each other.
3. Fresh points of contact are made between lap and work by constantly changing relative movement.
4. Both the lap and the work are improved in shape during the operation.

Lapping can be used to:

1. Remove surface roughness and save "running-in" time.
2. Give a superfine surface finish.
3. Provide liquid- and gas-tight joints without gaskets.
4. Remove errors from lead screws and gears that are noisy.

Laps may be made of cast iron, steel, brass, copper, lead, tin, aluminum, babbitt, or type metal. Wooden laps, charged with rouge or a similar fine polishing abrasive, are used for polishing hardened steel parts.

The abrasive may be either in bonded form or loose. Loose abrasive must be mixed with a vehicle, such as oil, grease, or soap and water. In general, hard abrasives are selected to lap hardened work; soft abrasives are for softer materials. The diamond is the hardest abrasive and is used for lapping precious stones. Next in hardness are the silicon carbides and aluminum oxides. Emery and natural corundum, which contain some impurities, are soft abrasives. Abrasives are graded by size of grain, from coarse at #120 to fine at #600 or higher. Grades finer than #240 are called *flours*.

The vehicle, or carrier medium, has a great deal to do with both the cutting action of the abrasive and the surface finish obtained. The abrasive must be suspended in the vehicle, which keeps the grains separated and lubricates the work to prevent scoring. Water is used for lapping glass, while oils of various consistencies are used for lapping steel. Grease is used for lapping gears and valves. The vehicle as well as the abrasive must be carefully selected for the type of finish required.

A #320 grain is good for most lapping operations where a high polish is not required. It will leave a matte finish on the surface. For a higher polish, use a finer grit, such as #800. The oil used as vehicle should be fine enough to keep the grains in suspension, or else they are liable to ball up between the lap and the work and cause irregular cutting. A lap works best when charged with the minimum of abrasive in plenty of vehicle.

The greater the pressure, the faster the lap will cut. High lap speeds reduce the rate of cutting. As a rule, the harder the metal to be cut, the harder the abrasives that should be used; but the lap itself should always be softer than the work. Soft laps cut faster, wear longer, and give a brighter surface finish. Hard laps give greater accuracy.

Specialized machines have been developed for lapping such items as bearing races, crankshafts, spherical surfaces, and flat surfaces. These are not found in a jobbing shop and so will not be discussed in detail.

Lapping both sides of thin material at the same time will make the two surfaces parallel, but they will not necessarily be flat. Flat surfaces are usually lapped against a true flat surface. As lapping cuts the lap as well as the piece of work, the work must be moved uniformly over the entire surface of the lap, so that the lap will wear uniformly and remain a true flat surface. However, this is very difficult to do when hand-lapping. Lapping machines are arranged so that work moves uniformly over the entire surface, which keeps the lapping surface true. To hand-lap a flat surface, use a small cast-iron lap, of heavy section so that it willl remain flat, and move it as evenly as possible over the entire surface, testing it on a true flat surface plate and lapping down any high spots shown up by the markings. This operation takes very careful work.

Cylindrical lapping is an easy method of producing a hole true to size and of the same diameter along its full length. The hole should be machined so true to size that only the tool marks must be removed by the lapping. Laps of cast iron, brass, or lead will become encrusted with the grit of the lapping compound, and points will be left sticking out to do the cutting.

Solid laps are sometimes used. These are turned to a size very slightly smaller than the finished diameter of the hole. The lap must be small enough to enter the hole while charged with the cutting compound. If it is too tight, it will bell out the end of the hole, while it is reduced to a size that will go through the hole. As the lap will then be smaller in diameter than it was when at the belled end, it will cut less while in the rest of the hole; and the result will be a tapered hole. By using several solid laps, each a little larger than the last, excellent work can be done.

An *expanding lap* can collapse so that it is small enough to enter the hole and move the full length before it expands to cutting size. The lap or the work should be revolved slowly; and the lap must be moved the full length at a uniform rate, so that it can cover the entire surface of the hole. So that the cutting can be felt, either the lap or the work should be held in the hand and moved until the resistance is felt to be uniform.

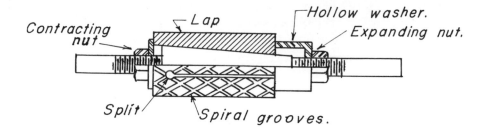

Fig. 75. Internal expanding lap

For lapping the outside of a shaft or other cylindrical piece, an adjustable *ring lap* should be made. This should be short enough so that it can be moved freely all along the length of the work, yet not so long that the abrasive will not be distributed evenly over the cutting surface, since it has no grooves on the inside. About 1 inch is a good length for this lap. The ring should be split clear through at one point and partially cut through at two other points so that it can contract uniformly over-all (see Figure 76). There should be contracting and expanding screws so that the size can be set accurately.

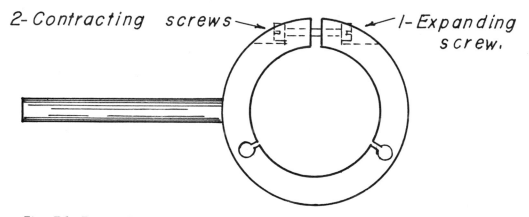

Fig. 76. External contracting lap

9

Hand-Turning Metal
and
Metal Spinning

HAND-TURNING

WHEN a curve is to be cut in the lathe, it is easier to use a hand tool and work as you would when wood turning than to try to work using the screw feeds of the lathe. It is possible to disconnect the cross-feed screw and fit a template to guide the tool to cut the desired curve. This method is used for production jobs where many parts must be made to the same contour, but it would not be worth your while in the home shop.

Tools for hand-turning of metal can be made from old three-cornered files. The teeth should be ground off the file to a point far enough back so that there will be no teeth bearing on the rest, as this would make the tool stick to the rest and prohibit its complete control. The point of the tool is ground to a cutting edge. One tool should be a round-nose, one a skew chisel, and one a narrow parting tool. A rest can be improvised by clamping a bar in the tool post and positioning it as a rest. The boring bar makes a good rest.

For wood turning, the chisel can be slid along the rest while cutting a long surface; and this will produce a cylinder with a uniform surface. In metal turning, the pressure is too great to allow the tool to slide. For cylindrical turning, use the round-nose tool, pick up the chip, and pivot the tool on the rest, making a continuous cut for one arc, then move along the rest and cut another arc. In this way you will cut a series of hollows, the combined diameters of which should not be less than the finished size of the work. To smooth out these hollows, use a broad mill file and file off the tops of the ridges between the hollows. This will show you where the high places are, and you can work them out by taking additional cuts with the swinging tool. When the file shows the surface to be nearly uniform, it can be finished with the file and emery cloth.

The same procedure is used to cut a curve. Turn the round-nose tool on its side so that it has a good deal of top rake in the direction of the cut, and it will almost feed itself. Swing little arcs until the curve is approximated. Then turn the tool so that it takes a scraping cut and finish down to the required contour. A template can be cut and filed out of sheet metal, and the curve is then worked to fit the template. Emery cloth on a curved wood form will remove the few remaining tool marks.

The hand tool is good for finishing fillets between two surfaces turned in the lathe. These fillets can be roughed out with the screw feeds, but a smoother job can be done with the hand tool. To finish the fillet with the screw feeds, the tool will have to be ground to give it a point radius equal to that of the finished fillet. A small-radius tool will leave over-lapping tool marks, which a large-radius tool will eliminate. But the large-radius tool is very liable to chatter and spoil the job. The hand tool can cut a smooth fillet and will not be subject to chatter. Care must be used to see that the tool does not take such a deep bite that it is forced out of control. Small cuts are best. Attach a long wooden handle to the hand-turning tool so that you will have good control of it.

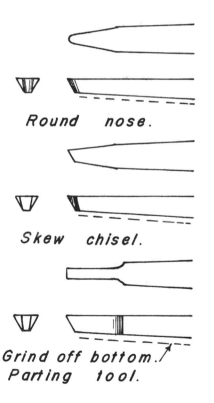

Round nose.

Skew chisel.

Grind off bottom.
Parting tool.

Fig. 77. Hand tools

For cutting steel, the point of the tool should have enough side clearance so that it can be turned on its side to give a good top rake. This will make the tool bite into the steel, and a good chip can be removed, but be careful that it does not try to feed itself too fast and get out of control. Revolving the tool back so that it has less top rake will curb its tendency to bite too fast.

For cutting brass, aluminum, and cast iron, the tool works best when held level so that there is no top rake. As these metals crumble when cut, a scraping cut works very well, with no danger of the tool getting out of control.

Parting, or cutting off, can be done with the tool, if you do not cut too deep. Cut a little on each side of the groove so that the tool will not strike both sides at once, which would make it bind in the cut. These tools are very brittle unless you retemper them to a yellow straw color, and a jam would surely break the tool.

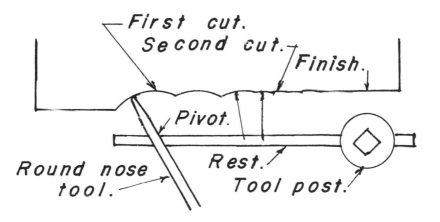

Fig. 78. Hand-turning

SPINNING

Sheet metal can be formed into various shapes by spinning it in a lathe. This requires a lathe with ample power and a wooden form, called a chuck, over which the metal is worked. The chuck has the exact shape and size as the inside of the finished work and is fastened to the face plate of the lathe. This chuck can be made from a suitable hard wood, but if many pieces are to be spun on the same chuck, it should be made of metal, usually of cast iron.

The sheet metal is cut into a circle large enough for the finished size. The center is marked, and a circle is drawn, to be used to center it on

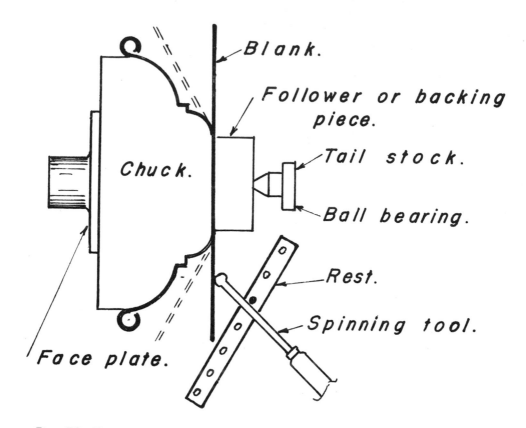

Fig. 79. Typical spinning setup

the chuck. The follower or backing piece is pivoted on a live tail center, as it requires heavy pressure from the tail stock to hold the work against the chuck. The tool rest is a horizontal bar with a series of holes for pegs, to hold the tool against while forming the work.

Spinning tools must be long, so that sufficient pressure can be applied to make the metal deform under the tool. The combined tool and handle is from 30 inches to 36 inches long. It is held under the right arm so that pressure can be put on it with the body. The tools, of various shapes, are of hardened steel and have a high polish.

The work is run at from 1200 to 1800 RPM, varying with the size and type of metal being worked. Exact rules for the speed cannot be set down, as there are too many variables, and so the operator must rely on his experience. You will have to experiment to find the best speed for the job you are doing. A lubricant must be used on the surface of the work. This can be ordinary yellow soap, tallow, beeswax, or one of the stiff greases that will stick to the work at high speed. A lubricant that flies off at working speed is of no value.

The spinning is started with a ball-point tool and gradually worked down to the shape of the chuck. Different tools are used to finish it tight against the chuck. The final edge is trimmed to size with the diamond-point tool. Beads are formed with a formed wheel tool, and the amount of stock to make the bead must be allowed for when making the final trimming to size. Spinning, which is cold working of the metal, tends to harden it very quickly. The work must be removed from the chuck and annealed at frequent intervals or it will become so hard that the metal will refuse to flow under the tool and will warp and crack. Before the work is removed for annealing, it must be worked tight against some part of the chuck, to center it and assure that it will run true when replaced on the chuck. For deep spinning, it is to your advantage to make a series of chucks, each one being nearer the final shape, so that work can be finished down tight to a solid chuck before it is removed for annealing.

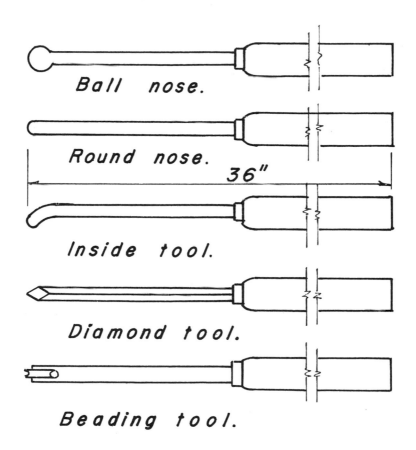

Fig. 80. Typical spinning tools

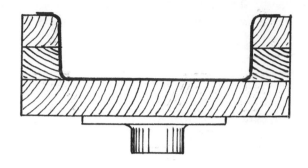

Fig. 81. Spinning an outside flange

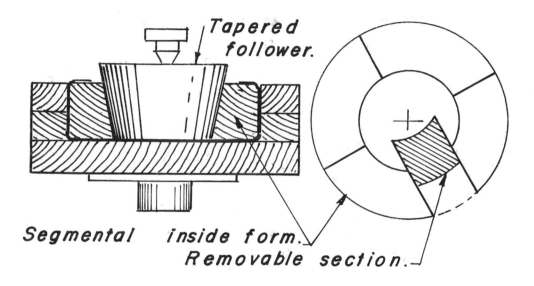

Fig. 82. Spinning an inside flange

When an inside bead is to be turned, a chuck must be used to work against. An outside bead can be formed with the same chuck used to spin to shape. An outside flange requires an outside chuck to prevent distortion as the flange is turned and to give a finished surface on which to form the flange. An inside flange calls for an outside chuck to prevent distortion and also an inside segmented backing piece for finishing the flange. The inside piece must be segmented so that it can be dismantled for removal through the smaller hole inside the flange.

10

Milling

MILLING is a process of removing metal by passing a stationary piece of work under a revolving cutter. This process is just the reverse of turning in a lathe, where the work revolves against a stationary cutter.

Milling machines can be grouped into four main types.

1. Universal milling machines.
2. Plain milling machines.
3. Vertical milling machines.
4. Manufacturing milling machines.

The *universal milling machine* can handle many kinds of work. It consists of a column on which a knee slides vertically. On this knee is a bed, or table, which can be swiveled to any angle and which has a longitudinal feed as well as a cross-feed. The milling cutter is held on a spindle above the work. The spindle has an outboard bearing held by an overhead arm and steady braces. Change gears regulate the speed of the spindle. Power feed is supplied to the table in any of its positions. Centers can be set up on the table so that cylindrical work can be held on centers. The head center can be geared to the feed train so that spirals can be cut. A dividing head is often used for the head center so that work can be divided accurately into equal spaces, as for gear teeth.

The *plain milling machine* is similar to the universal miller except that the table does not swivel and is limited to cutting in a straight line. It cannot cut spirals unless the spiral angle of the cutter is set off on a swivel table so that the cutter will have clearance in its cut.

The *vertical milling machine* is similar to the plain milling machine, except that the spindle is vertical instead of horizontal, and most of its work is done with end mills. Both the plain miller and the vertical miller are more rigid than the universal miller and can handle heavier work.

Manufacturing milling machines are generally of the solid bed type with the spindle rising on the column according to depth of cut. These machines are very rigid and can do very heavy work.

In addition to the standard types of milling machines, there are a large number of special machines designed to do a particular job, such as gear-cutting machines and tracer milling machines. For nearly every surfacing operation in the automobile industry, there is a milling machine designed to handle the work.

There are many attachments for milling machines that extend their use to work that cannot be handled in any other way. One is the plain vise, similar to a drill-press vise; another is the swivel vise. Such a vise has tongue strips under the base that register with the slots in the milling machine table. When clamped to the table, the jaws of the vise will be either parallel or at right angles to the travel of the table, and give you a quick way of setting up work that must be square with the machine.

The dividing head is used in jobbing and toolroom operations such as spacing, notching, grooving, and dividing, including the milling of flutes, plain and helical gears, cams, and a large variety of similar work. Plain dividing heads can index numbers up to 1000, and differential dividing heads can index up to 400000. The dividing head can be geared to the change gears of the table to revolve the work as it is fed under the cutter, thus cutting a spiral.

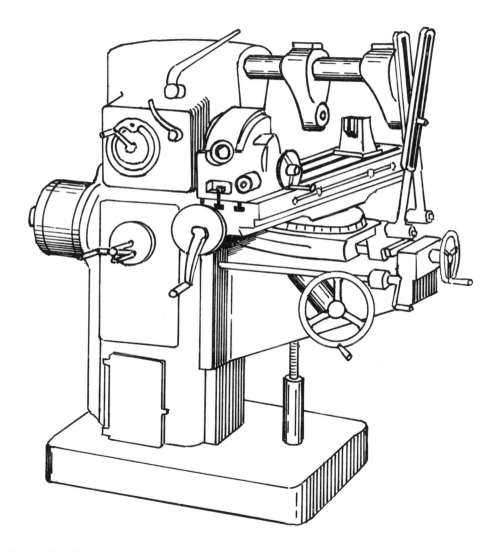

Fig. 83. Universal milling machine

Universal milling machine. The main table, on the knee, is light-colored, and the swivel table above it is dark-colored. Both table and spindle have individual motor drives.

Vertical milling attachment. A vertical, or end-milling, attachment is set to mill at an angle on a universal milling machine.

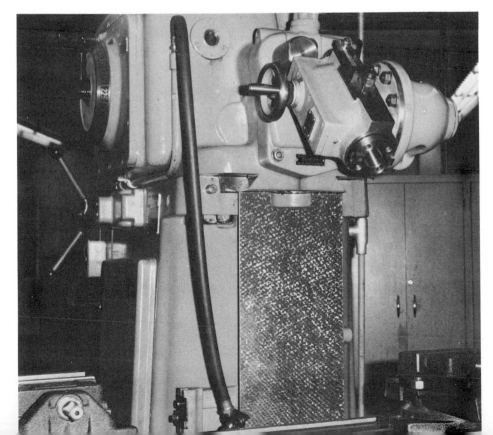

Rotary tables with an attachment for end mills enable you to cut circular work. The hand-operated rotary table has an indexing head for dividing work. The power-operated rotary table, the rotary motion of which is geared to the table traverse feed, can be used to cut a continuous scroll or flat spiral.

A swivel attachment is a device attached to the column and geared to the spindle that converts the machine into a vertical miller. The attachment can be swiveled at any angle as well as set vertically. A graduated base is used to set off the angle.

A universal head-milling attachment enables an end mill to be placed in any cutting position. The cutter is driven through gears from the spindle. It has two graduated bases at 90° so that vertical or horizontal angles may be set off to position the cutter. These universal attachments are made in three sizes, for light, medium, and heavy work.

A slotting attachment, giving a vertical, reciprocating motion to a cutter, can be used for slotting, such as making key seats. A rack-milling attachment is a device having an auxiliary spindle set parallel to the travel of the bed, so that grooves can be cut parallel to the cross-feed.

Precision measuring is required when milling to close tolerances. Micrometer measuring rods and micrometer stops are used where great accuracy is required.

The most important factors in doing good work are the speed of the milling cutter and the rate of feed against the cutter. Due to the many variables—the material to be cut and the type and condition of the cutter and milling machine—it is impossible to set down exact rules for speed of cutter teeth and rate of feed. Trial and error will soon indicate the best speed and feed for a particular job.

The following table gives approximate cutting speeds in feet per minute (fpm) for some of the more commonly used materials.

Alloy steel	25–45 fpm
Cast iron	50–65 fpm
Mild steel	50–65 fpm
Malleable iron	60–65 fpm
Bronze	130–165 fpm
Brass	160–200 fpm
Duralumin	980–1300 fpm
Aluminum	1300-1600 fpm

When using carboloy-tipped milling cutters, the above speeds may be doubled.

The approximate RPM of the cutter may be found from the following formula:

$$\text{Approximate RPM} = \frac{\text{Cutting speed (fpm)}}{\frac{1}{4} \text{ cutter diameter (in.)}}$$

Taking deep cuts is not always the quickest way to remove material. The strain this puts on the machine may cause vibration, and the excessive heat produced may ruin the sharp edge of the cutter. A poor finish will result; dimension tolerances will be hard to maintain. Taking more cuts, running the cutter as fast as possible, and removing less metal at each pass, will result in much better work. Do not force a milling cutter beyond the point of free and easy cutting. Using a cutter with the maximum number of cutting teeth, at a slow rate of feed, and taking light cuts, will give a smoother finish than will a coarse-toothed cutter fed at a faster rate, although the latter may remove metal faster. In any case, the depth of cut and the rate of feed must be such that the cutting teeth can bite deep enough to remove a good continuous chip. If the teeth are cutting shallow, the breaking away of the chip in front of each tooth may start vibration, and once this starts, it will build up to a destructive force that can ruin the work.

Milling cutters are of many types and forms. Some are used on an arbor and may be designed to cut either on the face or on the sides. Some have spiral-cut teeth: either right- or left-hand spirals. Some slotting cutters have staggered teeth. The narrow slitting saws are hollow-ground on the sides to give them clearance in the cut and let them do the cutting only on the face. Formed cutters, designed to cut a particular profile, do their cutting on the periphery. Cutters for milling gear teeth are of this kind.

An end mill is a combination tool, with a plain mill on the side and a face mill on the end. They are made right- and left-handed, with various combinations of straight or spiral side flutes. Most end mills have a dead spot at the center of the end where there are no cutting teeth. Such a mill cannot sink its own way into a cut, but must be started in a drilled hole, which will remove the material left at the center of the mill. There is a type of mill that has cutting teeth across the entire width of the end. This tool generally has only two teeth and will sink itself into the work like a drill. It is called a slotting mill and can be used to sink and cut a keyway slot.

Where a special job requires a formed cutter, and no standard cutter will do the work, fly-cutters can be quickly made to do the work. A fly-cutter is a single cutting tool formed to the desired contour and held in a jig similar to a boring bar. It cuts on one end only and is therefore slow in removing metal. The depth of cut and rate of feed are very critical factors. Fly-cutters may be either ground from hardened stock, like lathe cutting tools, or they can be filed to shape before the metal is hardened and thus carefully shaped to the required contour.

The teeth of a milling cutter must be relieved on the rear side of the cutting edge to prevent them from rubbing on the work. At the same time, the form of the teeth must be uniform, so that when it is sharpened the shape of the cutter will not be changed. When the cutter is working on a spiral, as for milling a thread, the table must be swung to the helix angle of the spiral, so that the cutter will be cutting on its true contour and will have no side motion, as it would if not set to the helix angle.

Setting up a complicated milling operation requires great skill, a complete knowledge of the machine, and very careful work. All adjustments should be checked, and all motions tried by hand, before using power. Where calculations are necessary, as in computing the change gears for indexing or cutting spirals, go over them again to be sure they are correct. Where possible, as in indexing, run through one cycle, marking the work with very slight tool marks to verify the setup.

Where depth of cut must be accurately measured, the point of zero cut of the cutting tool must be known in order to set the starting point on the measuring device. This can be found by placing a thin piece of paper under a cutter tooth and feeding the tooth against the work until the paper can no longer be pulled from under it. The cutter must be revolved by hand to find the point of starting cut for the tooth. Using a shim from a feeler gauge will do the same thing, and then the known thickness of the feeler blade can be used to correct the micrometer reading for the depth of cut. However, this may ruin the blade of the feeler.

The direction of rotation of the milling cutter with respect to the direction of feed has a great influence on the action of the cutter and on the surface finish. In standard milling, the work passes under the cutter in the opposite direction to that of rotation. The tooth starts its cut at a tangent to the finished surface, and the thickness of the chip increases as the work advances. If there is any backlash in the gibs or feed screw, the feed is opposed to the backlash, and the depth of cut remains constant. With "climb" milling, the cutter rotates in the same direction as the feed. The cutter starts its cut with the full width of chip and gradually reduces the chip thickness as it finishes the cut. If backlash is present, it can force the work forward a certain distance; when this is added to the depth of feed, the depth of cut is increased to danger point. Standard milling tends to lift the work, while climb milling forces the work downward. Any play in the gibs of the sliding ways will be reflected in the surface finish.

The Milling Attachment

With a milling attachment, many light milling jobs can be performed in the lathe. The milling attachment gives you a third direction of movement—vertical—so that work can be moved in any direction. Various devices are used to hold the work on the milling attachment, but the vise is the most useful. A flat plate or angle block fastened to the attachment, and to which the work can be bolted, is often used.

For most milling, an end mill, held in the three-jaw chuck, or better yet, in a collet chuck, is the best tool. This end mill can be used for finishing a vertical or horizontal surface parallel to the cross-feed of the carriage. For slotting, a circular cutter is held on an arbor. This arbor can be one that is held between centers and turned with a lathe dog, or it can be a one-ended arbor held in the three-jaw chuck. The three-jaw chuck is not perfectly accurate; the cutter will wobble and cut more on one side. This is hard on the milling cutter and makes it harder to produce a smooth surface. The collet chuck will hold the cutter so that it will run true.

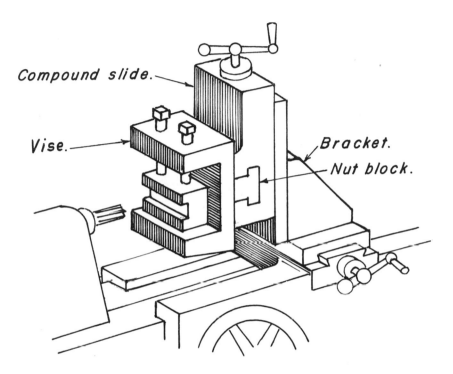

Fig. 84. Milling attachment

The End Mill

The end mill cuts best on its end, and so it should be used this way to remove large amounts of metal. Set the carriage stop to the depth of cut and take small cuts with the end of the mill, spacing the cuts close enough together so that you can roughly approximate the finished surface. If the surface being milled is a vertical one, it can be finished with the end of the mill after the carriage has been clamped to the ways, to prevent any movement while cutting. The end of the mill does not cut very well when fed sideways, so take a very light finishing cut. For removing the serrated surface left on a horizontal surface by the roughing cuts of the end mill, the mill can be fed to cut on its side flutes. As the mill will tend to spring away from the work with this kind of a cut, the flutes must be sharp, and small cuts should be taken so that there will be an even surface where the cuts overlap. If the end mill is held in a collet chuck, you will need a collet for each size of mill, as their shanks are not all the same size.

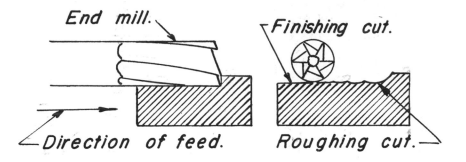

Fig. 85. Cutting with an end mill

Key Seats

Key seats are cut with a slotting mill. Special mills are available for cutting Woodruff key seats. The work is held in the vise of the attachment so that the place where the key seat is to be cut projects beyond the vise. Then center the cutter exactly over the shaft. This can be done by marking the sides of the key seat on the surface of the shaft and drawing a vertical line across the end of the shaft. The shaft can then be set vertically in the vise, and the cutter can be centered on the key-seat marks. The work is then run up until the cutter is just touching the work. Place a piece of thin paper under the cutter and adjust the height so that you can just pull the paper out. If the milling attachment has a stop on the vertical feed, set it to the depth of cut desired. If there is no stop, mark the zero point so that you can measure the depth of cut from it. It might be possible to clamp on a temporary stop with a "C" clamp. The work is fed up under the mill until the finished depth is reached.

For long keyways, the work is fed under the cutter with the cross-feed of the carriage until the required length has been cut. This will leave a curved bottom at each end of the cut. A long keyway can also be cut with an end mill of the correct size. In this case, the work is set up so that the keyway is facing the end of the mill. Start the cut by drilling a starting hole the same size as the mill. A drill must be used, because an end mill leaves a small tit at the center when it is fed lengthwise into the

Milling attachment. For milling a Woodruff keyseat in a shaft, the compound slide is set vertically on a bracket, and the work is held in the vise.

Collet chuck for milling cutters. The photograph shows the draw bar with hand wheel for closing collet, the outer sleeve, and the collet.

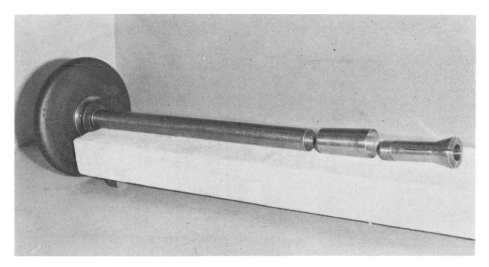

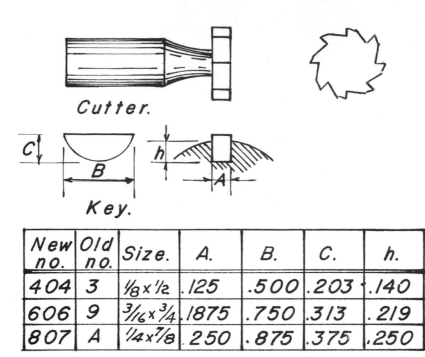

Cutter.

Key.

New no.	Old no.	Size.	A.	B.	C.	h.
404	3	1/8 x 1/2	.125	.500	.203	.140
606	9	3/16 x 3/4	.1875	.750	.313	.219
807	A	1/4 x 7/8	.250	.875	.375	.250

Fig. 86. Woodruff keys

work, and thus it cannot drill a hole. The end mill can then finish the slot, by roughing out with end cuts and finishing with a side pass.

When using the milling attachment, always turn the mill against the feed. As there is always some backlash in the slides and screws of the carriage, if the mill is turning with the feed, it may be forced in some distance by the backlash. This will jam the mill, causing a heavy cut that will either break the mill or damage the work.

Curved slots or surfaces can be milled by setting up the work on a pivot located at the center of the curve and clamping the work to hold it still during the cutting. By unclamping the work and advancing it a small cut each time, you can rough out the curve. If you attach a wrench or handle to the work you can make the finish cut, feeding by hand with this handle while the clamp is loose. The pivot must be a tight running fit so that there is no backlash, or it will not cut a smooth finish surface.

For milling out a closed hole, make the starting cut with a drill in one corner and then work out a slot with an end mill, always using the end of the mill and keeping the feed against the rotation of the mill. The design to be milled should be laid out with marking paint, using good bright lines, since you are feeding the work to cut to these lines and they are hard to see. Use a light on an extension cord to let you see the marks.

Milling a dovetail slot is done with a formed cutter similar to an end mill but with side-cutting flutes set at the angle of the finished slot. The straight center part is roughed out with the end mill, using end cuts, and then the sides are finished with the dovetail cutter, taking several passes to rough out the sides and then finishing with a full-width cut.

Milling of gear teeth can be done by using a set of formed milling cutters and a fixture to index the spacing of the teeth. Several formed cutters are required, as the shape of gear teeth changes with the number of teeth on a gear. Each cutter will approximate the shape of tooth for several sizes or number of teeth. With these cutters each tooth is milled to shape individually. The indexing must be exact, and the correct cutter must be used for each gear. It is not a practical way to cut gears in a home workshop. But there is a way in which very accurately cut gears can be made at home. This is by the use of a gear hob. The hob is a milling cutter that has teeth in the form of a rack and has straight sides. The teeth form a spiral like a thread around the hob, and the gear blank is revolved at the same pitch as the hob. As the hob is fed into the blank, the many cutters will generate a tooth shape correct for that number of teeth. Since a rack will mesh with gears of any number of teeth, the hob, which is a rack in the form of teeth spiraled around the hob, will cut the correct shape of tooth for any number of teeth. The hob and the indexing attachment are described in the chapter on Gear Cutting.

Milling flutes, such as on a reamer, is done with an edge-cutting mill with the edge formed to the curve of the flute to be cut. The work is set up in a fixture that has centers at each end and provision for setting up an indexing head. This indexing head can be one of the lathe change gears with a number of teeth that will divide evenly by the number of flutes to be cut. This gear is rigidly attached to the piece of work and has a stop so that it can be held in position after the correct number of teeth have been counted off between cuts. These teeth should be counted and marked before the gear is attached to the work.

When setting up work in the milling attachment, be sure to check the length of all the movements. The distance traveled by the slides is limited, and the method of fastening to the attachment may use up some of the length of the slide, so check to make sure that you can mill the **entire** job without disturbing the setting.

11

Planing and Shaping

THE tools used to machine a flat surface are the *planer* and the *shaper*. These two machines are similar in that, in both, the material is removed by a reciprocating motion while the cutting tool is fed across the work.

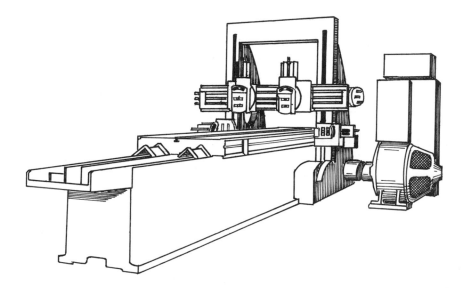

Fig. 87. Planer

THE PLANER

The planer uses a reciprocating bed on which the work is clamped and the tool is fed across the work on a rail supported by side columns (see Figure 87). Double-housing planers have side columns on each side of the table. The size of work that can be handled is limited by the width between the columns and the travel of the table. The tool is held in a head traveling on the cross rail, which has its own slides to give it a vertical movement in addition to the height adjustment afforded by the raising or lowering of the cross rail. This tool head may be swiveled and has a graduated base for setting to angles. On most machines the rail has two tool heads, each swiveling to the outside. Each head has its own feed, which can be controlled by hand cranks from either end of the cross rail.

Power feed to the cross motion is supplied by ratchet action from the reciprocating table.

In addition to the heads on the cross rail, some machines have tool heads on the supporting columns. These are similar to the heads on the rail, but have a vertical movement up the side column. They can be swiveled for angular cuts. More than one head may be set up to cut simultaneously.

Several methods are used to bring into action the reciprocating motion of the table. Belt-driven machines reverse the direction by shifting the drive belt to the reverse pulleys. This activates a set of belts and pulleys, causing a slower motion on the cutting stroke and a fast action on the return stroke. Some machines use a reversing motor, but the more modern machines use hydraulic feed. In all machines, the travel of the table is regulated by stops on the side of the table, which can be adjusted to reverse the travel when the table has reached the end of the stroke.

Work set up on a planer is usually long in one direction, and care must be used when clamping it to the table that the clamps do not spring the work. If it is sprung when clamped, it will spring back when released and thus will not be a straight surface. Shims must be used under the work at the point of the clamps to prevent this distortion. Due to the heavy end thrust of the cutting tool, the work must be prevented from slipping on the table by placing stop pins in holes provided in the table and having the work bear tightly against these pins. These stop pins sometimes have set screws or adjusting bolts so that they can be adjusted to fit against work with an irregularly shaped end. The table has "T" slots machined down its length for clamping the work. A bolt used in one of these "T" slots should have a head that will fit the slot to prevent the bolt from turning as it is tightened. Thus you may be required to have many bolts of various lengths, each with this special "T" head. A better way, however, is to have nuts that fit the "T" slot so that bolts of any length can be used. Where the work has a large overhang that may spring under the cut, special jackscrews can be placed underneath it to take up the pressure. Where the tool is cutting on only one side of the work, a large torque is produced, which may twist the work out of line on the table. To prevent this, set stop pins or stop blocks on each side, adjusted tight against the work.

THE SHAPER

On the shaper, the tool, not the work, moves with a reciprocating motion. The machine consists of a heavy base and column, on top of which are the slides in which the ram reciprocates (see Figure 88). Inside the column is the mechanism for imparting the motion to the ram. One of the most common of these arrangements is the crank and the connecting rod. The wrist pin of the connecting rod is offset from the center

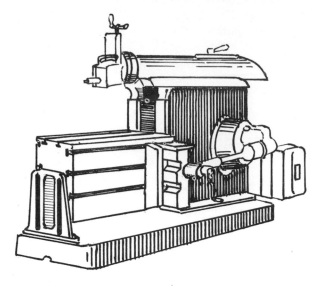

Fig. 88. Shaper

line of the crank so that the motion is slow on the cutting stroke and rapid on the return. The length of the stroke is regulated by moving the crank pin in or out from the center of the crank bearings. The position of the ram to adjust the cutting tool to the work is regulated by the point at which the wrist pin is clamped to the ram.

Another mechanism used to get the reciprocating motion is a vertical lever, pivoted to the frame at the bottom and attached to the ram with a short connecting rod at the top. There is a sliding cross head running in a slot up the center of this lever. The crank pin bears in this cross head, so that, when it is at the top of its circle and moving the ram on the cutting stroke, it is farther away from the pivot and gives a slower motion than when it is at the bottom on the return stroke. The length of stroke is regulated by the position of the crank pin; the position of the ram, by the place where the connecting rod is clamped to it.

On the front of the column are slides on which the cross rail can move vertically; and on the rail are slides which allow the table to move horizontally. The table is in the form of a box with "T" slots on each side and on the top. Work can be clamped directly to this box table or it can be set up in a vise fastened to the table. Machines with a long overhang to the box table have an outboard steady support.

The tool is carried on a swivel head on the end of the ram. This head has a short slide for the feed of the tool. The action of the cutting tool is somewhat different from that of a lathe turning tool. In a lathe, the tool is never exposed to reverse motion except in thread cutting, when it has to be withdrawn from the cut. In the shaper and the planer, the tool must be released from contact with the work on the return stroke.

Heavy-duty shaper

To accomplish this release of the tool, the tool post is attached to a swinging arm steadied by guides on each side and pivoted at the top so that the tool can swing out on the return stroke. This is called the *clapper box*. By revolving the clapper box on the swivel head, a position can be found so that the tool will swing out and away from the work as it returns.

A planer is used for work that is too large to be set up on a shaper. It is also used when multiple pieces can be set up in a row, and several parts are machined at one setting. By using the proper tools, the shaper can cut slots for either external or internal keyways. By the use of templates to guide the motion of the table, profile work can be done. There are also vertical shapers, or slotting machines, which are handier to use for slotting, with the work held in a horizontal position. A rotary table is often used on the slotting machine.

The action of the clapper box is illustrated in Figure 89.

Figure 89B, in which a straight tool is being used, shows how the cutting edge of the tool, which is forward of the pivot of the clapper box, has a tendency to swing downward on the cutting stroke and thus dig into the work. In Figure 89A a bent tool is being used; the cutting edge is behind the pivot point, and thus the tool will swing up and away from the work without tending to dig in. When there is much play in the gibs of the sliding members, the bent tool will give smoother work. Figure

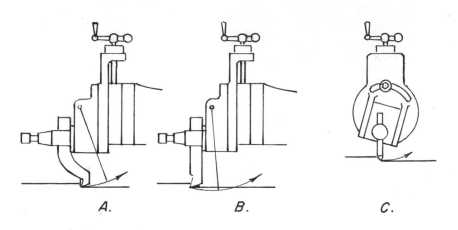

A.   *B.*   *C.*

Fig. 89. Action of clapper box

89C shows how, by inclining the clapper box, the tool can be made to swing away from a vertical edge. When setting the stroke of a planer or shaper, it is necessary to allow a little overtravel at each end. This allows the clapper to swing the tool into place for the stroke. About ½ inch is needed at the end of the cutting stroke, and ¾ inch is good at the start.

CUTTING FLAT SURFACES IN THE HOME WORKSHOP

A planer or shaper is not an essential tool for the small shop. Other means must be used for the few times a flat surface must be machined. Many times a piece of work can be set up in the lathe and faced off by turning. Sometimes an end mill and the milling attachment will do the work. But when the work is of such a shape that it cannot be turned, or when there is so much overhang that the milling attachment will not be steady enough, other means must be used.

The tool-post grinder does not put as much strain on overhanging work set up in the milling attachment, and this can often be used to do the job. You will have to make a bracket that will hold the tool-post grinder at the back of the lathe, while the work is reciprocated past the grinder when fastened to the carriage of the lathe.

The bracket can be welded up from scraps of angle iron and other pieces of steel, and must clamp on the bottom of the lathe bed so that the carriage can move without striking the bracket. The compound rest is to be mounted on this bracket to give the vertical movement to the grinder. The lathe longitudinal and cross-feeds give the other two movements. With the work set up on the carriage cross slide and the grinder mounted on the bracket, the arrangement can be used as a small planer to grind many flat surfaces. As you will be starting from a rough casting, arrange to use a coarse-grained grinding wheel to rough out the work and change to a fine-grained wheel for finishing. If the same wheel is used for roughing and finishing, it must be trued up with the diamond before taking the finishing cuts. As this arrangement has a long overhang on the grinder bracket, there is liable to be much spring to it, so slow feed and light cuts are necessary. It is a slow way to remove metal, but at least it gets the job done. If a large amount of metal is to be removed, it will be quicker to rough-chip the surface to nearly its finished dimensions before setting up for the finish grinding.

INTERNAL KEYWAYS

Cutting keyways inside the bore of a pulley can be done in the home shop. Large shops use a special broach for cutting such keyways, or they use a shaper. You do not have either of these in your home shop and it would not pay you to have them. You can simulate the action of a shaper by installing a cutter in a boring bar and moving the carriage back and forth until the keyway is finished. The carriage can be moved by means of the hand-feed wheel, but this is slow and tiresome work. A simple lever can be arranged to move the carriage with a handle.

The cutter for the keyway must be ground to the exact width of the finished slot. It is installed in a boring bar small enough to pass through the bore with the cutter projecting out far enough to make the full depth of cut. It is hard to reset the cutter to fit a slot partly cut if it is disturbed from its first setting. The outline of the end of the keyway should be marked on the end of the bore, and the cutter should be adjusted to it. The cutter is ground with very little face rake, because if it tends to bite in too deep at each cut it will jam. As the projecting boring bar will spring away from the cut, it cannot be advanced into the cut too rapidly. It must take scraping cuts, and each cut must be repeated until the full amount of the last advance of the cutter has been removed.

The layout marks on the end of the bore should be at the exact height of the lathe centers and on the side nearest to you. The cutter is adjusted to this height, and it should be level all the way across so that it will cut parallel to the sides of the keyway. If the length of the slot is to be limited, set the carriage stop to this length, keeping in mind that the cutter will leave a small part of the chip at the end of each cut, so that the end will not be a clearly defined line, but will be a series of little steps down to the depth of the slot. For this reason the stop must be set far enough ahead to allow for this unfinished end of the slot, if a full-length key is to be inserted. Set the inside calipers to the diameter of the bore plus the projection of the key, and this will give the depth of slot to be cut by measuring from the opposite side of the bore to the bottom of the slot.

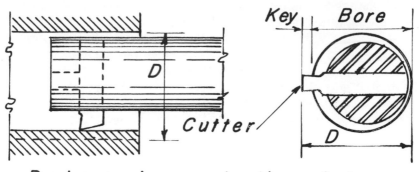

D = bore plus projection of key.

Fig. 90. Internal-keyway cutter

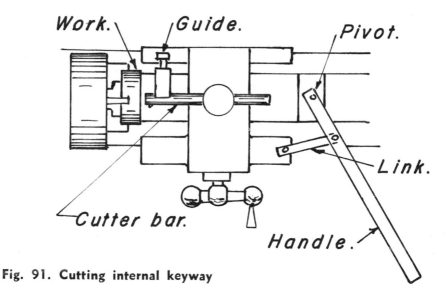

Fig. 91. Cutting internal keyway

To prevent the cutter from springing away from the cut each time, an adjustable bearing can be arranged to guide the bar into the cut. This is similar to a steady rest with one guide placed at the far side and on the center line of the lathe centers. Each time the cutter is advanced into the cut with the cross-feed screw, this guide is also advanced the same amount; it thus takes up the pressure of the cutter near the work and prevents the springing away of the tool (see Figure 93). On the face of this rest can be placed an adjustable stop to set the cutter for correct height and level. It is swung down out of the way after the cutter is set (see Figure 94, page 170).

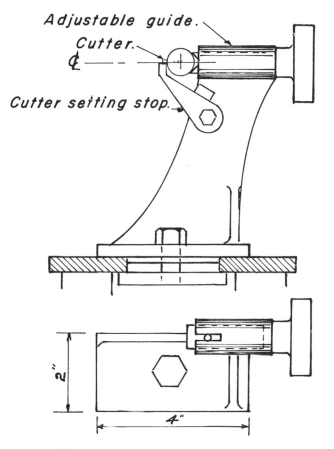

Adjustable guide.

Cutter.

¢

Cutter setting stop.

2"

4"

Fig. 92. Keyseat guide

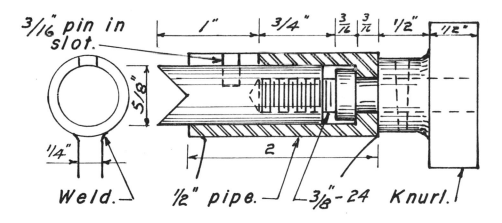

3/16" *pin in slot.*

1"   3/4"   3/16 | 3/16 | 1/2"   1/2"

5/8"

1/4"

Weld.   1/2" *pipe.*   3/8"-24 *Knurl.*

2

Fig. 93. Adjustable guide

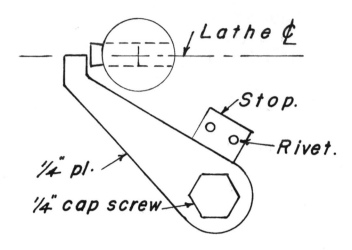

Fig. 94. Cutter-setting stop

12

Gear Cutting

GEAR-cutting shops use machines of various designs in the commercial manufacture of spur gears. These machines all employ variations on two basic methods of gear-tooth forming.

One method is to cut each individual tooth with a formed cutter, which, when passed through the final cut, gives the tooth the profile needed for a gear of that particular number of teeth. An indexing mechanism is used to space the individual teeth. As the profile of the teeth is different for gears with varying numbers of teeth, this method calls for a cutter of the correct profile for each size of gear. This would mean having a great many cutters for each pitch, very accurately made to give the correct profile to the teeth. It has been found that the variation of the shape varies so little for gears of approximately the same size that a given cutter can cut the teeth of a gear having a few more or less teeth than the number for which the cutter was designed. This allows the entire range of sizes to be cut with a series of eight formed cutters. The teeth are not exact, but if used at slow speeds and for light loads, teeth cut by this process serve very well. A milling machine with a dividing head is used; either the universal or plain milling machine can be used. This is a slow way of cutting gears, however, and is seldom used in the shops specializing in gear cutting. Its principal use is in the jobbing shop, where only a few gears are made at a time. Its main disadvantage is that so many cutters are required for each pitch. A modification on the process involves the use of a single fly-cutter in a suitable tool holder. These fly-cutters are much cheaper, but are slow in removing metal. The machine used is the milling machine, and the profile of the cutters must be just as accurately formed as for the rotary cutters.

For very large teeth, a cutter similar to an end mill with side flutes shaped to the profile of the tooth can be used in a machine that indexes the spacing of the teeth. These cutters are much cheaper to produce than some of the other, more accurate cutters.

The second method is the generating process, in which a series of cutting teeth, when passed through the cut, will remove a little metal from the center tooth and the several side teeth, thus generating the profile of the tooth. A rack will mesh with a gear of any number of teeth; since a rack has straight-sided teeth, it is easy to produce accurately. The involute form of gear teeth is preferred for most modern work. This tooth form produces a true rolling action between the teeth, which gives a smooth action with uniform angular velocity. This tends to produce a quiet-running gear.

There are two types of machines that use the generating type of cutters. One system uses a cutter in the form of a short rack with straight-sided teeth. This cutter is reciprocated past the gear blank, and the blank is slowly revolved as the cutter is moved in the same direction, so that the teeth being cut are always in mesh with the rack. This cuts a little off the sides of the several teeth in contact with the cutter. As the cutter is fed deeper into the cut, the shape of the tooth is generated. After one tooth is completed, the cutter is released from the meshing with the tooth just cut, and the blank is revolved to bring the next tooth under the center of the cutter; the operation is then repeated until all the teeth are finished. This requires that the machine be stopped each time the cutter is advanced to the next tooth. This stopping of the machine as well as the meshing of the cutter teeth are done entirely automatically by the machine.

Just as a rack will mesh with any number of teeth in the involute system of the same pitch and pressure angle, so will any other gear mesh with any other gear. This means that a cutter in the form of a pinion, when reciprocated past a gear blank, and when both the blank and cutter are rotated so as to keep them in proper mesh, will generate a tooth form that will mesh with any other number of teeth. This machine does not have to be stopped to advance the cutter to the next tooth, as the pinion shape of the cutter continuously presents the cutting teeth at the proper setting.

For cutting plain spur gears or helical gears, the hob method is the fastest and most accurate. The hob is a milling cutter with teeth in the form of a straight-sided rack, forming a helix, like a thread, around the hob. This helix can be either a single or multiple thread. In use, the gear blank is caused to revolve so that the teeth being cut are always in mesh with the pitch of the spiral thread of the hob. The hob can be fed into the work continuously until the gear is completed, without having to stop the machine at any time. The axis of the gear blank must be set at the helix angle of the hob so that the teeth of the hob will be cutting normal to the gear tooth.

Hobs cannot be used to cut herringbone gears, but can cut perfect spiral gears by combining the spiral angle with the helix angle of the hob. Herringbone gears consist of two identical spiral gears, each forming half of the herringbone gear, with the teeth cut right-handed on one half and left-handed on the other half.

Worm wheels can be cut by the hobbing method. This requires a hob of the same pitch and tooth form as the thread of the worm pinion. The worm wheel is then made to revolve at the correct speed, so that the teeth are kept in mesh with the cutting teeth of the hob. In this case, the axis of the gear blank is not set at the helix angle but at its running angle with the worm, normally at 90°. The hob will generate the correct form of worm-wheel tooth to mesh with the worm. Hobs can be used to cut splines on shafts, ratchet teeth, and sprockets, as well as gear teeth.

The teeth of bevel gears are of the same shape throughout their length but are smaller near the center than at the outside of the gear. For this reason they cannot be cut by any form of milling cutter that cuts a constant size of tooth. Special gear shapers are used that will generate and taper the tooth to be correct for its full length. All the elements of a bevel-gear tooth must pass through the common center where the two shafts meet. The gear shaper has the tool reciprocating on a guide that always passes through this center. At the same time a guide controls the position of the cutting tool, so that the shape will be generated by this guide.

Spiral bevel gears and hypoid gears both require special machines that will be found only in a specialized gear factory.

Gears that must be hardened are subject to distortion in the heating and quenching process and, unless trued up after hardening, are likely to be noisy in operation. Either grinding or lapping is used to correct any errors. Grinding of plain or spiral gears can be done with a formed grinding wheel or with wheels guided to generate the tooth form. Bevel gears can be ground on machines similar to the gear shaper, in which the grinding wheel generates the tooth form and the taper of the teeth. Herringbone and spiral, bevel, or hypoid gears cannot be ground. Lapping is employed for these gears.

In lapping gears, the hardened gear and pinion are run together

Gear-cutting attachment. Note the expanding gear train that drives the indexing gear.

with an abrasive between them until the irregularities of the teeth have been removed. As the teeth are hard, the abrasive action is slow. Gears lapped by this method must always be lapped and run together. The lapping will generate a modified tooth form typical only to this particular pair of gears, and they will not work with gears lapped with some other gear. A soft lap does not wear as rapidly as the hard work it is lapping, so that, if a gear is made from soft material, and the hardened gears are lapped with it, the finished hardened gears will have teeth approximately of the same shape and concentric with the gear axis and should run silently.

A lap similar to a hop and made from cast iron can be used to lap hardened gears. The lap is run at a slightly different helix angle than that used to cut the gear. This makes the lap touch the gear in a point contact and the abrasive gets a rolling action that cuts down the high points on the hardened gear with very little wear on the lap. The same lap can be used to true up several hardened gears, and the gears will mesh and run silently with each other. The sliding between the teeth due to meshing action is not sufficient to give good abrasive action. There must also be a reciprocating action that will cause the lap to travel the full length of the tooth. The running of the lap at an angle to the gear makes the point of contact travel the full length of the tooth and gives the required reciprocating action.

GEAR HOBBING IN THE HOME SHOP

To cut gears with a hob, you will need a fixture to hold the gear blank and a means of revolving it in mesh with the spiral of the hob. The fixture must have centers on which the arbor holding the gear blank can revolve. On the end of this arbor is mounted a gear of the same number of teeth as the one to be cut. This can be one of the change gears of the lathe. This indexing gear is driven by a worm of the same pitch as the pitch of the indexing gear, which revolves at the same speed as the hob arbor.

The teeth in the hob form a helix, or spiral, and the axis of the gear blank must be set at the same angle as the helix angle of the hob so that the teeth will be cutting parallel to the side of the gear tooth being formed as the blank is fed up to the hob.

Standard hobs are expensive and are made for larger machines, so a homemade hob should be used. There are two standard forms of gear tooth in general use. These have different pressure angles and will not mate exactly and run with a gear of a different pressure angle. The pressure angle is the angle between the line of action of the teeth and the common tangent to the pitch surfaces in the plane of rotation. A pressure angle of $14\frac{1}{2}°$ is satisfactory for all gears of over 32 teeth, but under that size the teeth of the mating gear tend to undercut the teeth of the small gear near the root of the teeth. The 20° pressure-angle system was developed to give a narrower tooth on the points and thus reduce the undercutting. These teeth do not start to undercut until there are fewer than 17 teeth. The teeth are also wider at the root and are therefore stronger. Both of these systems have many modifications to increase the strength and prevent undercutting. The stub tooth is the principal modification used.

The full-length 20° tooth is the more widely used. If you are cutting a gear to mate with one already made, such as an extra change gear, you must know which pressure angle was used. You cannot tell by examination. There are gauges for measuring the pitch of gear teeth. These are in the form of racks, and as a rack will mate with any other gear of the same system, it can tell which pressure angle was used. The 14½° rack is cut on one edge of the gauge; the 20° rack, on the opposite edge. Try both racks; the one that mates with the teeth of the gear will be the one with the correct pressure angle. The wrong one will not mesh the full depth with all the teeth in contact with the rack. As these gauges are expensive, and as you will seldom have to use one, you need not purchase a set.

Many of the catalogues of stock gear manufacturers have pictures of the exact shape and size of the various gear teeth. By placing the gear

Gear-cutting attachment. The spiral drive of the indexing gear is above; the hob that cuts the gear blank is below.

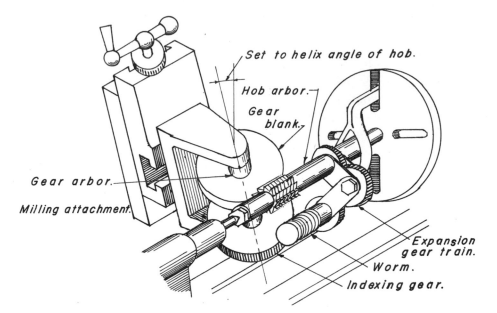

Set to helix angle of hob.

Hob arbor.

Gear blank.

Gear arbor.

Milling attachment.

Expansion gear train.

Worm.

Indexing gear.

Fig. 95. Gear cutting

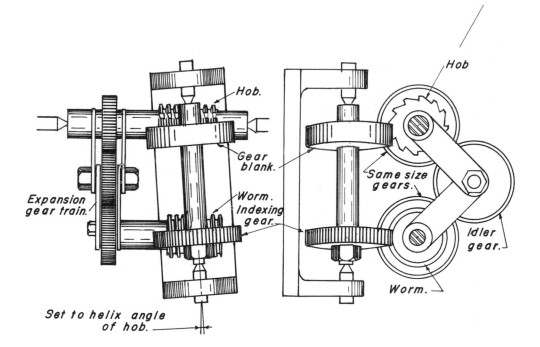

Hob.

Gear blank.

Hob

Expansion gear train.

Worm. Indexing gear.

Same size gears.

Idler gear.

Worm.

Set to helix angle of hob.

Fig. 96. Gear-cutting attachment

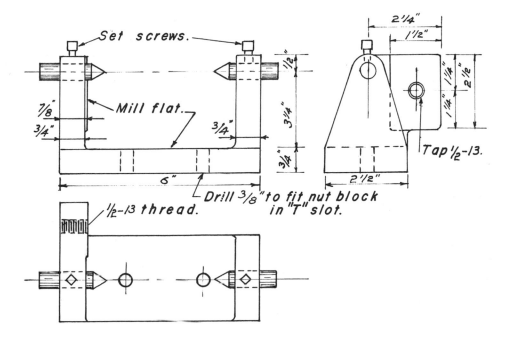

Fig. 97. Gear-arbor bracket

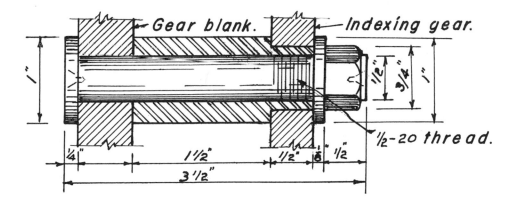

Fig. 98. Gear arbor

to be matched over one of these gear forms, you can gain a pretty good idea of the pressure angle used. If the teeth to be matched are badly worn, however, this may not work. The 20° teeth will be wider at the root and narrower at the point than the 14½° teeth. Both forms of the tooth are the same width at the pitch line.

There are two forms of the curve of the tooth face, the *cycloidal tooth* and the *involute tooth*. These names describe the action of the mating teeth as they roll in and out of contact. It is not necessary for your purposes in the home shop that you know just how these curves are arrived at. The cycloidal tooth was much used in the old days, but now the involute form is preferred, with modifications to fit special conditions. If you do not know what tooth form to use to fit a gear already cut, it is best to select the 20° involute.

To make a gear hob, bore a piece of tool steel to fit the arbor that works between the lathe centers. It must have a keyway; however, since it is too thin to allow you to cut a groove inside, mill or file a notch on the end to engage a pin driven through the arbor. The outside should be turned to some even circumference, such as 1½ inches or 2 inches, as it will be used for measuring the depth of the hob teeth. It is easier to subtract twice the root depth of the teeth from some even outside diameter and set the calipers to this, which is the diameter of the root of the teeth.

A special tool must be ground to fit the exact shape of the grooves between the teeth. This shape is the same as that of the teeth in a rack, and the dimensions are given in Table 9, *Spur-Gear Proportions*. The shape should be laid out very accurately on the top surface of the cutting tool, using marking lacquer and a sharp scriber. The width is very important, and this is measured at the pitch line of the teeth. The *addendum* is the distance from the point of the tooth to the pitch line, and the correct addendum distance must be marked on the tool for the particular pitch you are using. Mark the line so that, when the micrometer is set to the width of the tooth, the micrometer will go on the taper of the tooth only as far as this line. Use a good magnifying glass when laying out this line and when measuring to it with the micrometer.

The taper of the tool must be at either the 14½° or the 20° angle, according to the angle you are using. The tool-post grinder is used to make this taper accurately. Set up the cutter blank in the four-jaw chuck with the cutting end projecting out, so that the top is about ¼ inch above center. The grinding wheel, set at center, will then undercut the sides to give side clearance. Set the compound slide to the required angle (14½° or 20°) and grind the side to the layout mark. Now set the compound to the same angle, but *reversed*, and grind the opposite side. Test often with the micrometer set to the tooth width and stop when the micrometer reaches the mark for the pitch line. You can now remove the tool from the chuck and round off the corners slightly, to produce the fillets at the root of the teeth. During the grinding of the sides, the

Table 9

Spur-Gear Proportions

To Compute	When You Know	Rule	Formula
Diametrical pitch (P)	Pitch diameter and number of teeth	Divide number of teeth (N) by pitch diameter (D)	$P = \dfrac{N}{D}$
" "	Outside diameter and number of teeth	Divide number of teeth plus 2 by outside diameter (D_o)	$P = \dfrac{N+2}{D_o}$
Pitch diameter (D)	Number of teeth and outside diameter	Divide product of outside diameter times number of teeth by number of teeth plus 2	$D = \dfrac{D_o \times N}{N+2}$
Thickness of tooth (t)	Diametrical pitch	Divide 1.5708 by diametrical pitch	$t = \dfrac{1.5708}{P}$
Addendum (a)	Diametrical pitch	Divide 1 by diametrical pitch	$a = \dfrac{1}{P}$ or: $a = \dfrac{D}{N}$
Dedendum (b)	Diametrical pitch	Divide 1.157 by diametrical pitch	$b = \dfrac{1.157}{P}$
Total depth of tooth (H_t)	Diametrical pitch	Divide 2.157 by diametrical pitch	$H_t = \dfrac{2.157}{P}$
Root diameter (D_r)	Pitch diameter and dedendum	Subtract twice the dedendum (b) from pitch diameter	$D_r = D - 2b$
Outside diameter (D_o)	Number of teeth and diametrical pitch	Divide number of teeth plus 2 by diametrical pitch	$D_o = \dfrac{N+2}{P}$
Circular pitch (p)	Diametrical pitch	Divide 3.1416 by diametrical pitch	$p = \dfrac{3.1416}{P}$

cutter blank must not be moved in the lathe. Lock the spindle so that it cannot be moved accidentally.

Gear teeth are commonly designated according to their *diametrical pitch,* that is, the number of teeth on a pinion 1 inch in diameter. *Circular pitch* is the distance, along the pitch line, occupied by the width of one tooth plus the space between it and the next tooth. In order to make your hob, you will have to know the circular pitch, which will be the pitch of the spiral thread that you are to cut on the hob. To find the circular pitch, divide 3.1416 (π) by the diametrical pitch, as stated in Table 9. The result will be a decimal fraction, which will not fit any of the common gear combinations for the lead screw of your lathe. Use the formula given in Chapter 5, THREAD CUTTING (p. 92), to find the ratio of the stud gear to the screw gear. You will have to set up a compound train of gears in order to derive this ratio, using two or more gear combinations to give you the correct lead for the pitch of the gear to be cut.

When the lathe has been geared to the required pitch, turn a right-handed thread onto the hob blank, measuring the depth of the thread to the root diameter between the threads. Since you are cutting a thread very similar to an Acme thread, you may find it necessary to rough it out beforehand with a roughing tool. The finishing tool must be placed so that it is square with the axis of the hob. Since the clearance ground on the side of the cutter by the tool-post grinder may not be sufficient on its leading or cutting edge, it may be necessary to grind additional clearance to clear the helix of the thread. This extra grinding can be done by hand, if care is taken not to overgrind at the cutting edge and spoil the angle of the side of the tool. Of course, the compound slide should always be set to the angle of the side of the thread while the hob is being cut.

When the thread is completed, set up the hob on the milling attachment and mill the gashes to form the cutting teeth. The backs of the gashes should finish up close to the cutting faces of the teeth. After milling, the backs of the teeth should be relieved with a fine file until only a very small land is left at the cutting edges. If this relief is not given to the cutting teeth, they will rub against the work and refuse to cut. Only a little relief is needed. Be careful not to overfile and spoil the shape of the teeth.

The hob is now finished except for hardening. It must be uniformly heated to a cherry red and then quenched in water. Be sure that the color is the same over-all; see that it enters the water endways, so that cooling will be uniform and will not cause distortion. After hardening, the temper must be drawn to a straw color. See Chapter 14, the section on tempering.

When hardened, the teeth must be lapped to remove any distortion. Using a piece of soft cast iron, turn up a disk about 1 inch in diameter; bevel the edge to the same angles and width as the point of the tool used to cut the spiral thread. Mount this disk in a forked holder that will fit the tool post. The pivot of the disk should have a nut so that the

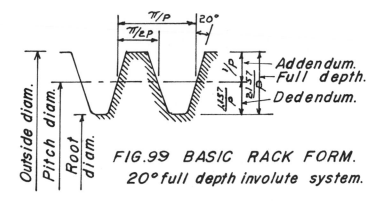

FIG.99 BASIC RACK FORM.
20° full depth involute system.

Fig. 99. Basic rack form (20° full-depth involute system)

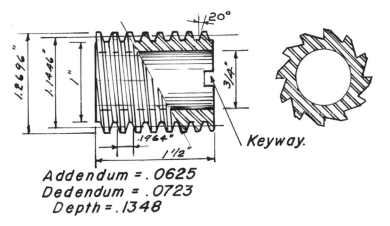

Addendum = .0625
Dedendum = .0723
Depth = .1348

Fig. 100. Hob for 16-pitch, 20° gears

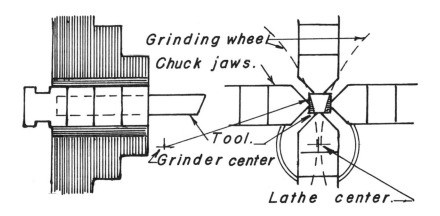

Fig. 101. Grinding a hob cutter

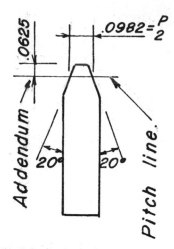

Fig. 102. Lathe tool for 16-pitch hob

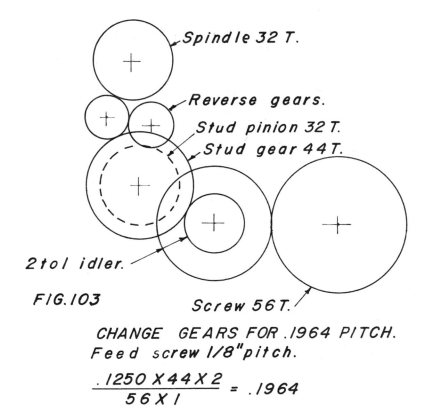

Spindle 32 T.

Reverse gears.

Stud pinion 32 T.

Stud gear 44 T.

2 to 1 idler.

FIG. 103

Screw 56 T.

CHANGE GEARS FOR .1964 PITCH.
Feed screw 1/8" pitch.

$$\frac{.1250 \times 44 \times 2}{56 \times 1} = .1964$$

Fig. 103. Change gears for .1964 pitch

friction applied to the disk can regulate its rate of revolution. The hob is then mounted in the running position on its arbor. The lapping disk is mounted in the tool post, square with the lathe centers; then, with the carriage geared to the pitch of the spiral on the hob, the disk is fed against the revolving hob, keeping a little abrasive between them. The friction pressure should be adjusted until the disk revolves more slowly than the hob. Continue lapping until all the teeth of the hob are bright, which indicates that they have all been cut true. The teeth of the hob must all be concentric; if a tooth wobbles, it will cut a high or a low place on the finished gear, and, since these variations from the true tooth form are not canceled out as the gear is cut, a wobbling hob will not cut an accurate gear. If the lapping removes much of the relief that has been filed onto the backs of the hob teeth before hardening, the outlines can be corrected with a fine stone in the high-speed hand grinder. It will be necessary to set the lapping disk to the helix angle of the hob so that it will not touch the wrong spot on the side and give an uneven shape to the teeth.

A worm drive is required to revolve the indexing gear. This device fits into an adjustable bearing bracket so that it can be adjusted to the size of the indexing gear. The pitch of the spiral must be the same as the circular pitch of the indexing gear; this again requires computing the gear ratio for a fractional pitch (see above, p. 179). The thread is the same shape as the thread of a straight-sided rack, and the cutter for it should be laid out and ground as described for the hob cutter (Fig. 101).

Since many sizes of indexing gears will be used, it will be necessary to have an expanding gear train between the pinion on the hob arbor and the gear on the spiral drive. These two gears must have the same number of teeth so that the gear blank will revolve in step with the spiral of the hob (see p. 182).

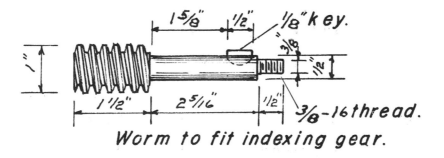

Worm to fit indexing gear.

Fig. 104. Spiral-drive worm

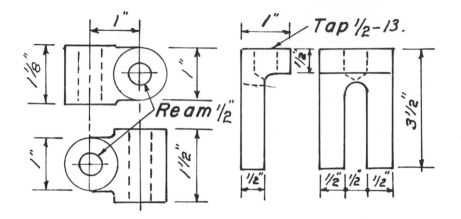

Fig. 105. Bearing for worm drive

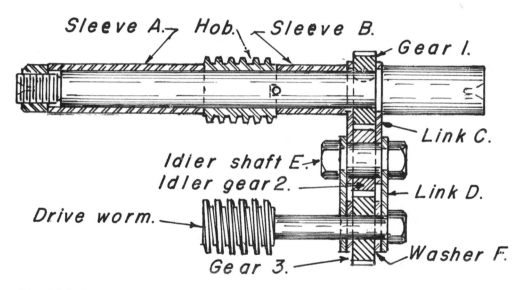

Fig. 106. Hob arbor

When the hob and the expanding gear train have been set up between the lathe centers, and the gear blank and the indexing gear are on the gear arbor, the bracket for the gear arbor must be set to the same angle as the helix angle of the hob. The teeth of the hob must cut parallel to the face of the tooth being milled, or else the cutting will not generate correctly shaped gear teeth. To set this angle, place a straight wire or rod between the teeth of the hob. When this rod fits tightly between the teeth, it will follow the helix angle of the hob. The bracket with the

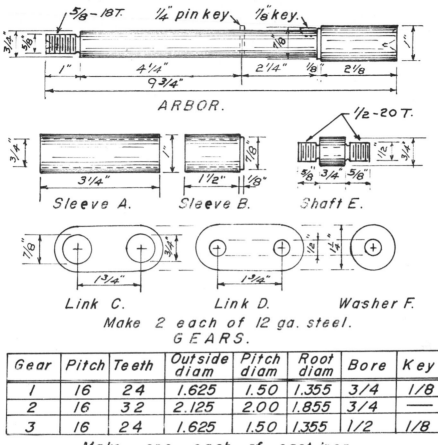

Fig. 107. Parts for hob arbor

gear blank can now be adjusted so that the tooth to be cut is parallel to this helix rod.

Feed the gear blank up to the hob and cut little notches, once around, to make sure that the proper number of teeth are cut and that the spacing is correct. Continue milling out the teeth, making several passes across the teeth until the root diameter, as measured with the calipers, is reached. As you approach the root diameter, take several small cuts; this will allow for any springing of the work or the hob arbor. You will find that the several teeth of the hob, each cutting a little on each gear tooth as it is fed into the work, will generate the exact shape of tooth for that number of teeth in the gear.

If you are cutting a steel gear, the hob will leave a burr at the finish side of the cut, which will have to be removed with a fine file. Cutting cast iron or brass will not cause so large a burr, and brushing with a wire brush should remove it.

It is not necessary that the indexing gear be of the same pitch as the one being cut. It is only necessary that it have the same number of teeth. Using the change gears of your lathe, with the appropriate hob for the pitch desired, you can cut gears of any pitch—but only those with the same number of teeth as your indexing gear. Of course, it is possible to devise a compound setup with an expanding gear train, so that the gear blank will revolve to cut a different number of teeth from that on the indexing gear. This operation is similar to setting up a gear train to drive a lead screw in thread turning. Since it may never be necessary, however, we leave to you the making of such a gear train and the fixture to hold it.

To cut helical gears with the hob, swing the axis of the gear blank to the angle of the gear teeth and feed the blank along this angle. The angle of the tooth is set off from the helix angle of the hob. Mating helical gears must be cut to be right- and left-handed. They will run more quietly than spur gears, but will cause an end thrust on the shaft that will require heavy thrust bearings.

Herringbone gears can be made with the hob by making a right- and a left-handed gear with identical diameters, placing them back to back, riveting or bolting them together, and then cutting a common keyway through both halves. As these right- and left-handed halves together will balance out the end thrust, heavy thrust bearings will not be required.

Worm gears are cut with a hob of the same size and pitch as the worm. It is common practice to use pitches of an even fraction of an inch so that the work can be cut with standard lead-screw setups. The hob is made with teeth higher than those of the worm so that it can cut some clearance at the root of the worm. The outer corners of the hob are rounded so that it will produce a fillet at the root of the worm thread. The shape of the worm thread is similar to an Acme thread; for single threads of not too great a helix angle, the Acme thread shape is very satisfactory. The pitch diameter and outside diameter of a worm wheel are similar to those of a spur gear. The worm wheel's outer face is not flat, however, like that of a spur gear, but is curved to match the radius of the root of the worm thread minus the clearance. The outside diameter is measured at the bottom of this curved face.

When helical gears are used to drive nonparallel shafts, they are called *spiral gears*. These gears can be cut with a hob, although their pitch diameter is not the same as that of a spur gear. The pitch of the hob, which fixes the width of the tooth, is measured at a 90° angle to the spiral or helix angle of the hob. To cut these gears, which have a tooth angle greater than 90°, the circular pitch of the gear teeth (measured on the pitch line, which is at a 90° angle to the axis of the gear) must be increased by the cosine of the helix angle of the gear. This increase in circular pitch increases the pitch diameter for a given number of teeth. To find the pitch diameter of a spiral gear: divide the *number of teeth* by the product of the *normal pitch* multiplied by the *cosine of the helix angle* of that gear. The helix angle of each gear depends upon the angle between the shafts and the speed ratios of the two gears. This angle must be determined by trial, either graphically or analytically, when the distance between the shafts and the speed ratios are known. Since the action of spiral teeth is a sliding one, the $14\frac{1}{2}°$ full-depth involute system allows the greatest amount of contact between the teeth.

Bevel gears—or any gears that do not have a straight or parallel tooth form—cannot be cut with a hob, but must be cut with a special gear shaper. This shaper has a reciprocating tool that generates the shape of the tooth and its tapering angle simultaneously. Such gears cannot easily be made in the home workshop.

Figures 95 and 96 show a gear-cutting attachment designed for a 10-inch lathe, and subsequent figures through Figure 107 illustrate the details of its various parts. The arbors should be made from a good alloy or tool steel. The shaft and sleeves are ground as described in Chapter 4. The hob and Gear 1 should be ground so that they are parallel on both ends. The nut should also be ground; this will prevent the arbor from springing out of line when the nut is tightened. If the hob is not ground accurately, it will revolve off center. Since the shape of a gear tooth is generated by all the teeth of the hob cutting continuously until the tooth is finished, a hob that is running off center will cut more on one side than on the other, and an uneven tooth shape will result. If you notice that the hob is not running true, it is useless to proceed; stop and correct it.

The data for cutting 16-pitch gears are given (Figures 100 and 102). For gears of any other pitch, similar data can be computed, using the same formulas.

Remember that the efficiency of a homemade gear depends on the accuracy of the home-constructed hob. It is not advisable to use your homemade gears for jobs where high speed and quietness of action are required. Get stock gears from a reliable manufacturer to use under such conditions. There are many jobs for which your homemade gears will be suited; and it is a great satisfaction to turn out a well-made article, as you can do in the home shop. Cutting the gears for the expansion train is a good project to start with. You can use some of the lathe change gears in the train temporarily and then duplicate them as you make the permanent one.

The following is an example of how a knowledge of gear cutting can save time and money for you. When a hedge trimmer finally broke down, after thirty years of faithful service, the trouble was traced to the bronze worm gear, which had worn out. This model of trimmer was no longer being made, and even replacement parts were not available. Since the rest of the trimmer was still in good shape, it was decided to make a new worm gear for the machine. A hob was constructed of the same size and pitch as the worm spiral gear, which had been hardened and showed no wear. Because this spiral was smaller than the hob arbor of the gear-cutting attachment, it was turned up from a piece of mild steel with an extended shank long enough to mount the driver gear of the expanding gear train. The hob was then case-hardened, giving the cutting teeth glass-hard cutting edges. Fitting an index gear of the same number of teeth completed the setup. The gear blank was made from soft steel, since bronze of the correct size was not available. Enough of the old gear remained so that it could be used as a pattern for the shape of the face and outside diameter of the new gear, although these could have been computed. When completed, the new gear worked perfectly with the existing spiral. The whole job was done in a little over half a day.

13

Sheet - Metal Work

IF you are a mechanic in a jobbing shop, you will seldom be required to do any sheet-metal work; when on repair or maintenance jobs, however, you will often have to work with sheet metal. Since you are not likely to have access to the equipment used in a sheet-metal shop, you will have to devise substitute methods and work with the tools that are at hand. A general knowledge of sheet-metal technique is therefore necessary.

The school shop should have several large benches or tables for layout work. Since layout is generally done directly on the sheet of metal to be used, the bench must be large enough so that you can reach all parts of the work easily. The stock is stored in flat racks, with a special shelf for each thickness of stock. There should be a small squaring shears and a small hand brake for bending. Bending rolls are necessary to bend cylindrical sections. Beading and flanging rolls should also be part of the sheet-metalworking equipment.

LAYOUT

Skill and accuracy of layout is very important in sheet-metal work. In most cases, you will be working with galvanized iron, and scriber marks show up well on its surface. If the edge of the sheet is straight, use it as a base line for laying out the rest of the design. Be sure to allow for the thickness of the metal when you are bending it to a line. If the bend is to form a sharp corner, scribe two lines as far apart as the thickness of the metal. If the scribed line is to be on the *inside* of the sheet after bending, place the mark exactly on the edge over which the metal will be bent. If the line is to be on the *outside*, you can scribe a second line as far below the edge line as the metal is thick. This second line will guide you when bending the sheet. A better method, however, and the one that is used by most sheet-metal workers, is to allow for the thickness of the metal when you are marking the layout and to scribe only one line, placing it on the bending edge, and marking next to it an arrow indicating the direction in which the metal is to be bent. Some complicated jobs can get quite confusing when there are many bends to be made; and unless the direction of bend is marked, it is easy to make a mistake. When a bend in the wrong direction has been made, it is almost impossible to straighten out the metal and rebend it. You should also mark the sequence in which the bends are to be made by numbering the scribed lines.

CUTTING

The power shears, shown in Figure 108, consists of a vertical traveling knife that makes a shearing cut, starting at one side and cutting across the sheet. The blade is actuated by power so that, when you step on the trip pedal, the shaft makes one revolution and causes the blade to make one stroke. The table of the shears has a guide at one side set at a 90° angle to the blade so that when work is placed against it, the cut will be square with that edge. Adjustable stops can be placed on the table for locating the work where more than one part is to be cut. On the bridge above the table there are a series of clamps that can be adjusted to hold the work firmly while it is being cut. The action of the shearing blade is such that there is very little stretching of the metal and both the work and the scrap will lie flat after cutting.

Sheet metal of the thinner gauges can be cut with tin snips. If you rest one of the handles on the bench and put all your weight to bear on the other handle, you can cut thicker pieces than could be cut by squeez-

Small sheet-metal shears

ing the handles manually. When cutting with snips, you will have to scribe a line that can easily be seen. The upper blade is placed directly over the line for each cut. The lower blade will line up the snips with the last cut, but the upper blade must be lined up for each cut. Since the tool will tend to work away from the cut, you must correct it for each cut, bending the waste piece away from the snips to clear the lower blade. Both the work and the waste will be crimped out of shape if the pieces are narrow. A wide piece will remain straight if the waste piece is sufficiently narrow to take up all the stretching of the metal caused by cutting.

Narrow pieces will have to be straightened after they are cut. This can be done by holding the piece on edge and hammering it along that edge, if it is possible to hold the work in that position. Or such a piece can be straightened by peening it along the inner arc of the curve while holding the piece flat on a flat surface. For this work, a ball-peen hammer is quickest, since it will expand the metal at each blow, but it will also leave hammer marks on the metal. An ordinary hammer will also expand the metal, but at a slower rate. Since peening also expands the metal sideways, the scribed lines may have to be corrected after the piece is straightened.

A thicker sheet can be cut to a straight line by holding it in the vise and cutting with a flat chisel along a scribed line set even with the top of the vise jaws. The chisel is held at a slight angle so that it will make a shearing cut. The base of the cutting edge should be held flat against the top of the jaw so that the chisel will cut exactly on the line. Since cutting in the vise will bend the top piece badly out of shape, the part above the vise should always be the scrap. Thus the work piece can be no wider than the depth of the vise jaws. Wide sheets can be cut by slitting them with a flat chisel held at a shearing angle and then cutting them against a soft piece of iron or brass. However, cutting with a chisel

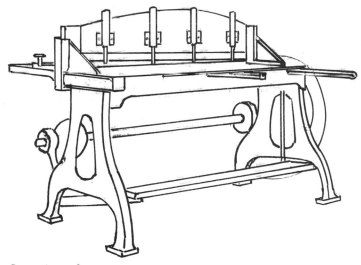

Fig. 108. Squaring shears

in this way will expand the work as the sharp edge wedges into the cut. This will cause the edge to buckle and put waves in the sheet that will prevent it from lying flat. Larger sheets can be cut with the chisel—a technique similar to shearing in the vise—if they are clamped between two angles. One end of the angles can be held in the vise; the opposite end is held with a ½-inch bolt. The angles should be about 2½ inches by 2½ inches by ¼ inch and about 30 inches long. They should be straight and have sharp edges where the legs meet. The outstanding leg of one angle can be rounded so that sheet metal can be bent over it when a round bend is needed. The work must be clamped so tightly that it will not move during the cutting. Keeping the scribed line toward you will enable you to see that it does not shift. If the chisel is not held with the cutting edge exactly at the tops of the angles, a little flanged edge will be left, bent away from the chisel, which will have to be removed with a file. Therefore, see that the tops of both angles are at exactly the same height by fitting dowel pins at the ends of the angles. The dowel holes should be placed so that the tops of the angles are aligned when the angles are back to back. When you turn one angle up to allow you to bend a round edge, the top of this leg should be even with the top of the other angle; to make the angles reversible in this way, position the dowels at the exact center line of each angle.

Sheet metal thicker than 16-gauge can be cut on the band saw if a 24-tooth blade is used. Place a piece of plywood under the sheet to give it a backing close up to the blade, since the clearance hole in the saw table is too large to support the thin metal.

BENDING

The hand brake consists of a table on which the sheet to be bent is clamped by a large vise jaw extending the width of the table, so that the sheet is gripped along the full length of the edge to be bent. The upper side of the clamping jaw slants backward so that bends of more than 90° can be made. The table has a leaf that is hinged to swing exactly over the edge of the table, and this bends the projecting edge of the sheet in a neat straight line, without causing any distortion of the metal. The swinging leaf is operated by hand; since it is quite heavy, the larger machines are provided with counterweights to make it easier to handle.

Work too heavy to be bent on a hand brake is bent in a press brake. This machine does not swing a leaf over a bending edge, as does the hand brake. The press brake is really a long power press. A stroke of the ram bends the sheet by squeezing it into a long die. Various shapes of dies are used, so that a great many straight or curved bends can be made on this machine (see Figure 111).

Cylinders are bent in a rolling machine, consisting of three rolls. Two rolls are on fixed bearings and are power-driven at the same RPM.

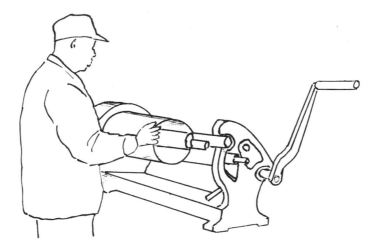

Fig. 109. Bending roll

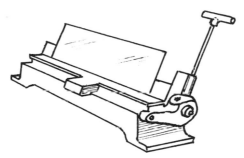

Fig. 110. Small hand brake

Small hand brake

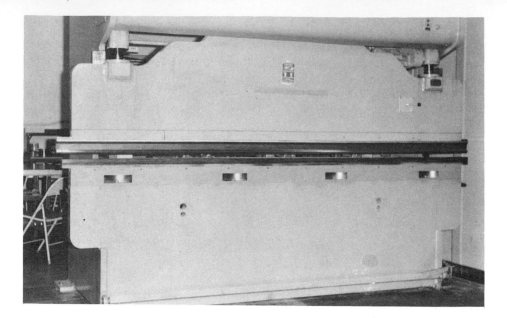

Small press brake

The third roll is on adjustable bearings and has one removable end bearing to allow removal of the finished cylinder. This third roll, which operates inside the cylinder, can be moved closer to the fixed rolls for a cylinder with a smaller diameter. The rolls cannot bend the sheet unless all three of them bear on the metal at once. This prevents them from bending up close to the edges of the sheet. These edges must be broken in a brake to the curve of the finished cylinder before the sheet is placed in the bending rolls. Tapered cylinders, or truncated cones, can be bent on the power rolls by moving one end of the adjustable roll closer to the fixed rolls, so that that end is bent to a smaller diameter. Since this feeds the work through the rolls in a line not parallel to the axis of the cone, after rolling a short distance, the rolls must be opened and the sheet moved to adjust the axis of the cone. It is a roll-and-try operation, which has to be done in short increments. The curve produced must be tested often with a template of the curve of both large and small ends.

Bending with the angles and vise is not difficult with metal up to about 20-gauge. Clamp the sheet between the angles with the scribed line exactly at the bending edge; then place a piece of wood (at least 8 inches wide and as long as the work piece) behind the work and use it as a form with which to bend the sheet. The wood must be kept in tight contact with the sheet so that the sheet does not wrinkle. Place one "C" clamp at each end of the board to hold it tightly against the sheet metal. Bending the sheet in this way will leave a rounded edge, the radius of the curve depending on the thickness of the sheet. The thicker the sheet, the larger the radius. If the bent part tends to spring away from the board, hammer the board enough to keep it tight against the metal.

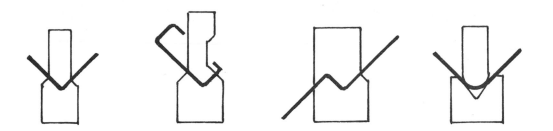

Fig. 111. Press-brake dies

To get a sharp corner, remove the bending board when the work is not bent quite to a right angle; then place a thick block of wood against the bent sheet and hammer it to the desired bend. This block of wood must be long enough that it will not dent the sheet, and it should be moved along the bend as you work the metal to the desired shape by hammering. If the sheet gets bent too far, it can be brought back by wedging under it with a wide chisel, taking care not to crimp the metal. A really sharp corner can be made by finishing the bend by hammering with a metal hammer directly against the corner of the angle over which it is bent.

Large press brake

Hammering against the metal angle with the metal hammer will expand the edge that was bent so that it will not be straight when it is removed from the angles. To prevent this expanding of the metal, use a non-metallic hammer or work with a piece of end-grain hard wood for this final hammering. Bending to a sharp corner loosens the galvanizing along the edge and weakens the metal, so that if you should try to

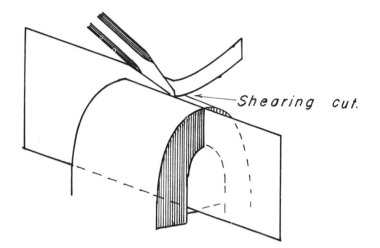

Fig. 112. Cutting sheet metal in a vise

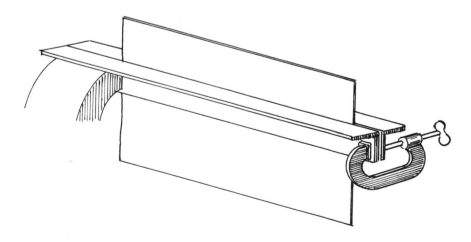

Fig. 113. Holding sheet metal between angles

straighten out the bend, not only will the metal be badly crimped out of flat, but it will be liable to crack along the line of the bend.

You should have two more angles, shorter than 30 inches long; these will be stiff enough so that you can bend heavier-gauge metal, up to 12-gauge. The 30-inch length is about the limit for handling sheet metal by this method. Longer angles are liable to spring enough to let the sheet slip near the middle. For bending larger work, take it to the sheet-metal shop where they have a brake large enough to do a good job.

BEADING AND FLANGING

Turning a bead or a flange on the edge of a thin sheet of metal can readily be done with the beading and flanging rolls. These machines bend the edge of the sheet to the desired shape as it is run through the formed rolls. A set of cutting rolls can be set up so that it acts as a rotary shears. When fed against a guide, a straight-line bend or cut can be made; when fed by hand to a scribed line, curved bends or cuts can be made.

For bending a round edge without bending rolls, turn up one of the angles' outstanding legs. File the outer edge of this leg to a half-round shape. Clamp the work between the angles, with the flat top of one directly on the scribed line, and the round edge of the other directly behind it with the top level with the flat angle. Now the sheet metal can be bent over this curved edge, even past the 90° point.

In scribing the line of bend, allowance must be made for the length of metal used to make the bend.

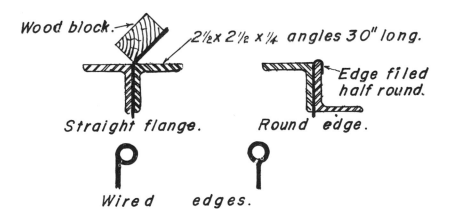

Fig. 114. Bending sheet metal

For bending a piece that is shorter than the angles and has a return bend that prevents its being clamped between them, it will be necessary to make a wooden form as long as the inside of the bend and as thick as the outstanding return bend, so that the metal can be clamped and has an edge to bend over. Unless the block is of very hard wood, it will be crushed under the bend and will give a round corner not true to the scribed line. It is also impossible to hammer such a piece to a sharp bend. When a sharp corner is required, cut a piece of scrap metal with a straight edge and screw it onto the edge of the wooden block, then bend over this metal edge. If the clamps holding the work are tight enough, this metal edge will stay in place long enough to complete the bend.

When you wish to bend a hem on the edge of the sheet, first bend it to a right angle, which is as far as you can go with the square corner of the bending angles. Then remove the piece from the angles and finish the hem by hammering it over a little at a time. Hammer on an anvil or some other wide flat metal surface. The metal will have been stretched by this hammering, and the edge will be bowed out of straight. Careful hammering on the anvil will straighten the edge. Be sure to allow for this double thickness of metal where there is a return bend. If the hem is on the inside of the bend, either cut away the end of the hem the amount of the thickness of the hem that will bend against it, or bevel both hems to a miter corner. If the hem is on the outside and is to be finished neatly around the corner, extra length must be added to the length of the hem to allow you to make a neat miter corner or to file it to a round corner.

Turning a wire into a round edge is a nice way to finish the edge. First compute the amount of metal needed to make the curve. You can easily make an error in this calculation, so cut a narrow strip of the metal and bend it around the wire with pliers. Mark the place to scribe the bending line and then straighten out the piece and measure the exact amount needed for the bend. Using the reversed angle with the round edge, bend a "U" as far as you can with the angle. Since this edge of the bending angle is thicker than the diameter of the wire, the "U" will be much larger than the wire. The wire should be straight, and any return bends should be formed in the wire. It is then placed in the "U" groove, and a piece of scrap is clamped on to hold it tightly in the bottom of the "U" as the metal is closed over the wire. Crimping the "U" closed with pliers will also hold the wire in place while the metal is worked down tight to the wire with a hammer, using a square-ended piece of metal to get into the close corner. All edges that are to receive the wire are to be bent to the "U" shape before bending any return bends.

Take as an example of bending the making of a sheet-metal box or tray with a round edge finished over a wire (see Figure 115). A wooden form must first be made, over which the sides and ends can be bent. Bend the "U" groove on all the edges, with the corners mitered or notched to allow for the thickness of the round edges. Next the flanges for making the corner joints are bent to a right angle. Then the sides and ends are bent. The corners are now soldered or riveted. The wire is formed to fit around the top edge and is placed in the "U" groove, and the metal is turned over it with pliers and hammer. Since the hammer cannot work into the tight corner under the wire, make a metal form to drive the edge in tight. After all this bending, the edge will be far from straight, so it must be carefully straightened over one end of the angles, held in the vise, to form a projecting surface that can get inside the box and on which the edge can be hammered straight. The straightness of the edges can be judged by sighting along the edge. Any curves will be clearly seen and can be corrected. The final straight edge is tested with the blade of the combination square, and the corners are checked for squareness. Figure 115 shows the edges finished with a hem, but the method is similar.

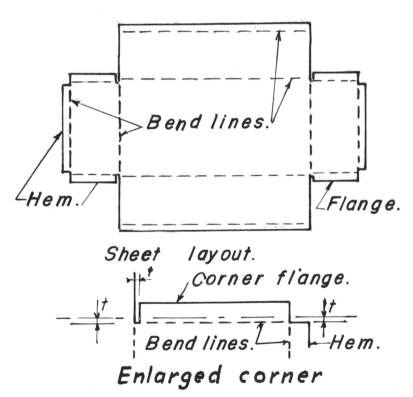

Fig. 115. Sheet-metal pan

FLANGING

A flange can be turned on a straight or curved edge. A flange on a straight edge is simply bent over a sharp 90° angle, as described. For the box above mentioned, where the flange is to finish on the inside of the box, the thickness of the flange and its round edge of bend must be allowed for and cut away before bending. A flange on a curved edge is quite another matter. If the edge is circular, try spinning the flange, as described in Chapter 9. If it cannot be formed by spinning, it is necessary to bend it over a form with a hammer. The form should be made of metal and should be the exact shape of the inside of the flange. This shape is also scribed on the top surface of the work. A cap piece is clamped on to prevent the center of the sheet from springing up as the flange is bent down. It also should be tight enough to prevent the work from shifting. The bending of the flange will tend to draw the work toward the flange, and the line scribed on the top will indicate any movement.

The width of the flange is marked and cut to the required shape before clamping onto the form, allowing for the thickness of the metal. The edge is now slowly hammered down to the required shape. You are now either stretching the metal or compressing it, depending on the curve. An inside curve will stretch the metal in the flange, while an outside curve will compress it. In either case, the metal cannot stand such treatment. Use a suitable torch to heat the edge to a red heat and bend it while hot. It can be worked to a small extent after it cools, but unless it is frequently annealed, it will crack or fold over in a wrinkle. If the form is made of wood, you cannot work the metal while hot, nor can you get a sharp corner. The work can be roughed out on a wooden form by removing it to heat it and then bending as it cools. The edge can be finished to shape by working it over the end of a piece of shafting of a diameter as near the size of the curve as possible. An outside curve can be worked over the edge of the anvil. This requires frequent annealing and hammering of the flat surface between the flanges to straighten it, as the flanging tends to bend it up. If the corner at the flange is to be round, the edge over which it is finished must be curved to the inside radius of the corner.

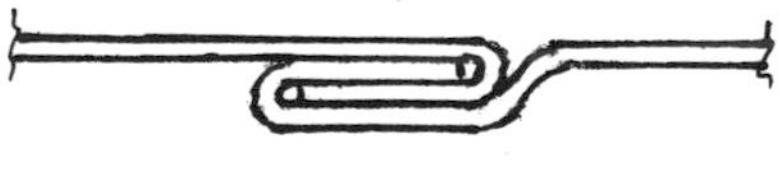

Fig. 116. Lock seam

FASTENING SHEET METAL

Edges of sheet metal can be fastened together by welding, spot welding, soldering, brazing, riveting, or by means of a lock seam. A lock seam is difficult to make with the home bending angles, but it can be done.

First, the edges are bent back as for forming a hem. Instead of closing them tight, place a strip of sheet metal a little thicker than the gauge you are using in the "U" of the edge to hold it open until the opposite edge is entered, then hammer the seam to a tight joint (See Figure 116). The edges may tend to work apart while you are hammering, so spot hammer it along the seam while the parts are firmly held in place. When thus locked, the rest of the seam can be hammered tight.

Soldering is easy with galvanized iron; however, since the best flux contains hydrochloric acid, the cut edges of the metal or any places where the galvanizing has been ruined by bending will eventually rust very badly. All traces of the acid should be removed by washing with hot water, and all places not covered by the zinc coating of the galvanizing should be covered with the solder. Any edges that are to be soldered must be perfectly formed so that the metal is in close contact and the seam is clamped in its exact position. Wide edges should be tinned with solder before being clamped in position. Then work with a large soldering iron having plenty of heat, so that the melted solder fed from the iron will melt the tinned edges and the solder will run into the joint by capillary action. If the joint is spot soldered, the clamps can be removed and the soldering completed. Care must be taken not to heat these spot-soldered places so that they will let go before the new solder has cooled enough to hold the joint in line.

Riveted joints should be clamped in place, then the rivet hole is drilled through both pieces at the same time. Try to get a rivet placed near both ends of the seam so that the clamps can be removed out of the way of the rest of the riveting. Copper rivets, or tinner's rivets, can be used. They should be just long enough to form the head on the riveted end when the plates are clamped tight. A rivet too long will bend, or hook, and will not expand in riveting. Be sure the two plates are held in tight contact before riveting. If there is any space between the plates, the rivet will expand in this space and prevent the plates being drawn into tight contact. A rivet set is used to draw the plates into tight contact before heading the rivet. This is a tool with a hole in the end that will fit over the protruding end of the rivet so that it can drive the plates down close to the rivet. Use a round peen hammer for expanding the rivet, as this will make the metal flow sideways more than a flat hammer will. The head of the rivet can be finished with the flat hammer or a formed tool having a cupped end. This formed tool is called a snap. For small rivets it is often combined with the rivet set to form one tool. The shape of the snap can be either conical or half-spherical. The end of the tool should be hardened (see Figure 117, page 202).

If you are working with black iron, it is difficult to make soft solder stick. It is better to silver-solder, braze, or rivet such joints. Welding with a gas torch is difficult on thin sheet metal, as it is easy to burn clear through. Spot welding is very quick, but it requires a spot-welding machine, which has no place in a home workshop.

Fig. 117. Rivet set

14

Heat-Treating of Metals

THE subject of the heat-treating of metals is far too vast and technical to be covered in a book of this type. However, there are a few fundamental practices that you should know how to use when the occasion arises. Annealing of steel and tempering of tools are both very important processes. Welding and brazing are often done in the home shop.

Commercial heat-treating plants have many methods of heating the material being treated and use various instruments to measure and control the temperature accurately. Gas- or oil-fired furnaces are used to a great extent. Electric induction is used to heat one part of an article while the rest remains at a lower temperature. In commercial plants, the quenching can be accurately controlled, and the quenching bath is designed to give the desired result. The small shop will not have any of this specialized equipment, but must rely on the methods and equipment used by blacksmiths, such as the forge and the tub of water. The gas torch and the fire-brick furnace have taken the place of the coal-fired forge. A torch is sometimes used with an air blast from a blower or with a self-inducted air supply. The former can produce higher temperatures.

Gas Torch

The basic tools for heat-treating are the gas torch and a furnace. The torch is a simple apparatus consisting of a mixing tube into which fuel gas and a blast of air are introduced to be mixed and burned at the end of the tube. An old vacuum cleaner can be used for the air blast. The hose used for the various attachments for the cleaner can be used to deliver the blast of air to the torch. You will have to make a fitting for attaching the hose at the dust-bag outlet and arrange the cleaner so that air can enter at the suction end (see Figure 125).

At the torch, a gate of sheet metal is arranged to regulate the amount of air entering the mixing tube. The fuel is supplied through a rubber tube of a size to fit the supply pipe and the fitting on the torch. The regular tube used to supply gas to portable appliances is ideal for this purpose. It has rubber ends that will fit on the gas nipples at each end. Any other good rubber tube can be used, such as a ⅜-inch garden hose (see Figure 121).

The mixing tube must be long enough so that the gas and air are thoroughly mixed by the time it gets to the burner end. Artificial gas will burn at the end of a plain mixing tube, but for natural gas there must be a special tip on the burner end to maintain the flame, or else the air blast will snuff it out. This special tip consists of a jacket fitted around the end of the mixing tube with several small holes drilled into the mixing tube. This gives a low-velocity supply of gas and air to the jacket. This will maintain a small circular flame around the end of the mixing tube, which will keep the mixture ignited as it comes out of the end of the main burner tube. The air blast tends to blow the main flame so far away from the end of the mixing tube that it will mix with so much outside air that it will no longer be a combustible mixture and will be snuffed out. This annular ring of low-velocity flame surrounding the outlet of the mixing tube will keep the main flame ignited unless so strong an air blast is used that the entire flame is blown away from the end of the mixing tube (see Figure 122).

When you start up the burner, shut off the air blast until the gas is ignited and then slowly open it until the desired flame is obtained. The flame should burn with a firm blue center cone, and the hottest spot will be at the tip of the blue cone. A yellow flame is not as hot and is very sooty. After the bricks of the furnace have become well heated, the air blast may be opened a little farther, and the heat will thus be increased. The flame from this torch is very hot and will heat steel to a white heat for forging, but it is not hot enough for welding. Welding must be done with the oxyacetylene torch.

The Furnace

Fire bricks can be stacked up on a metal table to form a furnace that will handle almost any job. You should have on hand about 24 bricks of the strong, hard variety used in commercial work, rather than the soft kind used to line fireplaces, which will soon crack and fall to pieces if used for the furnace.

The table should be made of small steel angles of the ¾-inch or 1-inch size, and it must be braced enough so that it does not wobble. The joints can be either welded or riveted. Fire bricks measure 9 inches by 4½ inches and are 2½ inches thick. The table top should be 3 bricks long (27 inches). The height should be 32 inches from the floor. Heavy-duty casters should be fitted to the legs. When it is not in use, it should be moved to some spot where it will not get in the way of other work. The top should be a piece of sheet iron reinforced below with cross-members of angle irons. On this sheet-iron top, place a layer of fire bricks laid on their sides. The joints between the bricks should be filled with fire clay, since a great deal of heat will get down through these bricks, and the fire clay will help shield the top. As the top will be warped by the heat in any case, make sure that there are sufficient cross-members below it to

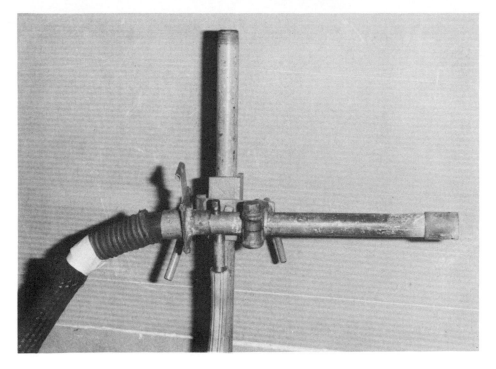

Gas torch

Furnace. Fire bricks are arranged to suit the work being heated.

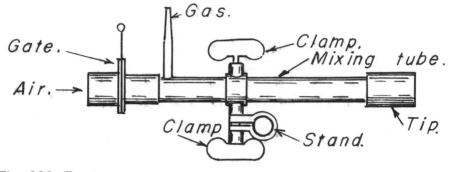

Gas.

Gate.

Air.

Clamp.
Mixing tube.

Clamp

Stand.

Tip.

Fig. 118. Torch

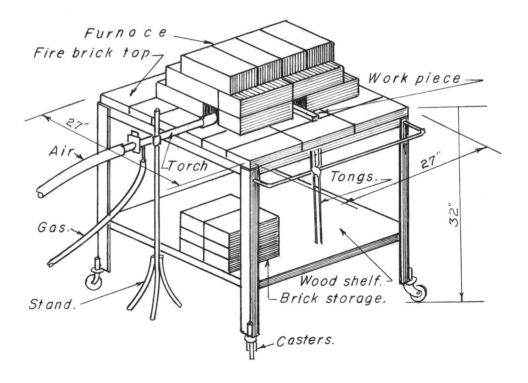

Furnace
Fire brick top

Work piece

27"

Air

Torch

Tongs.

27"

32"

Gas.

Wood shelf.
Brick storage.

Stand.

Casters.

Fig. 119. Gas furnace

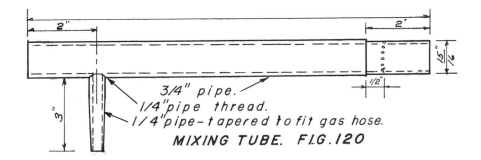

MIXING TUBE. FIG.120

Fig. 120. Mixing tube

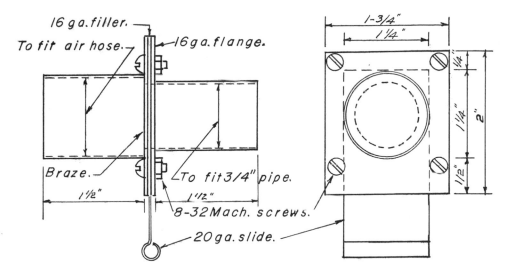

Fig. 121. Air gate

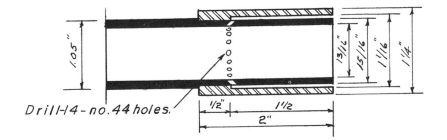

Fig. 122. Tip

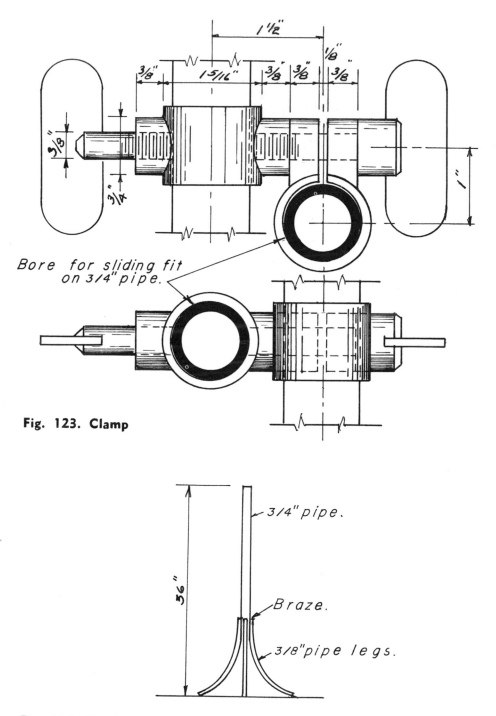

Bore for sliding fit
on 3/4" pipe.

Fig. 123. Clamp

3/4" pipe.

Braze.

3/8" pipe legs.

Fig. 124. Torch stand

prevent it from sagging and forcing the layer of fire bricks out of level. Hang a shelf of ¾-inch plywood under the table, about 8 inches above the floor, to store the fire bricks not being used. A ½-inch-round bar on one side of the table will form a rack on which to hang the blacksmith tongs (see Figure 119).

The fire bricks are stacked up to form a furnace that best fits the shape of the article to be heated. There must be an opening near the base where the flame of the torch can enter, and there must be another opening at the far end to let the products of combustion escape. The spaces between the stacked bricks will usually give enough of an outlet, or a space can be left when the bricks are placed.

To heat a large object like a crucible, arrange the entrance hole near the bottom so that the flame will spiral around the object and out a hole at the top. The bricks should be placed close enough to the work so that the flame is directed tightly against the work.

When forging and tempering a piece of work, first make a tunnel long enough so that the hot tip of the blue flame will touch the work. Leave openings on the sides so that you can place and remove the work.

The flame from the torch contains air mixed with the gas fuel, but it still requires air from the outside for combustion. The tunnel entrance for the flame allows the blast of flame to induce air into the tunnel for the combustion. The hot bricks at the entrance aid in maintaining the flame; and the air supply to the fuel mixture can be turned on fuller to give a larger flame, after the furnace is well heated.

FORGING

You will need an anvil, or other suitable metal block, on which hot metal can be hammered. The anvil should be fastened to a wooden stand to raise it to the best height for hammering: 27 inches is about the

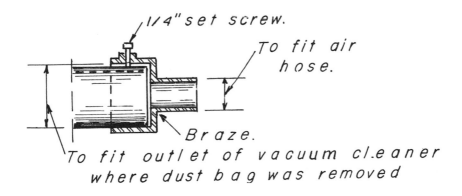

Fig. 125. Air-hose connection to vacuum cleaner

average height. A blacksmith has several hammers of various shapes, such as ball-peen and cross-peen hammers; for your home forge, a good 40-ounce ball-peen hammer will be the only one you will need.

Long-handled blacksmith's tongs are necessary equipment. These tongs come with various jaw shapes for gripping many different shapes of work. You should have at least one set that will grip around the circumference of a round bar and one that will grip bars lengthwise. You will also need a set of tongs that will open wide enough to grasp and move a hot brick while the furnace is running. It is frequently necessary to heat the jaws of the tongs and bend them to fit the shape of the work, to prevent them from slipping.

A fully equipped blacksmith's shop has many tools that require two men working together to use them, one to hold the tool and one to strike it. These tools have working faces shaped to give a definite contour to the work. When they are used to form a piece of work, they are called swages, and are generally used in combination with a similarly formed tool called a swage block. The smith places the work in the swage block and holds the hand swage while his helper strikes it. For drawing out a bar to a smaller size, a fuller is used. This tool has a round edge, so that, when it is driven into the metal, it forces it to the side. The fuller is also used to form a shoulder. A hardie is the tool used to cut off a piece of steel: this is a sharp chisel that stands up in the square hole on the top of the anvil. The work is driven down onto the hardie which cuts it. When there is a helper, the smith will also use a hot chisel on a handle, which the helper strikes as the smith holds the work on the hardie. In this way, he can cut both sides at once. For finishing into a corner, he uses a set hammer, a smooth-faced hammer on a handle, which he holds at the necessary spot while his helper strikes it on the head. For finishing flat work, a similar tool is used, called a flatter. To use any of these tools, except the fuller and the hardie, the smith needs the assistance of a helper, who strikes them. Thus the work a single man can do is limited to work that he can strike with a hand hammer. He can draw out work on the fuller, or across the corner of the anvil; and he can cut work with the hardie. He can hand finish only work that does not have a shoulder, as it is very difficult to finish neatly around a shoulder by means of hammer blows alone.

A clean hot fire is required to do good forge work, and the gas torch provides such a fire. Soft steel should be heated to a bright yellow for forging, and it can be worked until it cools to a dark red. When it is at a yellow heat, the grain of the steel has coarsened, and the metal will work easily under the hammer. The more it is hammered, the finer the grain becomes; therefore, hammering should continue until the red color has nearly disappeared. The metal should be heated as rapidly as possible, since prolonged soaking in the heat will make the grain too coarse, and much hammering will be required to refine it again.

After many grindings, a cold chisel will become too thick to use and will have to be forged to a thinner edge. This is done by drawing it out on the fuller or across the edge of the anvil, until it is roughed down to the required thickness; it is then finished under the flat of the hammer as it loses its red color. If the end seems to have split or cracked under the drawing-out process, cut off the spoiled end with the hardie and work it down again.

Small boring tools made of carbon tool steel will also have to be forged to a new shape after many grindings. First, hammer the cutting end of the tool to the correct shape while still straight. Then turn the end at a right angle over the edge of the anvil, being careful not to change its shape. After forming, a cutting tool must be hardened and tempered to suit the work it is intended to do. Before hardening, the cutting edge can be ground or filed to the desired shape and then sharpened by grinding after tempering.

To make a mark that can be seen when the metal is hot, use a center punch. This will make a little crater with a raised edge. When the metal is hot, the edge of this crater will be brighter than the rest of the metal; when it cools, it will darken before the rest.

The water tank is as important a part of the smith's equipment as the forge or the anvil. For the home shop, a bucket of water will do very well. Water is use to cool the tongs as well as parts of the work that are not to be heated, and it is needed for quenching during the hardening and tempering of metal. When a blacksmith has finished a forging and wants to free it of the scale that forms on steel when it has been heated, he dips his hammer in water and pours a little water on the top of the anvil. When the hot steel is hammered in this water, the resulting explosion of steam blows the scale off, leaving the metal clean.

When you are heating a long piece of steel, remember to support the piece at many places to prevent it from sagging when hot and becoming crooked. Work being forged can be straightened on the anvil afterwards, but work being annealed for turning must come out straight. To tell when a bar is straight, sight along its length. Any curves can then be easily seen, and the necessary corrections made.

To forge a round bar from a square piece, the corners are hammered until it is an eight-sided bar. If all eight sides are the same width, it indicates only that the bar has been evenly hammered. It still may not be round, however; it may have been hammered into an oval, all the faces of which are the same width. Check it with calipers. The corners of the eight-sided bar are again hammered until it is sixteen-sided. This is very nearly round, and the size and roundness can be tested with the outside calipers. A little finish hammering of the sixteen-sided bar will produce a round bar. Without swage blocks to finish on, the finishing must be done with light blows—and many of them.

A shoulder can be formed by drilling a hole in a bar of scrap and driving the work through the hole to finish the shoulder. The edges of the hole should be rounded to form a fillet on the shoulder. The bar is forged to the finished round size before driving the work through the hole. The larger part of the shoulder must be finished after it is driven through the hole, since this driving will upset it and change its shape.

To enlarge a bar, first upset it by hammering it on the end. The metal must be white hot at the place where the enlargement is to take place, and it should be cooled to a black color by quenching in water where it is to remain the same size. Since the hammering will distort it, it should be dressed back into shape after each end hammering. It tends to become beveled on the end, and this bevel must be corrected often, or it will get so bad that it cannot be corrected. Upsetting is tedius work and requires much hammering with a heavy hammer. You must work fast so as to cool the parts as necessary while keeping the hot part soft enough to work. It is much easier to work down a large piece of soft steel than to upset a smaller one. However, it may pay you to upset a piece of tool steel when a larger piece is needed, rather than to purchase a small piece separately, as the supply shops charge a high price for cutting small pieces of tool steel.

TEMPERING

In the tempering process, the steel is hardened; then the hardness is reduced to the point at which the tool will stand up to the work required. Very hard steel is brittle and will break under heavy work. To harden metal, the work is heated to a cherry red and then quenched in water or oil. Water is more liable to crack the work than oil, which cools it more slowly. The work must be heated as rapidly as possible, since prolonged exposure to heat will coarsen the grain; and, since it cannot be hammered to refine it, the edge could fail under work conditions. Have the furnace well heated, with the bricks a bright yellow color, and position the work so that it can heat uniformly. Placing small tools inside a white-hot pipe ensures a good distribution of the heat and protects the tools from direct contact with the flame.

To quench a piece being hardened, let the piece enter the cooling bath in such a way that it will be cooled evenly all over its surface. Most tools should be entered straight down into the bath. The cutting end, which is the end to be hardened, should be moved around in the bath so that it will cool quickly. If it is left in one place, the hot metal will heat up the water near it, and the water will not act as a coolant. This quenching during the hardening process will make the steel as hard and almost as brittle as glass, and it will break like glass if it is used when in this condition. The tool must therefore be reheated, but to a lower temperature, and quenched again when it reaches the correct temperature for the work the tool is intended to do. This second heating-and-quenching process is called *tempering, drawing the temper*, or simply *drawing.* Soft or mild steels cannot be hardened by this process, although the character of a steel can be changed and improved by proper heat-treating. Tool steels contain sufficient carbon so that they can be hardened by heating and quenching. High-speed steels contain ingredients, such as tungsten and cobalt, that alter their hardening characteristics. Most of these steels cannot be quenched, but harden in the air when they are heated to the correct temperature and then allowed to cool. It is not possible to harden these self-hardening steels at home, since the process requires the use of special furnaces heated to a specific temperature that can be controlled.

In your home shop, you will work as the blacksmith has always worked, gauging the temperature of hot steel by its color. As the metal grows hotter, certain colors appear on its surface; these colors can easily be seen in a good light. The colors are formed by the oxide on the surface of the steel, and change as the temperature of the metal changes. Table 10 lists the various colors seen in steel, with their corresponding temperatures; these indicate the points at which the steel is hot enough to be worked under the hammer and hot enough to quench. Table 11 lists the colors to watch for when you are tempering the steel. These temperature colors are very important and should be learned, since you must be able to act the moment you see the color specified for the tool you are tempering. You will have to work fast, for the colors change quickly, with only a few degrees of temperature between each color. They start at pale yellow and work up to blue and purple as the steel grows hotter. In order to see these colors, you must keep the hot metal polished, using emery cloth. When the required color appears, quickly quench the metal, thus fixing the temper. When you are quenching a piece that is being tempered, it is not as essential to enter the piece into the cooling bath as evenly as when you are quenching a piece during hardening. In tempering, the steel is not heated to such high temperatures, consequently, there is less strain on the steel, and so the danger of the metal cracking is not as great.

For tools like cold chisels and lathe tools, of which only the cutting end is tempered, quench this end until it is black cold, leaving the rest of the shank as hot as when it came from the fire. The heat from the shank will run down into the cold end, where the colors will begin to appear. The cutting edge must be kept polished and held in good strong daylight (artificial light will not do); it should be quenched when the correct color appears. If the colors are running too quickly to the quenched end, cool the entire tool immediately, but let enough heat remain in the shank so that it will continue to heat the cutting edge. If the colors are running down too slowly, hold the tool over some heat to speed up the process.

A tool that must be hardened over a large surface area, such as a reamer or a tap, is first hardened all over by quenching until it is cold; then it is slowly and evenly heated over the fire until the required color appears on the cutting edge. This even heating can be achieved at home

Table 10

Temperature Colors of Steel During Heating

Incipient red	977° F.
Dull red	1292° F.
Incipient cherry red	1472° F.
Cherry red	1652° F.
Clear cherry red	1832° F.
Deep orange	2021° F.
Clear orange	2192° F.
White	2732° F.
Dazzling white	2912° F.

Table 11

Temperature Colors for Tempering Steel Tools

Pale yellow	450° F.	Turning tools, scrapers, hammer faces
Straw color	460° F.	Milling cutters, taps, dies, reamers
Brownish yellow	500° F.	Hand planes, twist drills
Light purple	530° F.	Augers, cold chisels for steel
Dark purple	550° F.	Cold chisels for cast iron, saws, screwdrivers, springs

by making an oven of bricks and heating them to a good yellow heat, then withdrawing the fire and allowing the hot bricks to draw the temper of the tool. Place the tool in the center of the oven and turn it frequently, keeping it polished and watching for the correct color, then quickly quench it when it is ready.

When a cold chisel is being tempered, the drawing heat flows down from the hot shank; thus the inside of the shank remains soft and tough, and the tool is stronger after tempering. Reamers and taps, which have been cooled and hardened all the way through by quenching, require drawing heat from an outside source; therefore, these tools are brittle after they are tempered and can easily be broken.

ANNEALING

Steel that has been hardened or steel containing locked-in strains from some previous operation will have to be softened or freed from strains before it is machined. Hardened steel must be machined by grinding; in some cases, it can be cut with carboloy tools. Steel with locked-in strains will change shape as it is machined. Both these conditions can be remedied by *annealing*. In the annealing process, the steel is heated to a cherry red, then held at this temperature until it is thoroughly softened by the heat (from a half-hour to an hour). It is then allowed to cool very slowly.

To anneal a long piece of steel, such as a bar of shafting, first build a long tunnel of fire bricks, just wide enough to admit the work. Rest the bar on small shards of brick, which will raise it slightly so that the flame can get underneath it; make sure that the bar is solidly supported all along its length, however, to prevent it from sagging when red hot. The tunnel must have one opening for the tip of the torch and one at the far end, so that the flame can travel the full length of the bar and heat it evenly.

After the bar has been soaking in the heat for a sufficient length of time, remove the torch, close off each end of the tunnel with a fire brick, and allow the bar to cool off in the furnace overnight. The heating temperature required will depend upon the composition of the steel, but an average temperature of 1500° F. (when the steel shows cherry red) will be adequate for work done in your home shop. Heating steel at this temperature over a prolonged period of time will cause a heavy scale to form on its surface and coarsen the grain of the metal, weakening it. By subsequent cold working of the steel, you can refine the grain and restore the strength of the metal; but you should allow for scale formation in advance, by using a rough piece that can be cleaned off when it is machined.

The term *annealing* may include not only full annealing, or softening of the material, but also the various processes that change the structure of the steel in some way, such as normalizing. Since all these special annealing processes require precisely controlled temperatures and careful timing of the periods of heating, they should not be attempted in the small shop.

CASE HARDENING

Most mild steels do not contain enough carbon to enable them to be hardened by heating and quenching, as are the higher-carbon-content tool steels. However, if carbon is added to the steel, it can be made to harden upon quenching. There are many methods of adding carbon; commercial plants select the one best suited to their needs. In all these processes, the heated steel absorbs the carbon from the outside. The interior of the metal does not absorb the added carbon and so remains soft after quenching. A hard carbonous surface, or case, is formed on the metal, whence the process gets its name.

The only practical method for the home shop is one of the modified "cyanide" processes. Melted sodium cyanide is a very good carbonizing agent, but it is also very dangerous to use. There are several patented compounds on the market, such as Kasenit, that give the same results and are safer to use. The steel is heated to a cherry red, then covered with the hardening compound and allowed to soak in it. This will form a paper-thin case that will be glass-hard when quenched. The case will not be thick enough for grinding, however; to form a case that can be ground, the steel must be heated several times and let soak in the melted compound until cool after each heating. In commercial plants, the article is surrounded with the carbonizing agent—bone charcoal, molten sodium cyanide, or a nitrogen atmosphere—and held in a furnace at the carbonizing temperature until a case of the necessary thickness has formed upon it.

After the case has been thickened in this manner, the steel must be reheated to a cherry-red color and quenched in water. Take the same precautions against distortion as were outlined in the section on tempering. The surface of the steel will then be as hard as glass and covered with a thin scale. Since the metal underneath the case is soft and tough, the case-hardened bar can withstand as much strain as it could in its original state.

If the bar has become warped by the heating and case hardening, do not try to straighten it by bending, as this will cause the case to crack. It will have to be reheated until it is soft, then straightened out and hardened again, in hopes that it will remain straight. A piece of case-hardened steel may be annealed, worked on, then hardened again by heating and quenching. The case will be thinned somewhat by the annealing; however, if it was of sufficient thickness when first formed, further soaking in the carbonizing compound may not be necessary.

15

Welding — Brazing — Soldering

WELDING

THE high temperatures required for welding make an oxyacetylene torch an essential piece of home-shop equipment. Large commercial tanks of oxygen and acetylene are loaned by the supplier for a reasonable length of time, but demurrage is charged for any tanks returned after that period. Most suppliers also lease the smaller-sized tanks, and for these no demurrage is charged. Since you will not be using a great deal of gas and oxygen, you may find it more economical to lease the smaller tanks and avoid paying demurrage costs.

Your tanks should be equipped with regulators having gauges that indicate the pressure inside the tank and the working pressure at the torch. Since tank valves sometimes leak when only partly open, they should be opened all the way each time; this will bring a stop into position, which prevents leakage past the valve stem. When you have finished using the tanks, be sure to close the valves tight and relieve the pressure on the regulating diaphragm. The two tanks should be mounted on a two-

Welding tanks on a cart

wheeled cart that has a frame to hold them in an upright position. Since you can move the tanks close to the work, you will not need to provide long lengths of connecting hose. The short, flexible lengths of hose, known as "whips," which are used near the torch, will be long enough for your needs.

Your torch should be equipped with a #1 tip for welding and brazing small parts and a #3 tip for larger areas. A #5 tip is used to heat large areas, as for bending. A cutting attachment will be very useful.

Only the welding of mild steel should be attempted at home. Stainless steels and high-carbon steels require special techniques and special welding rods. Aluminum is also very difficult to handle. Only an experienced welder should attempt to weld these materials. When you have become proficient in handling the torch on the easier steel, you can attempt the more difficult jobs. For mild steel and malleable iron, a mild-steel welding rod is used. No flux is necessary. Cast iron and aluminum require cast iron or aluminum rods and special fluxes.

To weld steel, you must apply enough heat to fuse the parent metal properly, being careful so as not to burn clear through. Use a large-sized tip and turn the acetylene-pressure dial to about 5. The oxygen pressure should be about the same. Open the acetylene valve on the torch and ignite it. Reduce the pressure until it burns with a small yellow flame close to the tip. Now open the oxygen valve until the flame is burning with a bright white cone at the tip. This white cone is the hottest part of the flame and should be used to heat the metal. The rest of the flame, the blue part, will serve for preheating, but it is not hot enough to fuse the metal. A large weldment should be preheated with a gas torch, then reheated and annealed after welding and allowed to cool very slowly. This will prevent the weldment from being distorted by the high heat of the welding flame and possibly cracking open along a weld as it cools.

The torch must be kept moving in small circles over the spot to be welded so that the heat is distributed evenly to both pieces of metal, bringing them to a uniform temperature. This procedure will form a little pool of molten metal, and the welding rod can be melted into it. The rod should be kept in motion, so that the stirring of the rod and the motion of the flame keep the pool agitated. If the heat is not high enough, the metal will become sticky; the welding rod will stick to the parent metal and be hard to keep moving. When you are using thin metal, the rod will protect the metal from the flame and help prevent burning through. The edges of thick pieces that are being butt welded should be beveled so that the flame can penetrate to the center and not simply put a thin layer on the surface. If too much new metal is added from the rod before the pool of molten metal is well formed, it will be burned up and will form slag, which looks like molten metal but has no strength. You can tell when the added metal is joining with the parent metal, as they will both be the same color; as the work cools, there will not be a line between the new metal and the old. Slag resembles molten metal when it is hot, but gets darker as it cools, leaving a line marking the edge of the weld. Practice making welds and breaking them until you can produce a sound weld each time before trying your hand on something important.

BRAZING

Brazing steel and cast iron is a fairly simple technique and creates a strong joint. In many cases, it is easier to braze parts than to weld them. Since the heat required for brazing is lower than that necessary for welding, the metal is less apt to distort.

The work should be thoroughly cleaned and filed or ground until bright, and any scale removed. A flux is needed for brazing and can be obtained where you purchase your supplies. The flux is used, first to dissolve any oxides that may have formed on the metal surface after it was cleaned; second, to protect the surface with a coating, since additional oxides could form if the metal were exposed to air. Borax forms a good flux, but it is more difficult to remove after cooling than some of the prepared fluxes.

The brass rod that is melted into a joint being brazed is called a *spelter rod*. (Spelter is sometimes used in powder form as well, in which case the work is heated in a furnace or forge, and the powdered spelter is ladled onto the hot joint.)

The torch is moved evenly over both sides of the joint to bring them to an even light orange color. If one side is thicker than the other, it will have to be heated longer to bring it to the correct temperature. The end of the brass spelter rod is then heated in the flame and dipped into the flux, which will adhere to the rod. When the rod is applied to the work, the flux will melt and spread over the work. When the correct temperature has been reached, the spelter rod will melt and run like water into the joint and over the surface where the flux has protected the metal.

If the parts being joined are too cold, the brass rod may melt, but it will not adhere to the metal. If the joint becomes too hot, the flux will be burned off, and oxides will prevent the brass from adhering to the metal. It will then be necessary to cool the work, clean the joint down to bright metal, and start all over again. For brazing with brass or bronze, the two surfaces must be close together, but the joint must be open enough to allow the molten metal to flow into it. There is very little capillary action with brass spelter; nor can you make it bridge a wide-open joint. To fill up a hole or other open space, fit a block of carbon or asbestos underneath the opening; the brass can then be melted in until it fills the joint. It must be at the correct temperature to adhere around the edges. This method of brazing tight can be used to correct a drilled hole that is out of line or has had its threads stripped. By forming a mold of carbon or asbestos, an addition or correction can be made to a casting in this way.

The blue part of the torch flame can be used to braze with after the parts have been brought up to the correct temperature. This flame is hot enough to melt the spelter and to keep the parts hot enough to receive the brass. If you are brazing cast iron, be sure to use a neutral flame: that is, a flame burning with the little white cone very close to the torch tip. If the white cone spreads out from the torch, it contains too much acetylene and is a carbonizing flame. If there is a long blue streamer, the flame contains too much oxygen. Cast iron will pick up carbon from the flame if there is an excess of acetylene; as the metal cools, a hard spot will form around the braze that will be very difficult to machine.

Spot-welding machine. This machine is used to join thin sheet metal.

SILVER-SOLDERING

Silver-soldering, sometimes called "hard soldering," is a method of brazing at a low temperature that uses, instead of spelter, a wire or sheet of an alloy of silver and copper. Silver solder melts at about 1100° F., while brass spelter has a melting point of about 1700° F. It is difficult to braze brass with brass spelter; the work tends to melt almost as readily as the spelter rod, and can be completely destroyed in the process. To join parts made of brass, it is better to use silver solder, which is designed for brass, and which melts at a low enough temperature so that there is very little danger of the work being damaged.

A special flux in paste form is required for silver-soldering. It is essential that the parts be cleaned until bright and then covered with the flux before the oxides have a chance to form on the metal. Good capillary action is set up when this solder is applied and will cause the melted solder to be drawn into the joint. Leave a space between the parts of from .001 inch to .003 inch. Heat the work until a dark red color begins to be visible and the solder is melting and running like water. Then bring the heat up slowly. The solder will tend to melt before the metal is hot enough to make it stick; unless it is heated to the proper temperature, it will form balls, like drops of water on a hot stove, and run all over the work except into the joint. Both brass spelter and silver solder can be use to make very neat fillets after joints have been closed; melt a little over the joint and form it with the torch flame.

Silver solder can join either ferrous or nonferrous metals, but a special type is put out for use with brass or copper only, which is not suitable for iron or steel. Aluminum cannot be brazed; aluminum parts can be soldered with an aluminum solder: the process is about as difficult as welding aluminum.

Flat sheets of silver solder are used to join two wide surfaces. A piece of this sheet solder is cut to fit between the surfaces, which have been cleaned and fluxed. The parts are then clamped together and heated until the solder melts. This heating must be done in a furnace so that the work will reach a uniform temperature over-all; do not attempt to use an acetylene torch for this type of work, as the heat from a torch will melt the solder only in spots, and the surrounding areas will remain too cold to receive the solder.

Silver solder in wire form is very useful: it can be fed into the joint by hand while the parts are heated with the torch. Soldering a joint like that between a nipple and a flange can be done easily with this form of solder. Form the wire solder into a ring that fits tightly between the parts being joined, then flux and heat them with the solder in place. Capillary action causes the solder to flow into the joint, and the excess forms a neat fillet. The residual flux can then be removed by washing the parts with hot water.

SOFT SOLDERING

Soft or common solder is an alloy of tin, lead, and antimony with a melting point of from 300° F. to 400° F. It is melted onto the tip of a large copper bar, called a *soldering iron*; then it flows from the tip of the iron onto the work.

Constant heating will oxidize this copper bar, causing a hard scale to form on its surface. If the scale is not removed promptly, it will eat into the copper and form deep pits to which solder will not adhere. To remove this scale, file it off while the soldering iron is hot, then rub the iron over a piece of ammonium chloride (sal ammoniac) to clean it. To keep the copper bar free of scale, it should be rubbed in melted solder, coating all four sides of the bar—a process called *tinning*.

Soft solder is obtainable in several degrees of hardness. The harder types require more heat for melting. For general-purpose soldering, a 50-50 solder (50 percent tin and 50 percent lead) is best. For heavy work, use bar solder heated with a large soldering iron. Wire solder, heated with an electric soldering iron or soldering gun, is better for smaller work. Wire solder is available either in the form of plain wire or as wire with a rosin core (for electrical work) or an acid core (for general-purpose work).

A small gas stove placed on top of the bench is very handy for heating heavy solid copper soldering irons. A portable blowtorch can be used to heat the iron for work done away from the bench. An electric soldering gun is by far the best tool to use for any work that is not so large that the heat will be conducted away faster than the gun can supply it: the metal to which the solder is to adhere must be kept hot enough so that the solder will not cool and harden before the joining has been completed.

The parts to be soldered must be perfectly clean and free of rust or grease. A flux is required for all soft soldering. Diluted hydrochloric acid makes a good cleaning agent for tin and galvanized iron. A flux called *cut acid*, made by dissolving metallic zinc in hydrochloric acid, is one of the best for these metals. Cut acid should not be used near joints such as electrical connections, which would be damaged by corrosion. For such jobs, a flux with a grease-and-rosin base is used. There are several noncorrosive fluxes on the market, and you should have a supply of one of these in your shop. Liquid fluxes for general-purpose soldering are also available; keep some on hand to save yourself the trouble of preparing your own cut acid. Since any flux containing hydrochloric acid will cause steel or iron to rust, keep it away from the tools on your bench. Store flux in bottles with rubber corks. If any should spill on the metal top of the bench, be sure to wash it off promptly or neutralize the acid with baking soda.

Sheet tin and galvanized iron are very easy to solder; steel and cast iron are more difficult to work with. Stainless steel can be soft soldered when a special flux is used.

The edges to be joined should be held rigidly in position and clamped together. Since the heat will warp the sheet metal, the two parts must be clamped tightly to maintain the proper width of the joint to be filled. Capillary action will cause the soft solder to run into and fill a tight joint, provided the metal is hot enough. You cannot make solder bridge across a wide gap. When joining two edges, it helps to *tin* them, that is, to cover the edges with a thin layer of solder before clamping them together. The molten solder will then combine with the tinned layer on each edge to fill the joint.

Joining two large surfaces is called *sweating* them. Clean the two surfaces, then tin them; the tinned layers should be thick enough to melt and form the joint when heat is applied. Clamp the surfaces together so that the pressure is distributed evenly over the entire surface area. Then heat the joint until the tinned layers unite. The clamps should not be removed until the work has cooled and the solder has set.

Some copper pipe fittings are intended to be soldered to a pipe; such a fitting is bored to fit properly on the pipe, and there is a small hole on the top of the fitting. Clean the inside of the fitting and the end of the pipe and cover them with flux, then insert the pipe into the fitting. While the joint is heated with a torch, feed wire solder into the small hole in the fitting; this will melt and fill the joint. The parts can be tinned before they are assembled, provided there is enough space for the pipe to be inserted after the tinning has cooled.

16

Foundry Work

THE making of castings by pouring molten metal into sand molds, one of the oldest of the metal working arts, is also one of the most commonly used methods of producing parts for machines. Forming sand molds by hand and using them to cast some easily melted metal like brass or aluminum will give the student an insight into the techniques of pattern making and metal casting. For this purpose, a small foundry should be set up in the school shop.

Methods of making the mold vary according to the type of metal being cast. For general jobbing work, handmade molds and wooden patterns are most often used. When many castings of the same article are to be made, metal patterns and molding machines are used. There are several kinds of metal patterns. In one type, the two halves of the pattern are aligned on opposite sides of a single plate. When this plate is used between the drag and the cope (Fig. 129), it forms both parts of the mold and the parting surface at the same time. Two separate plates can also be used, with each half of the pattern on its own plate. Molding machines are much used in the modern foundry, especially in production work. These machines compact the sand either by slinging, squeezing, or vibrating it; and straight-draw the mold off the pattern.

Foundries also employ various methods of melting metals. Steel is melted in an open-hearth furnace or an electric arc furnace; iron is melted in a cupola furnace. Brass and aluminum are melted in a crucible or a tilting furnace. If the part you wish to make is to be of cast iron, it will have to be cast at an iron foundry. Aluminum and brass castings, however, can be made in the home workshop. The torch you use for forging can supply the heat; and a suitable furnace can be constructed of fire bricks, as discussed in Chapter 14. You will also need a crucible about 5 inches in diameter and 7 inches deep, which you can obtain at a foundry-supply firm. Set the crucible on the bed of the furnace and stack up the fire bricks about it; leave a space of about ½ inch around the crucible so that the flame can circulate. The metal will melt more quickly if the crucible is raised on some shards of brick or pieces of scrap iron to allow the flame to reach underneath it. Leave a small opening for the torch on one side of the base of the furnace; the flame should spiral around the crucible and out a vent at the top. Make a high enough pile of the bricks so that you can place several bricks across the top of the furnace as a cover (see Figure 126).

The metal should be cut into pieces small enough to fit inside the crucible, since any metal that protrudes will melt down the side and be

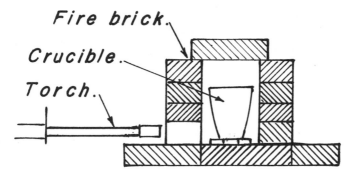

Fig. 126. Furnace

lost and may also cement the crucible to the bottom bricks. As the metal melts, more can be added to the crucible until a full *heat* (quantity of heated metal) has been melted. You will need tongs that open wide to move the hot bricks covering the furnace, as well as long-handled tongs to place the scraps in the crucible. You should have a pair of asbestos gloves to wear when working at the hot furnace and while pouring metal.

When all the metal has melted, test it for temperature by poking a dry pine stick into the crucible. The stick should burst into flame. If the metal is mushy, you will not be able to pour it. If it is too hot when it is poured into the sand mold, enough steam may be generated from the combination of the heat and the moisture in the sand to damage the casting. The metal must be just hot enough to be very fluid and remain fluid until it has filled the mold completely.

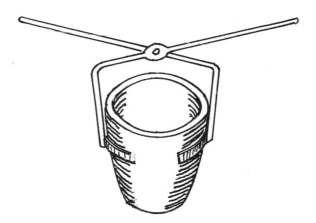

Fig. 127. Crucible tongs

When the metal is ready to be poured, shut off the torch, then remove the bricks from the top of the furnace. Lift out the crucible with crucible tongs and set it in the pouring handle. You can make both the tongs and the handle to suit your own crucible (see Figures 127 and 128). Before placing the crucible in the pouring handle, rest the handle on a bed of molding sand. Since the great heat of the crucible will set a wood floor on fire and will spall and crack a cement floor, you should always set it down on a sand bed. The slag must now be skimmed off the surface of the metal; here also the sand will protect the floor.

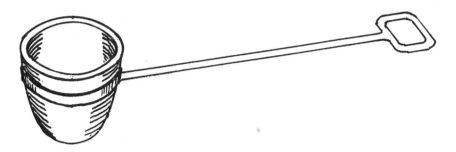

Fig. 128. Pouring handle

Molding Sand

Molding sand, also called *green sand,* is a coarse-grained sand mixed with a binder of clay or bentonite. There is a type of molding sand that best suits each metal. When you order your crucible at the foundry suppliers, tell them that you need a supply of molding sand for brass and aluminum. They will either have the correct mixture on hand or will prepare it for you. For your work you will need about two sacks of molding sand, one sack of core sand, and about five pounds of parting sand or parting compound. Core sand is a dry, coarse sand with no binder added; parting sand is a dry powder, usually made from crushed brick, that does not absorb moisture from the molding sand: when dusted onto the parting surface, it prevents the two parts of the mold from sticking together. You should have a pound of lycopodium powder, which is brushed onto the pattern to prevent sand from sticking to it. You will also need a *riddle,* which is a sieve about 18 inches in diameter; and a molder's trowel.

Before it can be made into a mold, the sand must be moistened, or *tempered,* as the foundry man calls it. The sand must be moist enough to cohere and hold its shape when molded, but not so moist that an excessive amount of steam will be produced when hot metal is poured through it. This steam is one of the causes of blow holes in castings, or *blown castings,* as they are called. No general rule can be given as to the correct amount of water to add to the sand; you will learn to judge this by experience. In the large foundry, a chemist takes a sample of the sand and specifies the correct amount of water to be mixed with it. The sand is screened and machine-mixed each night, after the day's pour, and is ready for the molders to use the next morning.

In your home foundry, you should also prepare the sand the night before you intend to use it, since it will become more even in consistency as it sets overnight. Spread the sand out on the floor, add a little water, and then turn the sand with a shovel until the water is thoroughly blended. Pick up a handful of the sand and squeeze it; if it holds its shape when jarred slightly, it is moist enough. Be very careful when adding water to the mixture: the sand soon reaches a critical point at which it is nearly saturated, when the addition of even a small amount of water will suddenly make it too moist. Reserve a little dry sand to add in case you get the mixture too wet. Sand molds that are too wet will not produce sound castings.

The Flask

The mold is made in a wooden box called a *flask.* You should build several flasks of different sizes so that you will be able to make a few molds and pour them all at the same time.

A flask is usually made in two parts (see Figure 129). The lower part is called the *drag*; the upper part, the *cope.* For some patterns a three-part flask must be used; the center part of this type of flask is

Foundry flask. The photograph shows the guide arms and cleats on one end and the shelf cleat around the inside of the cope.

called the *cheek*. The parts of the flask may be held in alignment by dowels on the upper part that fit into dowel holes in the lower. When making your flask, you can align the parts by means of a wooden guide arm at either end of the cope that fits between guide cleats on the drag. Do not center these guide arms on the width of the side, but position them off-center, so that the cope can be put down in one position only and not turned end for end. If the flask is 10 inches to 12 inches wide and 18 inches long, the parts should each be at least 4 inches deep. Run a small cleat around the inside of the lower edge of the cope to act as a shelf for the sand to bear on when the cope and the sand are lifted. A cope that is more than 10 inches wide will probably not be able to support the sand mold; when you must use a cope wider than 10 inches across, fit it with crosspieces, dividing it into smaller compartments that can support the sand. To prevent these crosspieces from interfering with the patterns, they must be fitted to each pattern as required. Leave space for an inch of sand between the pattern and the crosspieces. The flask must also have two mold boards, or bottom boards for the cope and the drag; they must be as wide and as long as the outside of the flask.

MAKING THE MOLD

Whenever possible, patterns are made in two parts, which are held together by two or more dowels. The part with *no* dowels projecting should be placed, parting side down, near the center of a mold board; the drag is then placed over it. Make sure that the top of the drag faces down, so that it will face up when the drag is turned over. Molding

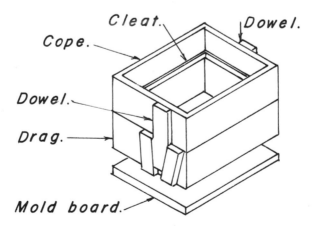

Fig. 129. Flask

sand is then sifted through the riddle onto the pattern until it is well covered. In commercial foundries, this *facing sand* is sometimes prepared to suit the kind of metal to be poured; for your purposes, special facing sand is not necessary.

Unsifted sand can now be used to fill the flask. It should be added layer by layer and rammed only enough to make the mold hold together. First ram around the edges of the drag, then hold the pattern firmly in place as you ram around it, being careful not to strike the pattern with the rammer. Then use the large round end of the rammer to compact the rest of the sand. When the drag has been completely rammed, strike off the top surface sand with a straight stick and sprinkle a little loose sand over the surface. Place the second mold board on the surface and embed it firmly in the sprinkled sand. This is an important step: the cope must now be rammed on top of the drag; and, if it does not bear solidly and evenly on the mold board, this ramming can damage the drag. Grasp the two mold boards and turn the drag over, so that the parting side faces up. If the drag is too deep to let you grasp the boards, clamp the boards together while you turn it, using wooden clamps with wedges.

Remove the mold board from the parting surface and set the other half of the pattern on the half already in the sand, after making sure that there is no loose sand between them. Place the cope on the drag and check to see that it is tightly seated and aligned. Insert a *sprue*, or a conical wooden peg; when withdrawn, it will form a gate through which the metal can be poured. A second spruc can be inserted to form a riser in which the hot metal will rise, providing a supply of molten metal to feed the casting as it cools and shrinks (see Figure 131). The riser will also form an escape vent for the gas and steam generated as the metal is poured.

Now sprinkle parting sand from its cloth bag over the entire top surface of the sand in the drag. Since the parting sand that falls on the pattern can collect in corners, which will prevent the molding sand from forming a good mold, blow off the excess sand, using a short length of tubing. If there are places on the pattern where the molding sand may stick, brush the pattern with some lycopodium powder on a soft brush.

Riddle facing sand over the drag, then fill and ram the cope. Level the top surface with the straight stick. Little vent holes must now be poked into the sand over the pattern with a straight piece of wire. Vent holes that are too close together may loosen the sand so much that it falls out of the cope as you lift it.

Withdraw the sprues and cut a pouring funnel around the top of the gate to aid you in pouring the metal. Now carefully lift the cope off the drag and place it on its side. The cope must be lifted straight up until the dowels in the pattern have cleared their holes, since any side movement will disturb the pattern's position in the sand. Any loose sand that has fallen down the gate should be removed. Place a mold board on the top side of the cope and turn the cope over so that the parting side is up.

The pattern must now be removed from the sand. This is usually done with a *lifter*, a tool similar to an ice pick. An ice pick will do very well for the home shop. Drive the lifter far enough into the pattern to allow you to hold the pattern steady. With the edge of the trowel, gently rap the lifter against all the sides of the pattern until the pattern is loose in the sand. This rapping must be done carefully, as it may break down any small or thin parts of the mold. To help you draw the pattern straight up out of the sand, place one of the fire bricks on the edge of the flask and rest your arm on it.

Runners are now cut through the sand of the drag between the mold and both the sprue holes in the cope (see Figure 131). The ends of the sprue pegs left holes in the drag that indicate where the runners are to be cut. The pouring runner should lead to a wide part of the mold and must be of sufficient size so that the mold will fill quickly before the metal chills. The vent runner can be from almost any part that is far away from the pouring runner. The gas and steam can escape through a small hole faster than the metal can enter through the gate. For a pattern with a large concentration of metal in the body, such as the hub of a sheave, position the riser directly over this concentration. The riser should be large, approximately the size of the part below, so that a large volume of molten metal can be stored before the metal in the mold solidifies, which can feed the concentration as the metal cools. If the riser is too small, the shrinkage of the metal as it cools may cause a hollow, called a *pipe,* to form in the casting. Aluminum especially is apt to shrink a great deal. Any loose sand remaining in the mold can now be blown out with the tube. Parts of the mold that may have been damaged when the pattern was removed can be repaired by wetting a little molding sand, plastering it on the damaged place, and shaping it with hand tools to conform with the pattern. A teaspoon with a wide smooth handle makes a very handy tool for cutting runners, and the back of the handle is good for smoothing. A professional molder has many small hand tools—trowels, spoons, gate knives, and other tools—that will enable him to work down deep into the corners of a mold and make many repairs. You can make some of these tools out of sheet metal: a flatter, which is turned on the end to be able to smooth the bottom of the mold; or a flat-sided tool for smoothing the sides of small places.

The cope can now be turned right side up and placed on the drag. When you pick it up and turn it over, do so away from the drag; then

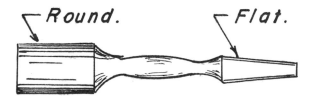

Fig. 130. Rammer

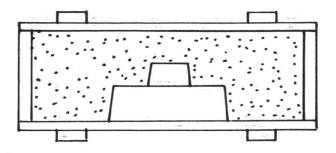

First operation-drag rammed.

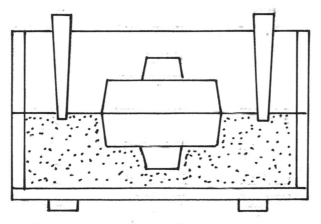

*Second operation-drag turned over-
pattern placed in cope-parting sand
applied-sprue for gate and riser placed.*

Gate— Vent. Riser.

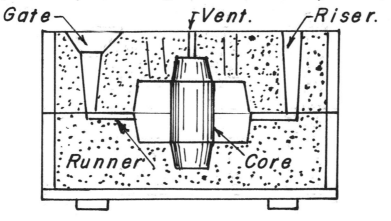

Runner Core

Fig. 131. Steps in making a mold

any falling sand will not get into the drag. If some part of the sand falls out, it is sometimes possible to place the pattern back in the mold and build the sand up around it to repair the mold. This repair sand must be wetter than the original sand, but not so wet that it sticks to the pattern, or the repair will not hold.

Be sure that the cope is tightly seated on the drag, since any opening will allow the metal to escape and ruin the casting. When iron is being cast, it is necessary to fasten the cope to the drag so that it will not lift when the metal is poured. Since the iron is much heavier than the sand, the cope will float if it is not held down.

With the mold complete and the metal ready for pouring, skim off the slag from the top of the crucible, using a metal bar or a small ladle. A small amount of slag remaining will do no harm if the gate and runners are large enough, since the slag, which is lighter than the metal, will float and will be washed through the mold and up the riser or the vent. Pour until the metal rises in the riser or vent to a level well above that of the top of the casting. After pouring, let the casting cool and harden for an hour or two before knocking it out of the sand.

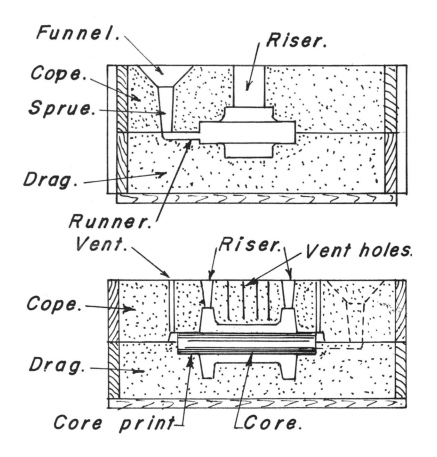

Fig. 132. Typical molds

CORES

For a hollow casting, a core must be made, the same size as the hollow space, and placed in the mold before the metal is poured. The core is made of core sand, molded in a core box, then turned out on a steel plate and baked in an oven until dry. Add flour as a binder to the core sand when it is moist; since the flour will burn out when the core is baked, add some linseed oil, which will bake hard and hold the sand together. Use no more than about one part to 50 parts of sand, as too much linseed oil will make the core stick to the steel plate, and you will ruin the baked core when you try to loosen it. Bake the core for about an hour at a temperature of 350° F. to 400° F. The oven of your kitchen stove will serve very well, although the baking oil will give off an odor. The steel plates on which the core is baked must be stiff enough so that they do not bend when they are picked up, or the surface where the two parts of the core are joined will be curved, and the core will be spoiled.

The two halves of the core are pasted together before being placed in the mold. Venting is very important when a core is being made. Since the gas formed by the hot metal can escape only from the end of the core where it fits into the mold, vent grooves must be cut along the center of the core before it is removed from the core box. These vents lead to the core prints, where vents to the outside of the mold are provided. Some long, slender cores require reinforcing wires to be placed in the sand, which are baked in the core. These wires must be so arranged that they can be easily reached to be pulled from the casting. Pieces of thin metal of a kind that will fuse with the molten metal, called *chaplets,* are placed under or over the core as it is placed in the mold. The heat of the molten metal will burn the core so that it crumbles and can be removed from the casting.

Sometimes the outside of a casting cannot be molded in green (molding) sand, because the green sand will be too thin to withstand the pouring of the metal. A dry sand mold must then be made and inserted in the green sand in the flask. This dry sand mold is made of core sand and is baked in the same manner as a core. In commercial foundries, in cases where green sand will not withstand the pouring of metal, a special binder is mixed with the facing sand, and then the mold is dried out with a gas torch. The binder is usually some form of plastic, and is not practical for home use. When iron is being cast in commercial foundries, the inside of the mold is usually faced with graphite or plumbago, to prevent the hot metal from cutting into the green sand. These facings are more refractory than the molding sand and so protect it from the intense heat. In home shops, where molten iron with its great heat is not used, satisfactory castings can be made without using these facings, although they will not be quite as smooth.

The groove of a pulley can be made by means of either a dry sand mold, as shown in Figure 133, or a green sand core. The upper drawing in Figure 134 illustrates the use of a two-part flask with a green sand core. The drag is rammed up; the place for the green sand core is cut out, and parting sand is sprinkled on it. The green sand core is then formed by hand, and another parting is made above the core. The cope is then rammed up and finished. The cope is removed, and the top part of the pattern is removed. The cope is replaced on the drag, and the whole flask is turned over. This holds the green sand core in place. The drag is removed, and the rest of the pattern is taken out, leaving the green sand core. The flask can now be assembled and poured in the usual manner.

The lower drawing in Figure 134 shows the green sand core being made in the third part, or cheek, of the flask. This also requires that the parting surfaces be shaped by hand, as the pattern cannot lie flat on the parting surface. With the three-part flask it is not necessary to place the parts together and turn them over to support the core, as it is supported entirely in the cheek and can be lifted off directly.

There are many jobs in a commercial foundry requiring complicated methods of molding; as these have no place in a home shop, time will not be taken to discuss them. You would do well to read through some of the many good books on foundry practice so as to be familiar with some of the problems.

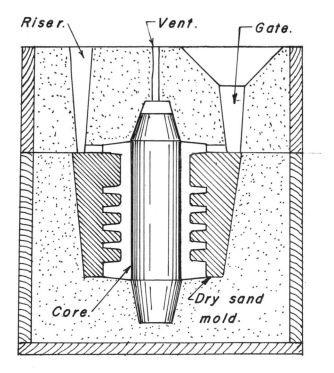

Fig. 133. Dry sand mold

Solid patterns, which are not split on a parting line, can also be molded, but it is more difficult and will increase the cost of the casting. There are two ways to mold a solid pattern. One way is to place the pattern on the mold board and ram up the drag, as when molding a split pattern. The sand will run under the overhang of the pattern; when the drag is turned over, this sand is removed down to a suitable parting surface. The cope is then completed on this irregular parting surface. The second way is to fill the cope with rammed sand and hollow out a place to receive the pattern. It is embedded down to a parting line and firmly tamped in place. The parting surface is then trimmed to the required shape and the drag is placed on it and completed. This first cope, or *odd side,* is now thrown away; and a correct cope is completed. This will all take a good deal of the molder's time; then, when he separates the mold, the mold can easily be ruined by any side movement. Do not use solid patterns unless there is no way of making a split pattern.

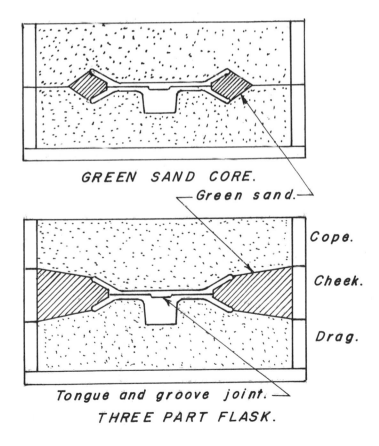

GREEN SAND CORE.

Green sand.

Cope.

Cheek.

Drag.

Tongue and groove joint.

THREE PART FLASK.

Fig. 134. Sheave-pulley mold

17

Pattern Making

Materials

THE best wood for making patterns is mahogany, but, since it is rather expensive, sugar pine is next best. Some of the varieties of white pine are also good, but as a rule they have more grain than sugar pine, and so are harder to finish to a smooth surface with no grain showing through. The wood must be thoroughly seasoned. You should buy one plank 2 inches by 12 inches and one 1 inch by 12 inches and have them surfaced on two sides as thick as they will finish. Wood over 2 inches thick may not be thoroughly seasoned all the way through, and this can cause trouble. Sections thicker than 2-inch should be made by gluing up laminations. You should have an assortment of clamps for gluing and use a good prepared glue. Let the glue set overnight before working further on the wood.

All dimensions of the pattern must be laid out and cut very exactly, working to a knife line. Since the hot metal will shrink as it cools, it is necessary to make the pattern larger than the finished casting. Cast iron shrinks about $\frac{1}{8}$ inch per foot, while brass and aluminum shrink about $\frac{3}{16}$ inch per foot. You can use an ordinary scale to measure the work and make allowances for shrinkage, but you would do better to purchase a shrinkage scale and use it for all measurements. These scales are graduated for the amount of shrinkage, so get a scale made for the kind of metal to be cast.

SPLIT PATTERNS

To illustrate several points about pattern making, we will outline the making of the pattern and core box for a simple cylindrical casting, such as the venturi (shown in Figure 135), a tube with flanges on each end. Since the pattern will be split on the center line, the stock must be glued up thick enough for each half and long enough to allow for turning. One edge and one face of each half is finished straight and flat. With a marking gauge, scribe the center line down the inside face of each half. Dowels are used to align both halves after they are separated. Some patterns are not the same on both sides, such as the pattern for a "T"-shaped piece; you must therefore decide which side of the pattern is to be up when it is placed in the mold. Since the bottom half of the pattern is placed on the mold board as the drag is being rammed, this half should have the dowel holes, and the top half will have the projecting dowels.

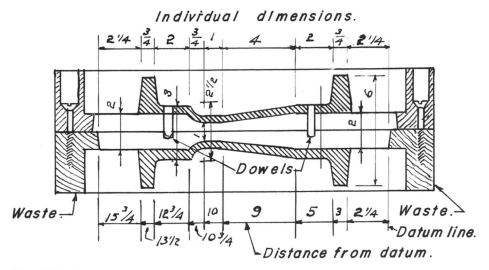

Fig. 135. Pattern

The Dowels

The dowel holes are bored from the inside of the top half, on the center line; they should be placed asymmetrically so that there will be only one way in which the pattern can be put together. These holes should be bored in the drill press so that they will be square with the face of the work. Clamp the two halves together, lining up the center marks on the ends, and bore the dowel holes in the bottom half through the holes in the top half as guides. The dowels are cut to the correct length and pointed. They should be long enough to completely fill the holes in the top half. Before driving the dowels into the top half, try their fit in the holes in the bottom half. So that the two parts of the pattern will separate easily in the mold, the dowels must be an easy sliding fit in the holes, but must still be tight enough to prevent side movement. Try sandpapering the end of the dowel until it slips easily in the hole. The point of the dowel should not be too long. As the cope is lifted off the drag, the sooner the dowels are free from the holes, the less danger there is of damaging the mold by moving the cope sideways and catching it on the dowels, thus tearing the pattern out of the sand. A projection of ⅜ inch with half of it in the tapered point and the rest full size to fit the hole is about right.

There are several methods of holding the halves of the pattern together while it is being turned. Long wood screws can be placed through the waste wood at each end. "U"-shaped metal dogs can be driven into the ends of the waste wood. Pieces of plywood can be screwed or nailed across the ends, and the center line transferred to it for centering in the lathe. Whatever method you use, make sure that it is fastened securely enough to stand the centrifugal force of spinning in the lathe.

The holes for the lathe centers must be accurately located at each end. Use a center punch to start the hole and drill small holes to receive the points of the centers. Be sure the work is held tightly on the centers and that the tail center is locked so that it cannot separate and allow the work to fly out of the lathe. Start with a slow speed until the pattern has been roughed down to the largest diameter of the pattern. Turn it the same diameter along the full length. Lay off the several lengths of the pattern with the shrinkage scale and spin the work while holding the point of a pencil against it to mark it all the way around. These pencil marks are just guide lines for rough turning. After roughing out the entire pattern, finish-turn one end as a starting point to make the final measurements.

In measuring the distances between points on the pattern, it is best to add up all the individual distances so that all measurements are made from one end as a datum. This way errors of individual measuring will be eliminated, and the over-all distance can be checked. Add up the distances and mark them on the drawing of the casting, being sure to add in the thickness necessary for finishing. Since the line on the drawing is the finished dimension, you must add the amount to be turned off in finishing the casting. The surfaces to be finished are usually marked on the drawing with a small "f" across the line representing the finished surface. One sixteenth inch is a good amount to allow for finishing, unless the shape of the casting is such that it may warp in cooling, in which case a greater amount must be allowed.

The Draft

Start at one end and finish-turn the first surface. If this is the face of a flange, be sure to allow for the taper of the draft. Without the draft, it would be almost impossible to remove the pattern from the mold. A draft of 1° is about right for most work, but some inside surfaces, where the sand would be locked between two ends, may require more. This draft should be set off on the bevel square and used throughout the work. The ends of the flange are probably end-grain wood, and these must be finished very smooth. Any roughness or torn grain will show up through the finish of the pattern and will make the sand stick and break the mold as the pattern is being withdrawn. Depending on sandpaper to smooth this end-grain wood is not the answer, as the sandpaper will wear away the soft spots faster than the hard ones, and the result will be an uneven surface far from the dimensions required. The end-grain wood must be turned smooth. Sharpen your flat chisel till it is very sharp and use a scraping cut. On sugar pine or white pine, this scraping cut will produce a smoother surface than a shearing cut, with far less danger that a slip of the tool will ruin the work.

The Core Prints

The core is supported in the mold in hollows made in the sand by the core prints. These are the same diameter as the core and should be about as long as the diameter of the core. The ends of the core prints are beveled to the draft angle. The core will have a vent hole down its center, and the gas and steam must be collected and carried out of the mold. Making the core print on the cope half about ¼ inch longer than on the drag, and then making the core the length of the drag half, will leave a ¼-inch space at the end in the cope to collect this gas. The core is made to fit the bottom half so that it will be accurately located in the mold. This extra space at the ends of the core in the top half makes it easier to place the cope over the drag when closing the flask.

Some cores must be located in the mold in one position only. To locate the core correctly, a flat place is left on the side of the core print and a similar flat place is left on the core so that there is only one way the core can be placed. When the casting must be set up for machining in one particular way, locating marks are built into the pattern. As an example, take an oval hollow on the inside of an otherwise round casting. The axis of this oval would be very hard to find on the rough casting, but the pattern maker had to know its location as he constructed the pattern, so he makes some mark, such as a raised line or a "V" notch, to indicate the location of the axis. There should be two such marks as far apart as possible. The guide marks should both be on the same part of the pattern, preferably on the drag, as there may be a shifting of the parts of the mold that would throw the guide marks out of line.

Fillets

All re-entrant angles should have fillets. When possible, turn these fillets in the lathe. Other places must have fillets fitted by hand. Pattern shops use several kinds of material for fillets. One form is a leather strip, beveled on the edges, that can be worked into the corner. Some use wax that is extruded from a machine in the shape of the fillet. Plastic wood is best for the home workshop. This is worked into the corner with a round-ended tool. Plastic wood will set too fast to be handled as it comes from the can, so have a small container of alcohol to dip the tool in. Alcohol is a poor solvent for plastic wood, but will keep it moist and slippery long enough for you to work it to shape. Putty is not good for fillets. It sets so slowly that it will be covered with the shellac finish before it is hard. This will stop its further setting so that it will be soft and apt to be damaged at the time when the pattern is to be used.

On completion of the turning of the pattern, it is sandpapered to a perfectly smooth finish, and all dimensions are checked. It can now be separated by removing the fastening in the waste wood at the ends. The lengths of the finished core prints are laid off, and the ends are cut on the saw table to the bevel of the draft. The table saw will probably not cut high enough to cut all the way through the core print, but it can be done on the band saw. It will be necessary to lay out a line on the top of the curved core print to guide the saw. This is best done by setting up a board to the required bevel and butting the end of the core print against it so that the print is exactly square with the board. Set the dividers or hermaphrodite calipers to the proper distance and scribe a line over the core print parallel to the board. Saw just outside this line and finish by sanding on the sand disk to the scribed line. Since the dowels projecting from the top half of the pattern will be in the road, a false bottom is made from a piece of wood with holes for the dowels so that the pattern will lie level on the table for sawing and sanding. The holes do not have to fit tight on the dowels (see Figure 136).

THE CORE BOX

To construct the core box, glue up a sufficient thickness of wood. Surface one side and the top and bottom. Scribe the center line down the top. If the core is symmetrical, only one half need be made, but when the two sides are different, both halves must be made. Lay out one end with the draft bevel marked on the sides. Saw this end to the bevel. It should be finished to the scribed line with the disk sander. All lines are to be marked with knife lines, and all surfaces are cut to the knife line. If the sawing is accurate, finishing with the disk sander is not necessary. Next lay off the length of piece #1. This is where there is a change in shape of the core. Accurately saw the box square across at this line. Before sawing off piece #1, make some identifying marks across the joint so that it can be assembled correctly. Now place piece #1 back against piece #2 and while holding them tightly together, mark off the length from the datum end to the far side of piece #2. Saw off piece #2, repeat this marking from the datum end, and saw off each piece where there are any changes in the shape of the core. Placing the pieces back together and marking from one end each time is done to eliminate the widths of the many saw kerfs.

Piece #4 has a large radius curve which can be formed best by turning in the lathe. Cut a separate piece with a thickness of the width of piece

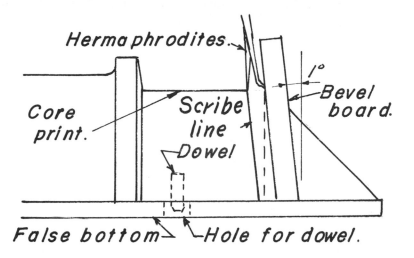

Fig. 136. Scribing line on end of core print

#4 and large enough to turn a complete circle. It would be difficult to
fasten this piece to the face plate in the lathe for turning so that its
center would be in exact line with the outside dimensions if it were cut
to size before turning. When it is in the lathe, spin it and mark the
center point. Then, without removing it from the face plate, lay off the
outside marks from this center point. After the piece has been turned,
it is cut in half, and the outside is finished to match the rest of the core
box. The other half is discarded. After all the pieces are cut to length,
the entire box is assembled, and the over-all length is checked by placing
the drag half of the pattern on top and comparing them.

It is very important that the core, where it fits into the place left
in the mold by the core print, be an exact fit to the core print. If other
parts of the core box are a little in error, it simply means a slight change
in the thickness of the casting, but if the core is larger than the core
print, it cannot be placed in the mold; and, if forced in, will break the
mold. If it is too small, the core will be off center, and the metal can run
in along the core print, possibly filling the vent space at the end, which
could cause a blown casting.

The width of the core is laid off on top of each piece, and the edge
line is scribed with a knife line. At the core prints check this width with
the actual width of the pattern. Place pieces #1 and #2 top to top with
the scribed lines in line. To be able to see the ends of these lines when
they are covered up, cut a little knife mark down the end of each line.
Clamp the two pieces together and, with the dividers centered on the
center-line mark, scribe a circle passing through the outside marks.
Now reverse the pieces and scribe the circle on the opposite end of piece
#1. Repeat this with all the parts of the core box, marking the circles

on the ends of each piece. The dividers used to make these marks should have sharp points so that the line will be cut into the wood like a knife line.

Each section is now carefully hollowed out with inside ground gouges, cutting exactly to the scribed lines. It is best to finish the cut to the two top lines at the side of the box. These can then be used to check the rest for a true half-circle. A right angle, when moved in contact with two fixed points, will scribe a half-circle with its apex. Rest your try-square on these two finished edges, and its point will be exactly on the finished circle. The point of the square will mark any high places and indicate where you should continue cutting. Also finish the two ends to the scribed circles so that the work can be tested with a straight edge between these finished ends (see Figure 139).

After each piece has been finished, they are all assembled on the bottom board (piece #7), with the side of each piece flush with the straight edge of the bottom board. The sections can be nailed and glued in place, and the end pieces (#6) fastened on. The outside of the box is now trimmed to neat lines, and the top edges are beveled so that the core maker can get under the edge to lift the box off the finished core as it is turned out on the metal plate for baking. Place the drag half of the pattern over the finished core box and check to see that they fit. Any error should be corrected at this time, or it will cause trouble in the foundry. Foundry men do not like homemade patterns, so you must be very careful to have yours correct.

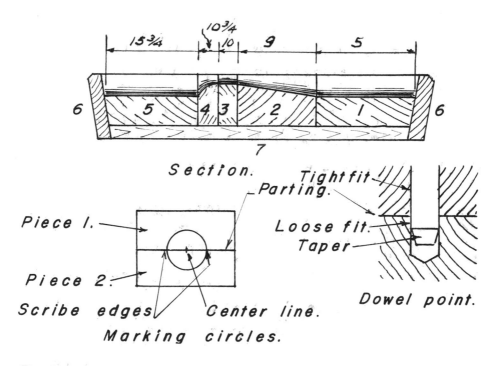

Fig. 137. Core box

PAINTING

The finished pattern and the core box are given several coats of orange shellac. Sand lightly between each coat until the surface is perfectly smooth, with no rough places that will catch on the sand. As a rule, the core prints are painted a different color from the metal part of the pattern. For cast iron, the prints are usually left natural color and the metal is painted black. For brass castings, the prints are black or red, and the metal is left natural color. The black is made by mixing some lamp black with the orange shellac. As too much lamp black will give a dull finish, use only enough to give a good black color. Use only fresh shellac, since shellac loses its drying quality with time. Old shellac will remain tacky and the sand will stick to it. It is usual to mark the outline of the metal section on the parting surface of the drag section of the pattern. This indicates to the molder the thickness of the metal and what the shape of the core is like. Your name and some identifying number should be painted on the pattern and the core box so that they will be used together in the foundry.

The core of the venturi that we have been using as an example is so long and slender that it will have to be reinforced with wires, and the molder will probably place a chaplet below it to support it and one above to prevent it from floating.

This example was fairly simple and illustrated many of the problems of pattern making. Some patterns are very complicated and must be carefully studied before deciding which side will be up and where the parting line will be.

Special Cases

Where there is a small projecting part, such as a boss, that would prevent you from removing the pattern from the mold, it can be made as a loose piece, held to the pattern with dowels or nails that can be easily withdrawn. A tongue can also be left on the loose piece that will fit in a mortise on the pattern. The dowel holds the loose piece in place until the sand has been rammed up to it. The dowel is then removed, and the sand keeps the loose piece in place until the pattern is removed. The loose piece is then removed through the open part of the mold. This means that there must be space enough opposite the loose piece for the molder to reach it and remove it. As the molder cannot drive a lifter into this loose piece, he must get hold of it some other way, such as by screwing a wood screw into the dowel hole of the nail.

Solid patterns can be molded without being parted into two halves, but this is more difficult for the molder and will add to the cost of the casting. In such a case, the molder must bed the pattern in sand down to the parting line at the center of the pattern. The drag is then rammed

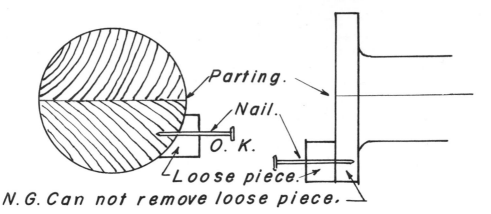

Fig. 138. Loose pieces

up on this "odd side," and another cope is made with the gates and vents. Or the pattern can be placed on the bottom board, and the drag rammed up; when turned over, the parting surface can be trimmed down to the center of the pattern, and the cope can be made up on this irregular parting surface. With a solid pattern, it is more difficult to lift the cope without damaging the mold by a slight side movement.

When a pattern is so thin that dowels cannot be used, matching tongue-and-groove faces can be made on the two parts to align them in the mold. The pattern for the sheave pulley shown in Figure 134 illustrates this condition. This sheave pulley could also have been made with a core print around the outside and a ring core used to form the groove of the sheave.

For large patterns, it is more economical to lag it up from 1-inch lumber than to glue up thick pieces. This is outlined in Figure 139. This figure also shows the use of the try square to test the core-box curve.

The dry sand mold for the pump impeller, shown in Figure 140, illustrates one way of handling a difficult pattern. Since the vanes of the pump are thin, if sufficient draft is used to make it possible to withdraw the pattern from the mold, they will be too thick for the tolerance called for in this design. If a mechanical drawing machine is used in the foundry, less draft can be used, but the deep width of the vanes makes it seem wise to resort to a dry sand mold. The vanes are sawed to the curved shape and are held in place in grooves in the core box. The sand is finished level with the top, then the loose top piece is fitted over the vanes and held tight with several wood screws. The vanes are then pulled up through curved slots in the loose cover. The cover prevents the core sand from being pulled up with the vanes. The cover is then removed, and the mold is turned out on the metal plate to be baked. As it is impossible to form the fillets by this method, the sharp corners of the dry baked sand are carefully filed off to form the fillets. This dry sand mold is then inserted in the flask in the usual way. Instead of using the loose cover plate to withdraw the vanes, the foundry can use a vibrating withdrawing machine to do it.

Sometimes it is desired to cast a piece of finished metal into the molten metal, such as the prefabricated vanes for the pump impeller. These can be placed in the grooves instead of the wooden ones and left in the dry sand mold. The edges will have to project enough to fuse with the molten metal. The inserts will have to be free from any dirt, oil, or scale, and even then they may not make a perfect union with the hot metal and will leave what is called a *cold shut joint*.

For production work in large foundries, instead of using split patterns and making a parting in the mold each time, each half of the pattern is rigidly attached to a mold board that has the same dowel arrangement as the flask. The gate runners will be part of the pattern. The drag and the cope are rammed up separately, usually on mechanical molding machines, and, when the two parts of the mold are put together, the mold is complete. Patterns and mold boards for this class of work are usually made of aluminum. Sometimes only one mold board is used,

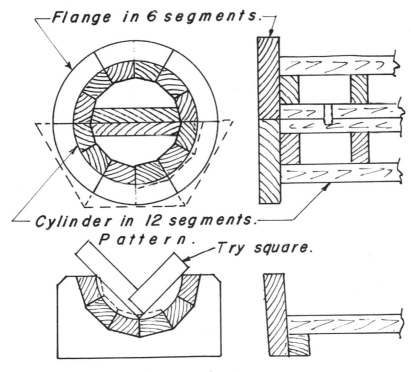

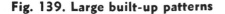

Fig. 139. Large built-up patterns

and the two parts of the pattern are accurately located on opposite sides. This match-plate pattern is placed between the drag and cope, and each side is rammed up. This forms the parting and the mold at the same time. None of these production methods are of any value to the home worker, where usually there will only be one or two castings made from any one pattern. Split wooden patterns are the ones to use.

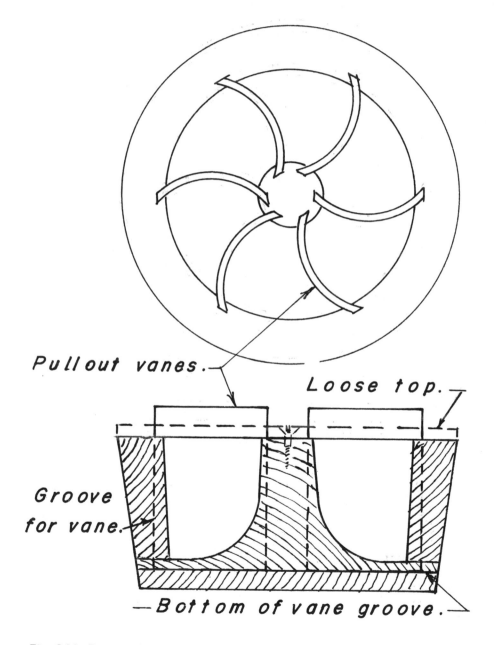

Fig. 140. Dry sand mold for pump impeller

18

The Magnetic Chuck

WHEN a thin piece of work is to be finished on the faces, it will often be impossible to hold it in any clamping device; it will either be sprung by the clamping, or the clamps will get in the way when you are machining the piece. A magnetic chuck is very handy for this sort of work. It can hold work firmly enough for grinding, but not for cutting with a lathe tool. In Figure 141 is shown a section through a simple magnetic chuck which can be made in the home workshop and that will take care of many of your small grinding jobs.

The core is a steel center piece with a flange welded to it. With the rough weldment held in the chuck, the inside is threaded to a good fit on the lathe spindle. Before removing from this setting, the back edge that bears against the collar on the lathe spindle is ground to a perfect alignment with the threads. The back face of the flange and the hub for the slip ring are also finished at this setting. It is now removed from the chuck and screwed directly onto the lathe spindle, and the front of the flange and the core are finished. This entire back piece should now be running perfectly true with the lathe spindle.

The outside is a piece of 4-inch double-extraheavy steel pipe. It is bored smooth on the inside and faced off to receive the face piece.

The face piece is made up of a center piece and two concentric rings, each brazed on the outside of the other. Use a $5/16$-inch steel plate to make these rings and rough-turn them all over so that they will be clean for brazing. These rings can be sawed out on the band saw by sawing the starting kerf from the outside, as shown in Figure 65. After finish-sawing the rings, the saw kerf is welded closed, melting the metal well down to the inside by working from both faces. After welding, the rings are turned on both faces. If the welding is not perfect when cut by this turning, repair it, since it should be a perfect surface, especially on the outside face.

There should be about a $1/32$-inch clearance all around between each of the rings at the joint. This clearance space is to be filled with brass to form the air gaps that enable the magnetic flux to hold the work. To center the rings before brazing, select a copper wire of the required diameter to form a spacer. This should be .0313-inch or #20 B&S gauge wire. Wrap this copper wire around the outside of each piece and solder the ends to hold it. Now bore the inside of the next ring to fit tightly over the copper wire. Assemble all the parts on the flat face of a fire brick and braze the joints. The copper wire will braze in with the brass, and the soft solder will melt and disappear.

The face piece is now faced on the inside surface, and a shoulder is turned where it fits onto the shell. This shoulder need be only deep enough to center the face on the shell. The face is now silver-soldered to the shell. Silver solder is used at this joint because the heat is low and there is thus no great danger of melting the ring joints, which are now finished on the inside. Another reason is that a silver-soldered joint can be made with less space than a brass joint; since each joint between parts in the magnetic circuit requires many ampere-turns of wire to

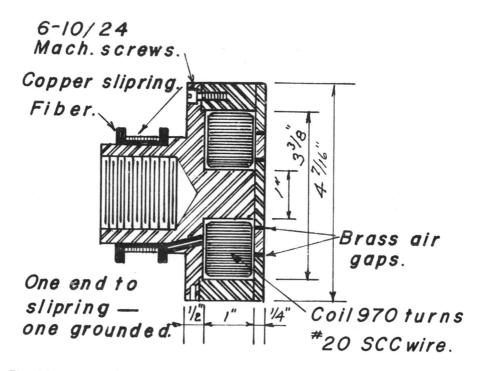

Fig. 141. Magnetic chuck

drive the flux across the air gaps, this joint, which is not used for holding work on the chuck, should be as small as it is possible to make it.

The shell is again set up in the four-jaw chuck, and a small cut is taken on the inside to eliminate any distortion that may have gotten in from the brazing. The core piece is screwed on the lathe spindle, and the shoulder is turned to receive the shell and face. The depth should be such that the inside of the face is tight against the end of the core when the shell is tight against its shoulder. These contacts are also air gaps and must be kept small to conserve the magnetic flux for useful work. Six 10-24 machine screws are drilled and tapped around the joint between the shell and the flange on the core. Between these, drill six ¼-inch holes so that a bar can be inserted, for screwing the chuck on or off the spindle nose.

The whole assembled chuck should now be screwed onto the spindle, and the outside, finished and polished with emery cloth. Drill a ¼-inch hole between the slip ring and the inside and insert a fiber tube with a $\frac{1}{16}$-inch hole in it to receive the hot end of the coil. Turn up two fiber washers of ⅛-inch fiber, making them a driving fit on the hub of the core. Drive on the inside washer and drill a hole through it for the lead from the coil. Wind gummed paper around the hub to a diameter .001 inch larger than the inside of the copper slip ring. If you cannot get a piece of copper tubing the right size to make the slip ring, one can be made by bending up a piece of sheet copper, or cutting down a piece of larger tubing and brazing the joint with brass. This slip ring should be bored to a true circle on the inside. You cannot hold it in the jaw chucks, as they would crush it; so soft solder it to a piece of brass plate that can be clamped to the face plate and centered. After boring, the soft solder can be melted off without damaging the slip ring.

The slip ring is heated to expand it so that it can be slipped over the paper insulation on the hub. You must not heat this copper ring till it is hot enough to char the paper insulation or melt open the brazed joint, so heat it in boiling water. This should expand it enough to let you slip it on. You can get it hotter by taking it to the kitchen and boiling it in the pressure cooker. If you cannot get the slip ring to fit tightly over the paper insulation, try cementing it on with Epoxy glue. It must be tight enough to be turned smooth after the coil lead is soldered to it.

The coil consists of 970 turns of #20 single-cotton-covered enameled magnet wire. Make a wooden form to wind this coil on. The form should have a center core $\frac{1}{16}$ inch larger than the steel core over which it is to fit. The length of the core must be $\frac{1}{16}$ inch less than the length of the steel core. The flanges of this winding form are held to the wooden core piece with at least two wood screws at each end and are turned on the outside to a diameter $\frac{1}{16}$ inch less than the inside of the steel shell. This $\frac{1}{16}$-inch clearance all around is to allow for the tape wrapping of the finished coil. Cut four small grooves at the quarter-points of the wooden core, lengthwise; cut radial grooves on the inside of the end pieces to connect with the grooves on the core. Place four pieces of string in these grooves and hold them there with cellophane tape while the coil is being wound. When the coil is completely wound, tie the strings tightly to hold the coil in shape as you remove it from the form. Drill a small hole through one of the end pieces near the core so that the starting end of the wire can be brought out and fastened while you are winding the coil. Fit a hub on the outside of one end piece that can be gripped by the three-jaw chuck and bring the tail center up to bear on the other end piece. Running the lathe at its slowest speed, wind on the wire until it is even with the outside edges of the end pieces. Wind it in even layers, if you can—or scramble-wind it, if you have to—but do not exceed the size of the end pieces, or else the coil will not fit in the shell.

Tie the four strings, remove the end pieces, and carefully work the coil off the core. Wind the entire coil with one layer of electrician's tape, removing the strings as you come to them. It is easier if you cut the tape into 12-inch lengths before winding. Fit the coil into the space inside the shell, bringing the inside end out through the fiber tube to the slip ring. File a groove big enough to receive the wire in the surface of the copper slip ring and solder this end to it. Solder the other end of the coil anywhere on the steel of the shell or core. Now turn the slip ring true with the spindle and press on the outside fiber washer. Put a little Epoxy glue under it to be sure it fits tight. Now turn the front face of the chuck and grind it to run perfectly true.

You will need a brush to run against the slip ring. Get a brush and its holder, with the spring, from an old auto generator or starting motor. You will have to build a bracket to take the brush holder to suit your lathe. The bracket must be insulated from the rest of the lathe.

For power, use a 12-volt auto battery. You should have a 12-volt trickle charger to go with the battery. An overnight charge will keep the battery in shape for your work. You cannot use alternating current with this chuck. Since it is made with solid metal, not laminations, in the magnetic circuit, it will get very hot from the eddy currents caused by alternating current. There is also a vibration caused by the 60-cycle current that will tend to make the work slip. Even with the direct current of the auto battery, the chuck will get hot. As the heat of grinding will also tend to heat it, after a long job of grinding, you should wait awhile and let the chuck cool down.

Work placed on the face of the chuck must be flat on the face next to the chuck. If there are any high spots on the work, it may pivot on these spots and slip. If the piece is thick enough to be grasped in a chuck, set it up in the lathe and face off the back. If it cannot be done in the lathe, file the back to a flat surface. Place the work so that it crosses the brass air gaps, as this is where the pull of the magnet is the greatest. For small parts that cannot span the air gaps, place little steel blocks, thinner than the work, across the air gaps, which bear against the work piece to steady it and keep it from slipping.

Take very small cuts with the grinding wheel, using the outside of the wheel. After each cut, shut off the current and remove the work to measure it with the micrometer. Before replacing the work on the chuck, wipe the face of the chuck and the work clean of any grinder dust. It is a good idea to take a roughing cut on one face and then turn this face to the chuck. This will give the work a good flat surface to fit against the face of the chuck.

The leads from the battery should have clips soldered on each end. One end can thus be clamped to the battery posts; one of the other ends can go to the slip-ring brush, and the other can be grounded on any part of the lathe. The brush to the slip ring will form a switch if you provide a means to release the spring and hold the brush off the slip ring.

19

The Milling Attachment

A MILLING attachment can be purchased with the lathe, or you can make one yourself as a work project. A milling attachment must have a vertical movement as well as the two horizontal movements. The carriage of the lathe gives the horizontal movements; if the compound slide is removed and mounted on a vertical bracket, it will give the required vertical movement as well.

Each manufacturer has its own method of fastening the compound slide to the cross-feed of the carriage, and you will have to make the parts to fit your own lathe. The lathe for which the following attachment was made used the cone-and-set-screw method.

Three iron castings are needed: the bracket (Figure 142), the nut block (Figure 143), and the vise (Figure 144). Draw up the details of the modifications for your machine, make the patterns, and have gray iron castings made.

The bracket must be set up on an angle block bolted to the face plate, so that you can face off the two flat faces at 90° to each other. Before bolting it to the angle block, lay out the center of each cone hole and make a small prick-punch mark. Then center the work with the wiggle bar and the dial indicator so that you can face and bore the holes at one setting. Since this setup will be badly out of balance, bolt on a counterweight onto the opposite side of the face plate.

The clamping cone should be made from a good piece of alloy steel, which you can get as scrap from your local machine shop. If you cannot get alloy steel, make it of mild steel and case harden it. The two pins under the set screws must have beveled ends to fit the bevel of the cone. These pins should be made of tool steel and hardened, and the temper drawn to a blue color. The set screws used to set up the clamping pins should also be hardened.

Set up the casting for the nut block in the four-jaw chuck and finish the outside all over. With the compound set up on the bracket you have just finished, bolt the nut block to it and mill the two edges to fit the "T" slot of the compound. Use a ½-inch end mill in the three-jaw chuck and mill both edges at the same setting so that they will be parallel. The nut block should fit snugly in the "T" slot, yet be free enough to slide out easily.

Set up the casting for the vise in the four-jaw chuck to face off the back. You will find that two of the jaws will clamp on solid metal, but that the other two will be in the open space. Fit a piece of heavy scrap across each of these openings and set up these jaws against the scrap pieces. After the back is faced off, it can be set up in the four-jaw chuck so that the ends can be faced off square with the back and parallel to each other.

Drill the clearance hole for the two ⅜-inch socket-head cap screws that hold the vise to the nut block. There should be two rows of these

Milling attachment. The bracket supporting the compound slide and the dowel screw to maintain position are shown. The thread-cutting dial is at the end of the carriage apron.

holes so that the vise can be adjusted for height within the limits of the compound-slide movement. As these two holes must be exactly the same distance apart in each row, make a drilling template from some scrap metal. Have one edge of the template straight as a reference edge for laying out the holes and placing the template for drilling. The template must be firmly clamped in place to prevent any movement. This drill template or the holes drilled in the vise can be used to start the tap drill in the nut block. These holes should be tapped in the drill press, as explained in Chapter 5, so that they will be perfectly square with the work. The holes in the vise must be countersunk for the heads of the cap screws. When countersinking these holes, allow for the thickness of metal to be milled off the inside of the vise.

Bolt the vise to the compound, using the just-finished nut block. Then, using an end mill in the three-jaw chuck, mill the inside of the bottom and the back face true with the back of the vise.

Nothing is more aggravating than to have something slip and throw the work out of line when it has been only partly machined. Most of the work you will mill in this attachment will project far from the center of the carriage, and this will put a heavy strain on the cone or other clamping device that holds the bracket. The two dowel screws

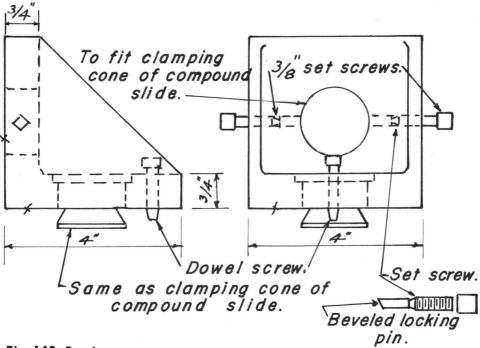
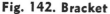

Fig. 142. Bracket

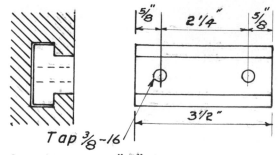

Tap ⅜-16

Sliding fit in "T" slot of compound.

Fig. 143. Nut block

are provided to take this twisting torque. These dowel screws have tapered points so that they will enter the dowel holes easily. You must find a place on the carriage and the compound where these dowel holes can be drilled without injuring the slides or screws. Be sure the bracket is set exactly square with the lathe when you are drilling for these dowel holes. Since the tapered points of the dowel screws must be exactly concentric with the threads of the screws, you should turn and thread these screws in the lathe so that the points can be tapered at the same setting as when cutting the threads.

Any looseness in either the cross slide or the compound slide will make it difficult to do accurate milling with the attachment. As all the movements made in milling are slow, the gibs for adjusting these slides can be set up more tightly than usual. After you have finished milling, the gibs can be set back to slide easily for turning.

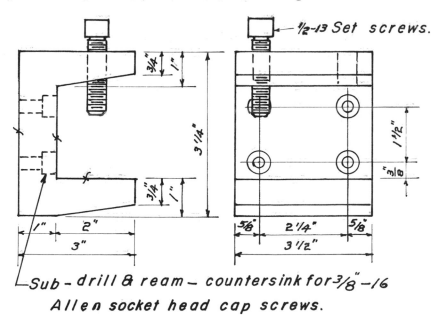

½-13 Set screws.

Sub-drill & ream — countersink for ⅜-16 Allen socket head cap screws.

Fig. 144. Vise   VICE.

20

The Tool-Post Grinder

IF really efficient grinding is to be done, two tool-post grinders will be required—a large one to handle jobs that need more power and a small one with a high-speed motor to take small mounted grinding wheels for small internal holes. The building of the small grinder will be outlined first. Figure 145 shows the completed small grinder.

THE SMALL TOOL-POST GRINDER

Since the grinder is built around the motor, the small grinder must have a high-speed motor. The small universal motors used in vacuum cleaners run at very high speeds, from 15000 RPM to 20000 RPM, but have very little torque. Such a motor is very well suited to a constant load, such as operating the fan of a vacuum cleaner, but to use it on a variable load, as for heavy grinding, will easily cause it to slow down and start heating badly. It works very well on the light load of the small mounted wheels.

Visit your appliance dealer and pick up a used vacuum cleaner that is in good shape. Take the motor apart and clean it thoroughly. True up the commutator and undercut the mica. Fit new brushes and new bearings if these are needed. The appliance shop, or a small motor repair shop will put the motor in shape for you, but it is interesting and easy to do this work yourself.

If the armature shaft has centered ends, mount it between centers in the lathe and take a small cut off the commutator, being careful not to cut into the slots where the wires are soldered. Each armature bar should be examined to see that the wires are well soldered to them. There are two wires in each slot. If the soldering looks doubtful, you should scrape the slot clean before resoldering. To do this, grind the end of an old hacksaw to a blunt end and grind the teeth on the side enough so that the saw is narrow enough to enter the slots. Scrape the entire end and interior of the slot and, of course, the wires themselves, until it is all bright copper. Use a noncorroding soldering paste and plenty of heat to melt the solder down to the bottom of the slot. The solder will probably spread over onto the next bars, and this must be cut through so that there will be no short circuit between the bars. Be sure you do not injure any of the wires in doing this.

Some vacuum-cleaner motors do not have the centers reamed in the shaft ends. In this case, use the steady rest and drill and ream the centers so that you can turn the commutator. To cut the copper bars, use a narrow pointed tool, since any tool with a broad point will chatter as it jumps from bar to bar. The surface can be finished with a fine-toothed file and fine sandpaper. Never use emery cloth on a commutator. Emery is a conductor of electricity, and some of it may become embedded in the mica and cause arcing between bars, which will soon ruin the commutator. If the commutator shows sign of excessive arcing between bars—that is, if the edges of the bars are burnt—there are damaged coils in the armature. Do not use it, as it will soon need a rewinding job, but get a better motor.

After the commutator has been turned to a smooth surface, the mica will spring up enough to hold the brushes off the bars. The mica must then be cut down, or *undercut,* below the surface of the bars. Electrical repair shops have a special machine for undercutting mica, but you can do it in your lathe. Take an old hacksaw and grind a cutting point the width of the mica between the bars. This is mounted flat with the cutting edge toward the head end. Mount the armature in the three-jaw chuck and the tail center. The cutter should be at the center height. Put the head stock in back gears to give slow motion and to hold it steady. Turn the armature until the tool is centered on a mica. Take a few passes with the cutter, operating the carriage as for cutting internal keyways (described in Chapter 10). Set the carriage stop so that the tool can not run over into the wires and damage them.

There should be no looseness in the bearings. If they are bronze bearings, you may enjoy making new bushings for them. Be sure the shaft is not worn before fitting the new sleeves. If ball bearings are used, get some new ones. Be careful when removing the old bearings from the shaft. The inner race was probably pressed on the shaft and will have to be removed with a puller. Too much pressure from a puller can bend the small shaft of the armature. Do not try to drive the bearing off the shaft. You will surely ruin it. Take it to a motor repair shop where they have the proper equipment to remove the bearings and replace them.

New brushes can be purchased from the appliance firm to fit your motor. These should be fitted to the curve of the commutator by gluing a piece of fine sandpaper to the commutator and revolving it under the brushes until they are formed to the curve. Since the brush holders are not always the same, the brushes should be marked so that they will always be replaced in the correct position.

Most vacuum-cleaner motors are covered with an aluminum jacket. This jacket should be retained if it can be made to fit. Some motors have a flange on the end that is bolted to the fan housing. This will be in the way. If it cannot be cut off, discard it and make a sheet-metal cover to suit the new conditions. This cover must be open on the ends enough to let the draft from the cooling fan of the motor have free circulation through the motor.

With the jacket for the motor completed, a mounting must be made to fit that particular motor. It will consist of a seat with a curved top that fits the contour of the motor and some means of fastening the motor to it. Machine screws coming up from underneath can be used, if there is a satisfactory place on the motor where you can drill and tap for the screws. This would have to be some place where the windings will not be damaged. If the screws from below cannot be used, a band of strapping can be arranged around the outside of the motor to hold it tight to the seat. You will have to work out the motor mount to fit your motor. Figure 146 shows details of the base of the grinder and motor mount.

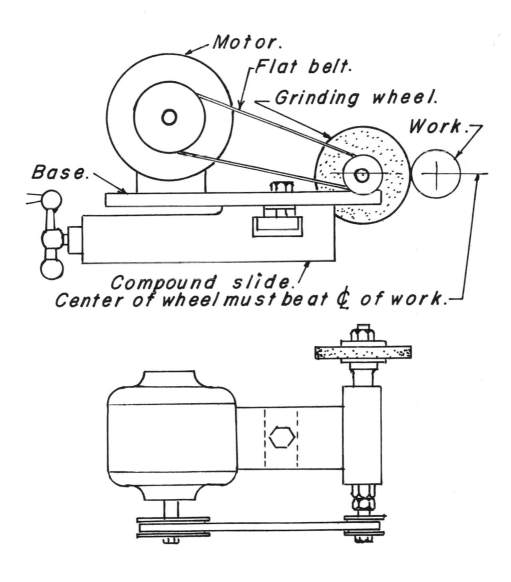

Fig. 145. Small tool-post grinder

The base of the grinder is a piece of ⅜-inch cold rolled steel 7 inches long and 2½ inches wide. There is a ⁷⁄₁₆-inch slot cut down the center under the motor so that the motor seat can be adjusted for belt tension. The motor seat has a ⅜-inch–16 cap screw up through this slot from underneath. The head of this screw may have to be cut thin if it strikes the top of the compound slide. There are two ⅛-inch-by-¼-inch guide bars riveted to the underside of the motor seat to guide it when moved along the base. These should be fitted to the width of the base as you rivet them. The base also has a guide block, riveted to the underside and fitted to the "T" slot of the compound slide. This is done so that the base will always be placed on the compound in the same position. The ½-inch–20 cap screw used to bolt the base to the "T" slot has a special square nut that will slide easily in the "T" slot but will not turn.

Figure 147 shows details of the spindle and its housing. The spindle should be made of a good piece of alloy steel that has been annealed to relieve it of all locked-in strains. A shoulder is turned at the wheel end, and the threads are turned in the lathe to be concentric with the spindle. The two seats for the ball bearings should be ground to a push fit in the inside races. If you do not have a grinder to finish for these bearings, a good turning job will do.

The bearings are New Departure #77502, double-shielded and permanently lubricated. These bearings, when new, will run without any vibration, but with use they may loosen up a little and need adjusting. This is done with the ½-inch–20 nut and lock nut at the pulley end. A little side pressure will make the balls run on a new part of the races that is not worn. Do not put enough side pressure on the bearings to make them run hard. If they will not run smoothly with a little side adjustment, discard them and install new ones.

The bearing housing is made from a piece of mild-steel shafting, bored and turned as indicated. This piece cannot be held in a chuck while boring, as it projects too far out, so hold the head end in the three-jaw chuck and support the tail end in the steady rest. This means that the ends must be centered and the outside finished before you bore and finish the inside. The recess for the bearings should be a good push fit on the outer races. The underside, where the housing fits on the base, must be milled to a flat seat, leaving enough thickness to take the ⅜-inch–16 flat-head machine screws fastening it to the base. Since the grinding wheel should be at the same height as the lathe centers, it may be necessary to fit shims under the housing to adjust this height.

The pulleys are made from mild steel. Since it is desired to use a flat belt, they should have a crown turned on the face under the belt. A flat belt always tries to run on the highest place on the pulley; if there is a crown in the center, making it the highest place, the belt will run there and not need the flanges on the sides. These are only to help if the belt stretches out of shape and one edge gets longer than the other, in which case it will run to the side off the crown. When the belt starts to do this, discard it, as it can start to whip at the high speed and cause vibration.

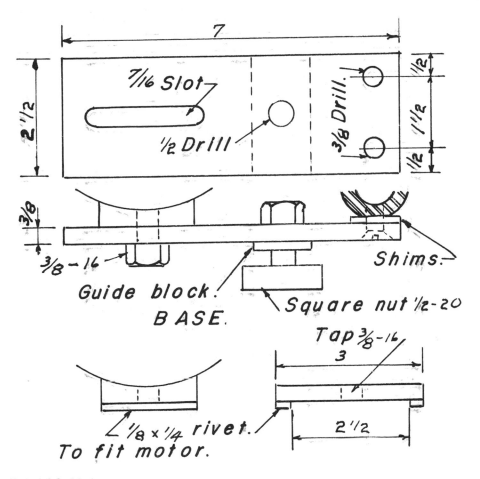

Fig. 146. Motor seat

Make a pulley for the spindle, as shown, and a similar one for the motor, but fitted to the motor shaft. As these very small mounted grinding wheels must run very fast, you may have to make several sets of pulleys to find the maximum speed you can run it. This will be limited by the belt action.

Because of the high speed required, it is not possible to use a belt of much weight, such as a "V" belt. Such a belt would stand out away from the pulleys, due to centrifugal force, and would not only do very little work but would be apt to start whipping. The small flat rubber belts, made for some floor-polishing machines, work very well at this speed. Get several from your appliance dealer. Since the total length of the belt is about 16 inches, you should get one before making the base of the grinder. Then, when the pulley diameters are known, the distance between pulley centers can be worked out. This will govern the length of the $7/16$-inch slot and the position of the bolt to the "T" slot of the compound slide.

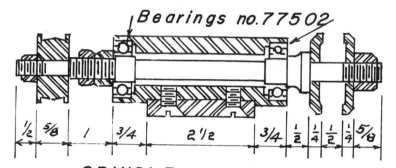

SPINDLE ASSEMBLY.

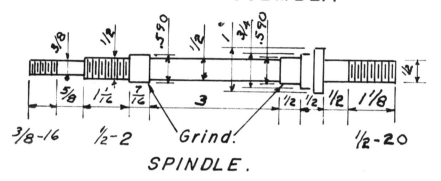

SPINDLE.

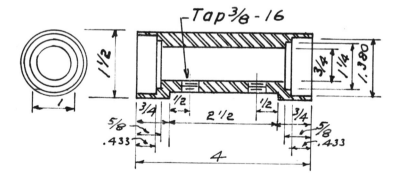

Fig. 147. Spindle for small grinder

Make up two collars with parallel faces to grip the grinding wheel. After boring and reaming the hole, mount them on a mandrel and finish both faces at the same setting. Use very light cuts so that the collars will not slip on the mandrel. The face of the collar that bears on the grinding wheel is relieved so that pressure on the wheel is concentrated well out on the wheel. A layer of blotting paper should be placed between wheel and collar to equalize the pressure. If the collars are not relieved, one

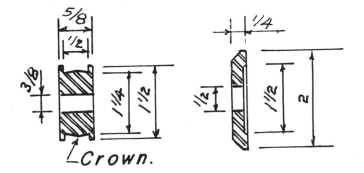

Fig. 148. Pulley and collars

collar may put pressure on the wheel near the shaft while the other bears near the rim. This could put a bending strain on the wheel that might crack it.

For grinding small internal holes, the small mounted stones are held in a collet chuck mounted on the end of the grinder spindle. Figure 74 shows a section through such a collet. Since these small stones come mounted on ⅛-inch and ¼-inch shanks, you will need a collet for each size. These collets must run absolutely true, and great care must be used in constructing them.

For the body of the collet, use a piece of good alloy steel. Mount it in the chuck and drill and bore the inside to the size of the root of the thread on the end of the spindle. This should be finish-bored with the small boring bar so that it will run absolutely true. Then turn the inside thread to fit snug on the spindle. The thread should be long enough so that the end of the collet can fit up tight against the shoulder on the spindle. Before removing it from this setting, set up the grinder and finish-grind this end to a perfect fit against the spindle shoulder. Repeat for the second collet.

Set up a piece of scrap and turn and thread a spud that is an exact duplicate to the thread and shoulder on the spindle end. The collets can now be screwed on this spud, and the outside can be finished and threaded for the collet-closing nut. The hole through the center must now be drilled exactly at the center. Start the point of the drill with the combined center reamer held in the tail-stock chuck. Drill very carefully with the small drills so as not to spring them. Place the dial indicator against the drill up close to the work and watch to make sure that the drill is not wobbling. Do not put enough pressure on the side of the drill to spring it. Drill with an undersize drill and then ream it to size with the finish drill. With the ¼-inch size, finish with a ¼-inch reamer. If the drill does not start true in the center-reamer starting hole, it will be necessary to turn off the poor hole and start another. Drill the ⅛-inch size first so that, if it does not come out, you can work it over for the ¼-inch size.

Turn up four nuts to fit the thread on the end of the collet. Two of these are to be finished for closing the collets and should be knurled on the outside. The other two can be rough; these are to be used to hold the jaws of the collet as they are being split with a hacksaw. To split the jaws of the collets, saw down on the center line the depth of the collet nut. Use the narrowest hacksaw you can get, with at least 24 teeth: 32 teeth is even better. You will be able to make the first cut, sawing all the way across both sides while the end of the collet is in the open. Trying to make the second cut at a 90° angle to the first one, while the jaws are in the open, may spring the jaws, which would ruin the accuracy of the collet. After screwing on the rough nuts, the second cuts can be made by sawing through the nut and the collet at the same time, and there will be little danger of bending the collet jaws. After sawing, the burr left on the inside of the jaws will have to be removed. If you have a set of needle files, you can reach in with a small three-cornered file and file off the burr. Or you can make a small end scraper, shape it to a "V" on the cutting end, harden it, and fit a handle to it, then use it to scrape out the burr. The finished hole must be a snug fit on the shank of the grinding stone.

The grinding wheels must be trued up with the diamond each time the grinder is set up. If the face of the wheel is not parallel to the feed across the diamond, more of the wheel must be cut away to make it parallel. Putting the guide block under the base plate, to fit in the "T" slot, assures you that the grinder will always be positioned correctly relative to the compound slide. The compound can then be set to the same angle each time, and a minimum cut can be taken off the wheel when dressing it.

With small-diameter grinding wheels, this grinder is suitable for grinding small work. Its small power limits it to very small cuts. An old ⅛-inch cutoff wheel, which has worn down to a diameter no longer suitable for cutoff work, makes a very good wheel to use. With this larger-diameter wheel, the very high speed of the spindle is not needed. A larger pulley can then be used on the spindle, and a smaller one on the motor. This will increase the torque applied to the wheel and enable you to do light grinding. When this larger pulley is on the spindle, it will foul on the tail stock when grinding small diameters between centers. To reach this small work with the wheel, the compound can be set to some angle, such as 10°, that will set the wheel in closer to the work. Each time the grinder is set up, set the compound to 10° before dressing the wheel.

THE LARGE TOOL-POST GRINDER

For larger grinding wheels and heavier work, a motor with more power is needed. For this, get a new ¼ H.P. split-phase motor running at 1725 RPM and that has a balanced armature so that it runs without vibration. It may be necessary to try out several motors before finding one that is free from vibration. Have the dealer test them for you before you buy.

The general construction of this grinder is similar to that of the smaller grinder, but the method of mounting the motor may be different. If the motor is one with a swinging base, it can be mounted rigidly in one position, and the belt tension can be adjusted by swinging the motor in its mount. Most of these inexpensive motors have rigid bases and sleeve bearings. These are all right. The motor can be made to fit a sliding base similar to that on the small grinder.

Since this grinder will be doing internal grinding in larger bores and at some distance in, it will need an extended spindle. As it will also be used to grind cylindrical work between centers and parts set up on the face plate, it also should have a short spindle with collars close to the bearings at each end, so that the grinding wheel can be placed at either end to reach the many positions needed. As this grinder is designed to use grinding wheels about 6 inches in diameter, it will not be necessary to set it at the 10° angle to clear the tail stock. However, for the use of cup wheels, which work better when set to have as small a cutting arc as possible, it will be necessary to set the grinder at an angle.

There are times when it is necessary to feed the grinder with the screw of the compound slide, such as when grinding tapers or truing up lathe centers. This means that the guide block under the base that fits in the "T" slot must be at 90° for most cylindrical grinding, but parallel when a taper is to be ground. The guide block should not be riveted in one position, as with the small grinder, but fitted with two ¼-inch cap screws to hold it in either position.

The spindle is made similar to the small grinder. On the pulley end, cut a left-handed thread and make a nut to fit it. A right-handed thread at this end will not stay tight, since the torque of the grinding wheel will turn a right-handed nut in a direction to loosen it.

The bearings are New Departure #77503, double-shielded and permanently lubricated ball bearings. The housing to support the bearings is a piece of extraheavy 1¼-inch pipe with the ends bored to fit the bearings. Standard-weight pipe is not thick enough to bore for the bearings unless filler pieces are brazed into the ends large enough to bore out for the bearings. Silver solder will be best for this brazing, as it will run into the joint better than brass spelter. It is not possible to mill the flat on the underside to bolt to the base plate, since the pipe is too thin. A ⅜-inch plate bracket is welded on the side to take the bolts to the base plate (see Figure 150). Before welding on the bracket, the pipe should be set up on the large cone-pipe centers, and the outside should be finished so that it can be held in the steady rest when you bore the inside for the bearings. The bottom of the bracket should be milled to fit on the base plate.

Since the motor runs at a much slower speed than that of the small grinder, and more power must be transmitted to the spindle, a "V" belt will work very well on this machine. Make a 1½-inch pulley for the spindle and a 4-inch pulley for the motor. These should have ⁵⁄₁₆-inch set screws bearing on flat places on the shafts. Since you can get these ⅜-inch "V" belts in almost any length, you can lay out the centers between pulleys to suit the base plate.

The motor will come with a saddle on its bottom. This hollow saddle will not work well with the slide on the base plate. It is possible to fit

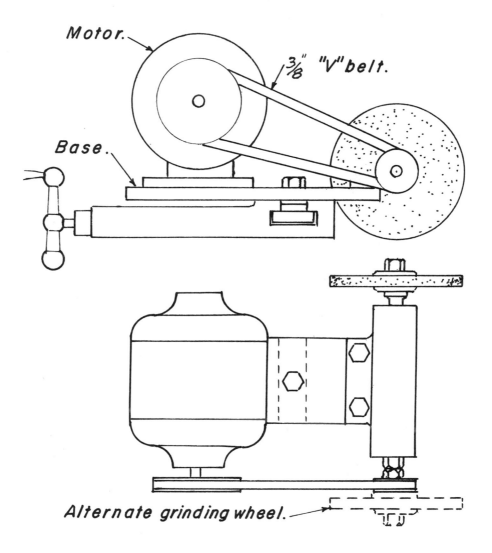

Fig. 149. Large tool-post grinder

a piece of ¼-inch plate under the saddle and have this form the slide. The ⅛-inch-by-¼-inch guide cleats can be riveted to it. Otherwise, make a whole new saddle for the motor that will work with the base plate.

If the motors on the grinders do not have built-in switches, install one at a convenient place on the motor or in the cord leading to it. A small-appliance switch mounted in a sheet-metal housing makes the most desirable installation.

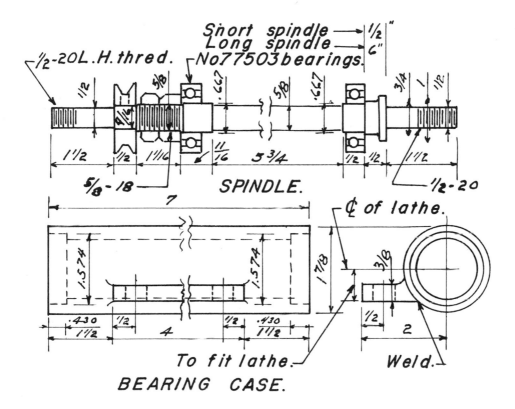

Fig. 150. Spindle for large grinder

21

Special Tools

Reamers

A SET of reamers made by some well-known manufacturer and in the most often used sizes should be part of your equipment. When an odd-sized reamer, one that will be used very seldom, is required, it is more practical to make a tool to do the job rather than to spend a large amount for a temporary tool. Such a reamer would be a king-pin reamer, used to ream an oversized hole to fit new king pins to a front axle. An expanding reamer would do the job, but the cost would be more than the job is worth, and a reamer of the size needed can be made quickly. Another example would be a large reamer to remove a scored mark in an engine cylinder.

For these "one-time" reamers, excellent tools can be made of mild steel, case hardened to give sharp cutting edges. These case-hardened tools will last quite a long time. When they need sharpening, they can be annealed, sharpened with a file, and again case hardened. An interesting work project would be to make your own set of standard-sized reamers. These reamers should be made from a good grade of tool steel, tempered, and ground to size.

The steel should be annealed to remove any strains and then turned between centers. Turn the flutes and shank about .010 inch larger to allow for grinding. You will need a fixture to hold the blank while you are milling the flutes; that is, a base piece that can be bolted to the nut block of the milling attachment. This should be a steel bar, 3 inches by ½ inch and 12 inches long. At each end of the bar, bolt on a bracket that will take a 60° center. These brackets can be cut from ½-inch-thick steel angles. The outstanding leg should be 3 inches long. The centers are held in place with set screws, as shown in Figure 152, which illustrates the indexing gear-arbor bracket. The other leg of each bracket should have two ⅜-inch–16 threads tapped at 1-inch centers. Down the center line of the 3-inch-by-½-inch bar, drill a series of ⅜-inch holes on 1-inch centers. The brackets for the centers can then be bolted on at 1-inch intervals, to accommodate work pieces of different lengths. The fixture will be used quite often and is well worth the time it will take you to make it. It is similar to the bracket shown in Figure 97, but has adjustable ends.

To use this fixture for milling flutes, the centers are first adjusted for the length of the work. A lathe dog is fastened to the work and locked to the fixture with a "C" clamp, or other device, so that the work cannot turn while being milled. Where the spacing of the flutes does not have to be accurate, as for straight-fluted reamers, the spacing can be marked on the work, and the indexing can be done by loosening the lathe dog and resetting it by eye for the next cut.

Where the indexing must be accurate, make a center for one end that will take one of the lathe change gears and also a small dog driving plate similar to the drive plate of the lathe. This has a slot to take the end of the lathe dog and a set screw to clamp the end of the dog so that there is no movement to it. The indexing gear and the driver are keyed to a bushing that revolves on the center at the indexing end. There is an index locking arm at the indexing gear. The indexing gear is one with a number of teeth that will divide evenly for the number of slots to be milled. These teeth are marked on the indexing gear, and the stop is set to these marks at each move. This entire indexing fixture is mounted on the milling attachment so that its length is parallel to the cross slide of the carriage. A milling cutter of the required shape is mounted on a single-ended mandrel held in the head-stock collet. A double-ended mandrel, held between centers, cannot be used, as it would interfere with the indexing fixture.

Since it is not possible to mill spiral flutes with this setup, an odd number of straight flutes will be used. If these are not perfectly evenly spaced, chatter will be reduced. After hardening and drawing the temper to a straw color, the reamer is ready for grinding. The reamer is first ground, for its full length, to the exact size of the hole it is to cut. Since you cannot accurately measure the diameter over the points of the flutes, the shank is ground to size where the measurements can be made. After being ground to size, the lands of the flutes must be relieved, or they will refuse to cut. Relieving is done by mounting the reamer between centers and fitting a spring finger stop that will hold each flute in the same position. Use a lathe dog on the reamer to hold it to the slot in the driving plate of the lathe. Put the lathe in back gears, so that the reamer can be turned against the spring stop and held there while grinding. There are two ways the relief can be ground on the flutes. Figure 153 shows the use of a cup wheel. A saucer wheel will also work very well. Since the cup wheel will have to be mounted way above the lathe centers, mount the grinder on the milling attachment so that the height can be adjusted. With an odd or irregular spacing of the flutes, the spring stop, if placed as shown in Figure 153, will not bring the flute being ground into the correct position, and the relieving will have to be done by eye. The stop finger must be on the flute being ground each time, as shown in Figure 154.

In Figure 154 the use of a regular grinding wheel is illustrated. The stop finger is adjusted so that the flute being relieved is a little below center. This will make the wheel undercut a little on the top side. It must be adjusted so that the wheel does not strike the flute above it. With this arrangement of the stop finger, it can be set once, then all flutes can be ground alike by setting them on the stop. The relief should be ground until there is only a very small land left at the cutting edge.

If the reamer has a starting taper, as a hand reamer does, this taper must be ground and relieved at the same setting for the taper. It would be very difficult to get the same setting for this relieving of the taper if it is moved after the taper has been ground. Grind the taper and relieve it, either before the straight part is ground or after it is finished. If the reamer is to be a rose reamer, the starting bevel is ground and relieved in the same manner as for the hand reamer.

Before hardening the reamer, select a place on the shank and stamp its size deep enough so the figures will not be obliterated by the grinding.

A temporary reamer can be turned to exact size from mild steel while still soft. The flutes can either be milled, as described above, or they can be cut with a hacksaw and filed to shape. The backs of the lands are filed for the relief with a fine file. The reamer is finished completely while still soft. It is then hardened by heating it to a cherry red and soaking it in the case-hardening compound until the color is black. This is repeated several times to give it a good thick case of hard steel. Quenching from a bright cherry red will give a glass-hard surface deep enough to do good work for quite a while. A reamer made by this method may not cut to the exact size intended, as it may warp a little when hardening. Test it before using it on an important hole. When an exact size is required, use a reamer that has been ground to the exact size. But there are many jobs for which a smooth hole is required, but where the exact size is not so important when the mating member can be fitted to the reamed hole. The large reamer for the scored engine cylinder mentioned above is an example. It can be quickly and easily made from soft steel. It is not very likely that you would have a piece of tool steel large enough to make this reamer, but mild steel of that size is easy to get.

Another type of soft steel reamer is a rose reamer with inserted cutting teeth. The rose reamer does all its cutting on the beveled entering end while the body of the reamer acts as a guide in the finished hole. This type of reamer is made by drilling 6 to 8 holes for cutters where the

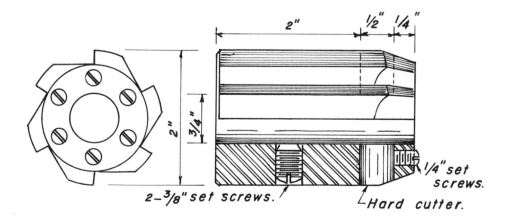

Fig. 151. Inserted-tooth reamer

bevel is to be made. The cutters can be made from ½-inch-round tool
steel, hardened and tempered to a straw color. These cutters are short
and are held in the drilled holes with ¼-inch set screws. Flutes can be
cut with the hacksaw, or the band saw, passing through the center of
the cutters. These flutes allow the cuttings to escape from the cutting
edge. The cutting face of the inserted cutters is ground back to the center-
line of the cutter. This can be done with the saw before the cutters are
hardened. The bevel for the cutting end is turned while the outside is
being roughed out. The body of the reamer is left large enough to be
finish-ground. With the hardened cutters in place and firmly held by the
set screws, the outside of the flutes is ground to the finish size, and then
the bevel on the cutters is ground. The bevel edge of the cutters must
be relieved so that they will cut. This can be done by hand, if care is
used not to overgrind. The flutes are not relieved; so, if an even number
is used, the size can be accurately measured with the micrometer. This
type of reamer will cut a very smooth hole to the exact size intended.
Figure 151 shows an inserted-tooth reamer, intended to finish a 2-inch
hole. It can be either mounted on a ¾-inch mandrel or on a ¾-inch bar,
being held by the set screws.

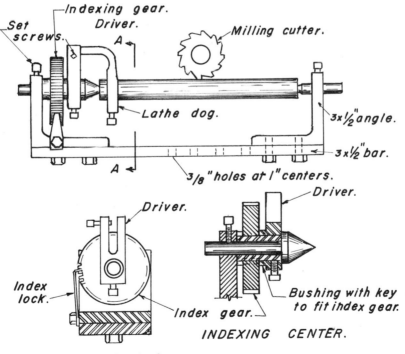

Fig. 152. Indexing fixture

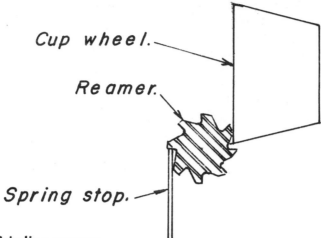

Cup wheel.

Reamer.

Spring stop.

Fig. 153. Grinding reamers

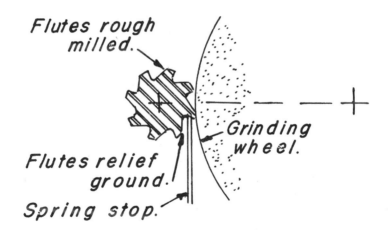

Flutes rough milled.

Grinding wheel.

Flutes relief ground.

Spring stop.

Fig. 154. Grinding reamers

Countersinks

A countersink is similar to an end mill with a pilot added. It is sharpened on the end to do the cutting and has flutes on the side for the cuttings to escape. The pilot is the same size as the hole to be countersunk. Since the tool is seldom used, it can be made of mild steel and case hardened. The tool is turned to size, and the hole is bored for inserting the pilot. The end teeth are shaped by sawing and filing. They can be filed to a sharp cutting edge while soft. The pilot must be inserted, as it would not be possible to form the end teeth if a solid pilot were used. Drill the hole for the pilot first and use it as a center to turn the outside. In this way, the pilot will be concentric with the outside.

As the length of the countersink is short, it is very easy to saw and file the grooves for the flutes on the sides. The lands of the flutes do not have to be relieved, since they do no cutting. The shank is made intregal with the cutter and should be ½ inch in diameter for a good grip in the drill-press chuck. One countersink can be used for several sizes of holes if the pilot is changed. The pilot must be a good running fit in the drilled hole, as the countersink cannot get a good start with a pilot smaller than the hole. To be able to change pilots, which are a driving fit in the countersink, a hole is drilled the full length of the shank so that a knockout pin can be used to extract the pilot.

If the countersink is made of tool steel, it is set up, after tempering, in the three-jaw chuck, and the face of the teeth are ground straight across so that they will all be the same length and do equal cutting. This must be done before the pilot is inserted. After facing, the teeth must be relieved. This can be done with a small wheel in the high-speed hand grinder.

Spot Facers

A spot facer is similar to a countersink. Since it does not cut a hole any deeper than the depth of the face teeth, it does not need the side flutes for the cuttings to escape. This tool is intended merely to true up the surface around a bolt hole, but not to cut deep. Of course, a countersink can be used as a spot-facing tool; if you make up a series of countersinks for the usual size of cap screws you will be using, they can be used for both purposes.

Large-Hole Drills

These tools are similar to countersinks, but, rather than having an integral shank and an inserted pilot, they are made to be fastened to a ½-inch drive shank that projects through to form the pilot. Use at least two ⅜-inch set screws to hold the cutter to the shank and provide a flat place on the shank to receive the set screws. To use these large drills, drill a ½-inch pilot hole where required and enlarge it with the large drill. The drill must be turned at a slow speed and frequently withdrawn. While the side flutes allow the cuttings to escape from under the cutting teeth, they will not remove them from the hole. The tool must be withdrawn, so that the chips can be cleaned away

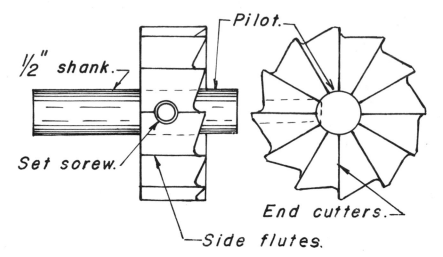

Fig. 155. Large-hole drills

Taps

Special taps, like left-handed taps, or taps that are so seldom used that it would not pay you to purchase them, can be made by this case-hardening method with little trouble. The thread is turned in the lathe, as for making a bolt, using a nut of known size as a gauge. If you do not have a nut as a pattern, as when turning a left-handed thread, compute the depth to the root of the thread and turn this size on the end of the blank. Then cut the thread until the point of the threading tool just marks this root diameter. The grooves for the flutes are milled, and a fine three-cornered file is used to remove the burr left on each tooth by the milling cutter. Grind or turn the starting taper. It is not possible to relieve all the teeth, as would be done on a commercially manufactured tap, but the backs of the teeth on the tapered part can be relieved. As all the cutting is done on this tapered part, the tap will work very well. This relieving of the teeth can be done with a file while the tap is soft. Mill or file the square end for the tap wrench and stamp the size on the shank. If you are using mild steel, case harden the tap, but if using tool steel, temper it to a straw color.

Plug Gauges

It is difficult to set calipers to an exact dimension unless you have something solid to set them to and can feel the resistance as they are removed. Your inside micrometers will not measure diameters smaller

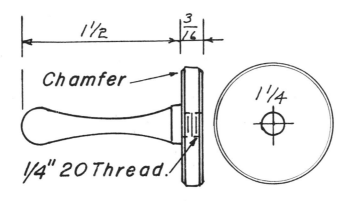

Fig. 156. Plug gauge

than 2 inches. Over the 2-inch size, you can set the outside calipers to dimensions set up on the inside micrometers. Under 2 inches, a set of gauge blocks or plug gauges will be a big help. Ring gauges are not so necessary, as you can set your inside calipers to the micrometers for anything under 2 inches. For over 2 inches, set the vernier calipers, which are rigid, by the inside micrometers, and then set the inside calipers to the vernier caliper.

Plug gauges ranging in size from $\frac{3}{8}$ inch to $1\frac{15}{16}$ inches in steps of $\frac{1}{16}$ inch should be made from tool steel that can be hardened. Case-hardened soft steel will not do, since the outside must be ground after hardening, and the hard case on soft steel is not thick enough for grinding. Use tool steel.

Rough out the disks to a thickness of $\frac{3}{16}$ inch, leaving .005 inch to be ground after hardening. With the disks set up in the three-jaw chuck, drill and tap a $\frac{1}{4}$-inch–20 center hole to fit on the handle. A nice finish can be given to the sides of the disks by grinding them on the magnetic chuck.

Harden the disks and draw the temper to a blue color. Put a piece of scrap in the chuck and turn up a spud with $\frac{1}{4}$-inch–20 threads on which the disks can be screwed for the outside grinding. Provide a shoulder on the spud to screw the disks against and do not remove the spud until all the disks are ground to size.

Make a handle with the same thread to screw the disks onto while you are using them. Make a hardwood box with slots for each disk. Stamp the size of each disk on an aluminum strip opposite each disk.

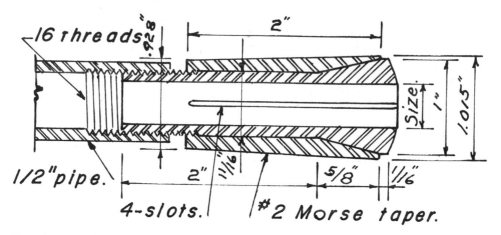

Fig. 157. Collet chuck

Collet Chucks

For holding the milling cutters, which must run perfectly true, a collet chuck is more accurate than the three-jaw chuck and it does not take up as much room. You can also reach into a smaller space with a collet chuck.

The chuck consists of a sleeve fitted to the Morse taper of the head-stock spindle. The inside of this sleeve has a tapered part to close the collet and a straight part to guide it. The collet is a split sleeve with a tapered end to close it; the other end is threaded to take a draw bar made from a piece of ½-inch pipe. The pipe extends through the length of the head-stock spindle and has a hand wheel or "T" handle rigidly fastened to the outer end.

The sleeves should be made from tool steel and tempered to a blue color. Make the inside sleeve, or split collet, first. Drill the inside hole ¹⁄₆₄ inch smaller than the size of the finished collet. Mount it on a mandrel and finish-turn the threads and rough-turn the outside, leaving .002 inch for grinding. The four slots should be cut: use either a slotting saw in the milling attachment or a hacksaw.

The outside sleeve is drilled and bored in the three-jaw chuck, leaving enough space for finish-grinding both the inside and outside of the sleeve, and allowing the .002 inch for grinding.

Both sleeves are now tempered to a blue color. Mount the outside sleeve on its mandrel and grind it to a fit in the head-stock taper. This taper can be fitted when the part is rough-turned, and the setting of the compound slide can be left without moving it until the taper is ground. It should be ground until the end of the sleeve is flush with the end of the spindle.

Put the split collet on its mandrel and grind the outside and the taper.

The burrs from the slotting should be removed before placing it on the mandrel and it should be driven on just tightly enough to hold it for grinding but not enough to enlarge it beyond the amount to be ground from the inside. The solid part under the thread should be placed on the large end of the mandrel.

Firmly seat the outside sleeve in the Morse taper of the spindle, after you have wiped out any chips. Grind the straight part of the inside, using the small mounted wheels in the small high-speed tool-post grinder. During this operation, the angle of the compound should not be changed from that for grinding the outside of the closing taper on the collet. As the grinding wheel must be on the same center as the lathe spindle, the small grinder cannot be set up directly on the tool post, as the guide block riveted under the base plate would force it to the angle of the compound and not parallel to the centerline of the spindle. Mount an angle block on the compound with its face parallel to the lathe. This may require making large square nuts for the bolts at the "T" slot so that they will not turn in the slot. Since these large nuts will be handy for many other setup jobs, you should make them.

The grinder can now be mounted vertically on the upstanding leg of the angle block, and its height can be adjusted as needed. This internal grinding is tricky. You cannot see what the wheel is doing. You can only test the results after each cut. Test very carefully with the inside calipers, which were set to the inside of the micrometer measuring the outside of the collet sleeve. The inside must be ground to an easy sliding fit with no play. Be sure to oil the inside each time and wipe it clean before entering the split collet to test it. For the straight grinding, the longitudinal and cross-feeds of the carriage are used. The angle block should now be loosened and turned to the angle of the angle of the compound, which has been left at the angle of the closing taper. This taper is now ground until the end of the collet projects $\frac{1}{16}$ inch.

Put the split collet back on its mandrel with the big end at the threaded end. Insert it in the outside sleeve and tighten it with the draw-bar pipe. Do not tighten it so tight that the mandrel cannot be driven out. Drive out the mandrel and remove it from the draw-bar pipe. True up the small grinding stone and grind the inside of the collet to a tight fit on the shank of the milling cutter for which this collet is being made. The long parallel shank of the cutter is a poor gauge to test the ground hole. These small stones wear very quickly; if you have forced the grinding, you may have ground a slightly tapering hole. Use the correct plug gauge to test it and also check with the cutter shank. The inside of the collet must be ground so that the cutter shank is a good sliding fit at the solid end under the threads; when the split end tightens on it, the cutter should run true to the lathe centers.

The slight angle of the Morse taper to the outside sleeve will give it a good grip on the spindle and prevent slipping, but the steeper angle of the collet may allow it to slip. Before the two sleeves are hardened, therefore, a $\frac{1}{8}$-inch-square keyway should be cut on the outside of the collet and the inside of the sleeve. These keyways should be deep enough to allow for grinding. After grinding, fit a square key to this keyway, making it tight in the collet and sliding in the sleeve. For the same reason that the head-end lathe centers are marked so that they will always be replaced in the same position, the outside sleeve should also be so marked.

Cup Chucks

Where one side of a work piece must run true to the back side, which has been finished first, a cup chuck can be used. It is not possible to set up such a piece in a jaw chuck and be sure that it is running true to the back side when this side is covered by the chuck and when the dial indicator cannot be used.

A cup chuck is a piece of metal thick enough to turn a recessed place to receive the part to be finished. This piece is bolted to the face plate for turning. The recess is turned to an easy driving fit for the work piece. The back face of the recess is countersunk so that the work bears only on the outer edge. The bottom corner should be undercut a little so that the sharp corner of the work will not be obstructed by a slightly rounded corner. The work must be seated tightly against the back face and tightly around the outside. To be sure the work is seated properly, four observation holes are drilled around the outside edge before the center is bored out. At least three ejection screws should be tapped in from the back to force the work out after completion. These screws must be in line with the slots in the face plate so that they can be reached without disturbing the setting of the chuck on the face plate. This is only necessary if the chuck is to be used again to finish a second piece. If the chuck is to be used only once, it can be held in a jaw chuck, and the ejection screws can be placed anywhere. The observation holes will still be required.

Since this type of chuck is very accurate, but has very little gripping power, heavy turning cuts cannot be used. It is best to rough-turn the work while it is held in a jaw chuck, and then place it in the cup chuck for finishing with very small cuts or by grinding. Before taking the finishing cuts, check the setting of the work in the observation holes to see if it is held tightly against the back.

Spuds

Spuds are used to hold internally finished work, and operate on the same principle as cup chucks. The work is held by friction on an accurately centered fixture. The observation holes are not needed, as the rear face of the work can be seen. Undercutting of the rear shoulder is required to allow for a tight fit into the corner. The ejection screws are required, as with the cup chuck, or pry-off holes can be provided, as described in Chapter 4, under *Arbors*.

A similar type of spud is used for facing a nut or other internal threaded piece. The shoulder should be undercut, and the thread must be a tight fit.

Care must be taken, when making both cup chucks and spuds, that the work does not fit so tightly that it must be driven on, as this will disturb the setting of the fixture in the lathe. Its accuracy depends on making a fixture to hold the work that is perfectly concentric with the lathe and being able to hold the work on it tightly against the guiding surfaces of the fixture.

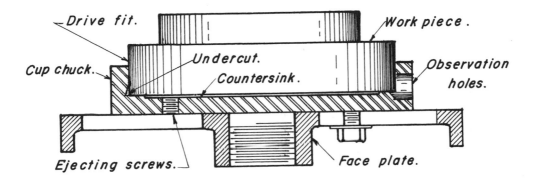

Fig. 158. Cup chuck

Special Milling Cutters

End mills will do most of the work in the home shop, but special cutters are sometimes required. These can be homemade in the same manner as the large-hole drills. Use mild steel and turn them to the shape required. Mount them on the indexing fixture (shown in Figure 152); then, with an end mill and an indexing gear, cut the teeth. Sharpen and relieve the teeth with a file and case harden the tool. These cutters are very useful for milling the flutes of reamers, and are mounted on a ¾-inch arbor while the work is held in the indexing fixture. When they get dull, the cutters can be sharpened by grinding or they can be annealed and filed sharp. They will have to be hardened after sharpening, since the grinding will penetrate below the hard case.

22

Electric Motors

THERE are four kinds of motors suited for use in the home shop: *split-phase, capacitor-start, repulsion-start,* and *universal.* A brief description of the uses, advantages, and disadvantages of each type of motor follows.

Split-Phase Motors

Split-phase motors are the cheapest of the four kinds. They have a fair amount of starting torque, but are not suited to starting a heavy load, such as an air compressor or a lathe while it is cutting. This is the type of motor used in most washing machines. The motor has two windings: heavy wire for the running winding, and fine wire for the starting winding. The high resistance of the starting winding throws the current in it out of phase with the main current, which flows through the low-resistance running windings without much change of phase. In effect, starting it up makes a two-phase motor out of it, of which the two phases are less than 90 electrical degrees apart. This splitting of the phase will give enough starting torque to bring the motor up to its "pull-in speed," if it has very little load attached.

The starting winding will get excessively hot very quickly, and must be disconnected from the line when the required speed has been obtained. This is accomplished by means of a centrifugal switch on the armature. If the motor is trying to start too heavy a load, it will be pulling a very heavy current through the starting coils when the centrifugal switch opens. This will cause heavy arcing at the switch points, which will cause them to burn out very quickly. The motor will then have to be dismantled, and new switch points installed.

These motors are suitable for use on the bench grinder, the wire brush, the tool-post grinder, and the band saw. A good used washing-machine motor can be bought cheaply. After having it overhauled to clean it up, and the bearings and the centrifugal switch checked, it can be used for many light starting jobs in the shop. When getting a used motor, examine it to see that the coils have not been overheated. If the insulation has been roasted and is brittle and easily cracked, do not buy the motor.

Capacitor-Start Motors

The capacitor-start motor is similar to the split-phase motor in that it divides or splits a single-phase current into two currents out of phase with each other. In this type, the second winding is not a fine-wire high-resistance coil, but is nearly the same as the main winding and has a condenser in series with it. This condenser causes the current in the secondary winding to lead the current in the main winding. By the use of the proper size of condenser, the two currents can be separated by nearly a full 90 electrical degrees apart. This gives the motor a very strong starting torque as well as making the power factor nearly unity.

These motors usually use more capacitance when starting than when running and so have a centrifugal switch to cut out part of the condensers after they come up to speed. This type of motor is expensive, but its high power factor makes it economical to operate. Its high starting torque makes it suitable for any machine in the shop.

Repulsion-Start Motors

Repulsion-start motors have a wound armature and a commutator. The brushes are short-circuited on themselves and are set very slightly off center in the direction of rotation. A very heavy current is induced in the armature windings, giving a good starting torque. When the motor is up to speed, a centrifugal governor throws out the brushes and short-circuits all the commutator bars on themselves, so that the motor runs under load as a straight single-phase induction motor.

The heavy starting current will overheat the armature windings if they are not disconnected. With so great a load that the motor cannot get up to speed, it will soon get very hot.

This type of motor is larger in size and cost more than the capacitor-start type of motor; as its power factor is low—that of a single-phase induction motor—it will cost more to operate. These motors also have the disadvantage of not being reversible, unless the position of the brushes is shifted. This cannot readily be done except by unfastening the brush holder and shifting them to the other side of center. This does not interfere with installation of the motor or adjustment of its direction of rotation; but it makes the motor unsuitable for quick reversal work, as for driving a lathe. This type of motor can be used for any of the machines in the shop except the lathe.

Universal Motors

The fourth type of motor used in the shop is the wound-armature commutator motor, designed to run on alternating or direct current. These motors, used on most portable power tools, are similar to direct-current motors, but have laminated fields so that they can run on alternating current without heating excessively. Alternating currents set up a heavy eddy current in solid castings, and these eddy currents heat the castings. With the laminated field, these eddy currents are broken up into small ones in each lamination, resulting in very much less heating.

The universal motor will run on direct current of the proper voltage and will develop a little more power than when used with alternating current. They can be designed to run at very high speeds, and, with the proper reduction gears, will put out quite a lot of power for a small motor. If such a motor is overloaded to the point of slowing down, it will draw more current and start to heat, like any electric motor. It should be taken apart periodically and cleaned; the commutator should be trued up, if necessary; and new brushes should be fitted when needed.

Reversing a Motor

Split-phase and the capacitor-start motors can be reversed by reversing the connections to either of the two windings. There are four leads to these windings, and these leads can be brought to a reversing switch, which will reverse one of the windings and thus reverse the direction of rotation.

The reverse switch can be incorporated with the starting switch, as on a drum switch. One movement of this switch connects the line current and the windings for either direction. Two separate switches can also be used. One is the line switch that turns on the current; the other is a two-pole, double-throw switch, to which the starting winding is connected, that will reverse the starting winding but does not start or stop the motor. A drum switch is very convenient in that it lets the motor start and run in either direction, depending on which way the handle is moved. With two switches, the reversing switch must be set for the direction of rotation before the starting switch is closed. Moving the reversing switch while the motor is running has no effect on the motor, since the centrifugal switch in the motor has disconnected the reversing switch. It must come to a standstill before reversing.

If toggle switches are used, see that chips of metal do not get into them. Either cover them or turn them on the side so that any chips that fall on them cannot work down around the handle and cause a short circuit of the electrical parts or jam the mechanical workings.

Index